Bad to Good

Achieving High Quality and Impact in Your Research

As the editor of a respectable academic Marketing journal, I identify very closely with the research issues pointed out by Professor Woodside, and also strongly believe that he is moving in the right direction to ameliorate the identified problems. Woodside is a hugely experienced researcher and editor, immensely respected in the management and marketing world. His insights and wisdom are ignored at a researcher's peril – there is a strong wind of change blowing through business research, and this book offers a clear guide to help weather the storm by conducting genuinely useful research.

– *Professor Roger Marshall, Auckland University of Technology, New Zealand*

A highly practical and readable book on bad practices in research and how to fix them. I particularly appreciated the focus on the following: mismatch between theory and research; non-response bias; and single outcome dependent variable. *Bad to Good* is a must read for scholars of any age and especially for doctoral students.

– *Jagdish N. Sheth, Charles H. Kellstadt Professor of Marketing, Emory University, USA*

The book is a 'must read' for all business researchers who want to stay on top of recent developments in quantitative research methods. Based on complexity theory tenets, the book illustrates the flaws of mainstream use of regression analysis and structural equation modeling in the development of useful theories. Examples from various fields impressively demonstrate the increase in quality of research findings coming with the use of configurational analysis.

– *Dr. Hans Mühlbacher, Professor of Marketing, International University of Monaco*

This is a landmark contribution to the renewal of research methodology. The bulk of research in business and management is still misguided by the positivist paradigm from the 1600s, dominated by surveys and hypothetico-deductive techniques and the claim that such research is 'rigorous'. Unfortunately it is better characterized as 'rigid' and 'ritualistic' and it seldom has relevance for practitioners. Arch Woodside is a brave thinker who advocates a move to a complexity paradigm and that we need cases to do so and to generate theory on a more general and abstract level.

– *Evert Gummesson, Emeritus Professor, Stockholm Business School, Stockholm University, Sweden*

Bad to Good

Achieving High Quality and Impact in Your Research

Edited by

Arch G. Woodside
Boston College, Chestnut Hill, MA, USA

United Kingdom – North America – Japan
India – Malaysia – China

Emerald Group Publishing Limited
Howard House, Wagon Lane, Bingley BD16 1WA, UK

First edition 2016

British Library Cataloguing in Publication Data
A catalogue record for this book is available from the British Library

ISBN: 978-1-78635-334-4

Printed and bound by CPI Group (UK) Ltd, Croydon, CR0 4YY

ISOQAR certified
Management System,
awarded to Emerald
for adherence to
Environmental
standard
ISO 14001:2004.

Certificate Number 1985
ISO 14001

INVESTOR IN PEOPLE

Contents

List of Contributors

Roger Baxter	Auckland University of Technology, Auckland, New Zealand
James Po-Hsun Hsiao	National Yunlin University of Science and Technology, Douliou, Taiwan
Tzung-Cheng (T. C.) Huan	National Chiayi University, Chiayi, Taiwan
Chyi Jaw	National Yunlin University of Science and Technology, Douliou, Taiwan
Alexandre Schpektor	Queen Mary University of London, London, UK
Arch G. Woodside	Boston College, Chestnut Hill, MA, USA
Pei-Ling Wu	Chienkuo Technology University, Changhua City, Taiwan
Richard Xia	Shanghai University of Finance and Economics, Shanghai, China
Shih-Shuo Yeh	National Quemoy University, Jinning, Taiwan

The Editor, Arch G. Woodside, expresses gratitude to Andy Boynton, Dean, Carroll School of Management, Boston College, for substantial course-teaching release during 2014−16 for research and writing resulting in this book.

Bad to Good is dedicated to my colleagues, the Carroll School of Management, Boston College, and to my wife, friend, and colleague, Carol Murphey Megehee.

Preface

Most of the articles in most of the scholarly journals in finance, management, marketing, and organizational studies include empirical positivistic methods and findings – and each of these empirical articles likely includes 3–10 or more bad practices that this book describes. The introductory chapter includes how to design-in good practices in theory, data collection procedures, analysis, and interpretations to avoid these bad practices. Given that bad practices in research are ingrained in the career training of scholars in sub-disciplines of business/management (e.g., through reading articles exhibiting bad practices usually without discussions of the severe weaknesses in these studies and by research courses stressing the use of regression analysis and structural equation modeling), this book is likely to have little impact. However, scholars and executives supporting good practices should not lose hope. The relevant literature includes a few brilliant contributions that can serve as beacons for eliminating the current pervasive bad practices and for performing highly competent research.

1

Moving away from Bad Practices in Research toward Constructing Useful Theory and Doing Useful Research

Arch G. Woodside

ABSTRACT

The introductory chapter includes how to design-in good practices in theory, data collection procedures, analysis, and interpretations to avoid these bad practices. Given that bad practices in research are ingrained in the career training of scholars in sub-disciplines of business/management (e.g., through reading articles exhibiting bad practices usually without discussions of the severe weaknesses in these studies and by research courses stressing the use of regression analysis and structural equation modeling), this editorial is likely to have little impact. However, scholars and executives supporting good practices should not lose hope. The relevant literature includes a few brilliant contributions that can serve as beacons for eliminating the current pervasive bad practices and for performing highly competent research.

Keywords: Bad; competency; complexity; configuration; good; incompetency

Introduction

Across several decades scholars (Inman, 2012; Lutz, 1991; Mick, 2006; Pham, 2013; Sheth, 1982; Wells, 1993) bemoan the low relevancy/impact of most articles in the leading journals in research in business, management, and marketing — the number of citations in the literature is the stable proxy for both relevancy and impact. Though scholarly, empirical, journal articles do appear that have high impact but low usefulness, and vice versa, most articles high in impact also have high usefulness. In a study of the impact of articles appearing during 2004–2008 in the *Journal of Consumer Research*, Pham (2013, p. 412) reports that "very few articles — less than 10% — get very well cited, and the vast majority — roughly 70% — hardly ever get cited [by anyone, ever]. In other words, the vast majority of the research that gets published, even in our top [ranked] journals — perhaps 70% of it — hardly has any measurable scholarly impact in terms of citations." Consequently, Pham (2013, p. 412) describes "seven sins of consumer psychology" as "the roots of our relevancy shortcomings." However, Pham's (2013) proposal of seven sins in journal articles do not get to the roots of the low impact of most articles in ranked journals. The present article reframes, broadens, and deepens the discussion of the lack of relevancy/impact of the *JCR* and most (likely all) journals related to the business sub-disciplines. Rather than low relevancy, the claim here is that the deeper issue is the pervasive use of bad research practices appearing in most articles in most of these journals and all journals related to the sub-disciplines of business/management research.

With the objective of reducing the high volume of bad practices in research, this chapter offers propositions for improving theory construction and empirical testing of theory especially by early to mid-career scholars in the sub-disciplines of business/management. Here is a brief summary of four of these propositions. (1) Most articles appearing in most of the ranked (i.e., A*, A, B, and C rankings in the ABDC, 2013 listings) journals of the business/management sub-disciplines exhibit 3 + bad practices in theory construction and research procedures. (2) The use of bad practices contributes to the low usefulness/relevancy/impact of most of the articles appearing in the leading the journals. (3) The prevalence of bad practices is likely a result of the training focus of doctoral students that is almost exclusively on the use of symmetric tests (e.g., regression analysis including structural equation models of collecting verbal responses to five- and seven-point scaled questions) and the reading of literature exhibiting a plethora of bad practices. (4) Additional training and planning is possible to avoid the use of bad practices and embrace the use of good practices; early to mid-career scholars should do both: train and plan to adopt readily available but ignored good practices.

This chapter describes 22 bad practices prevalent in the sub-disciplines of business/management; most of bad practices appear pervasively among most articles among the ranked journals. A summary of the 20 bad (and good) practices appears in Table 1. The discussion of each bad practice includes suggestions of steps useful to take to avoid or eliminate such practices. The references in the discussion are particularly useful sources for learning how to avoid bad practices in business/management-related research and how to embrace good practices. The list and discussion of bad practices is incomplete; discussion of research by scholars "breaking bad" in a few studies may help decrease your use of bad practices and increase your use of good research practices. This chapter does not include the accusation that many scholars seek to use bad practices purposively in designing and implementing their studies; the lack of training and the mental stance of asking what is bad and good practices are likely to be principal causes of the current domination of bad practices.

Recipes of antecedents to using bad practices are likely to include combinations of the following features: lack of experience (most scholars submitting most papers are likely to submit twenty or fewer studies based on completing twenty different data files in their lifetimes); lack of training beyond building and testing theories centering on the net effects of independent variables on a single dependent variable; modeling their own research behavior by reading published studies exhibiting several bad practices; and having zero to very limited exposures to the relevant literature on adopting good practices in behavioral/business research (e.g., here are some primary sources that include exceptional insights and advice for designing and implementing good practices in research and data analysis: Armstrong, 2012; Campbell & Stanley, 1963; Dillman, Smyth, & Christian, 2014; Eskin & Baron, 1977; Feldman & Lynch, 1988; Gigerenzer & Brighton, 2009; Golder, 2000; Howard & Morgenroth, 1968; Levitt & List, 2007; McClelland, 1998; Nisbett & Wilson, 1977; Ordanini, Parasuraman, & Rubera, 2014; Ragin, 2008; Sawyer & Ball, 1981; Shadish, Cook, & Campbell, 2002; Whyte, 1984).

Table 1: Recognizing and Shifting Away from the Bad Practices Pervasive in Research in Business.

Topic/Issue	Bad Practice	Good Practice	Shifting to Good
1. Theory to data analysis/type of models/ "controlling"	Mismatch/ex ante modeling/controlling by adding terms into regression models	Match/*a priori* modeling/controlling by examining different recipes	Case ID theory and case ID data analysis/no use of stepwise regression analysis
2. Validation	Testing fit validation only	Testing for fit and predictive validity	Test for predictive validity with additional samples
3. Contrarian cases	Ignore	Recognize and model	For continuous variables, create quintiles and crosstabs
4. Reporting findings	Using t, p, F, r, R^2	Reporting consistency and displaying XY plots	Compute consistency and show XY plots
5. Focus of findings	Net effects of variables	Recipes of antecedent conditions	Construct and test predictive accuracy of recipes
6. Type of data/response metrics	Verbal self-reports only/5- and 7-point scales to measure processes	Observation and nonobtrusive methods/natural responses	Direct research – getting into the context; triangulation
7. Study of dynamics	No, cross-sectional study	Yes, longitudinal study	Collect data across 2 to 20+ time periods
8. Persons interviewed per firm, household, unit	One	Two to three	Interview 3 separately and examine and segment by answer consistencies
9. Useable share of respondents	5–30%	50% plus	Use four attempts to reach respondents, apply Dillman et al. (2014) tenets

10. Measuring nonresponse bias	Compare demographics of early versus late respondents	Compare attitudes, brand involvement, and use of early versus late respondents	Cross tabulate attitude/behaviors by responses for each contact attempt
11. Type of modeling/recognition of the causal asymmetry tenet	Symmetric only/no recognition of tenet	Asymmetric modeling separately of high and low outcomes	Estimate asymmetric models for high score and low score cases separately; a
12. Experimental control group	Use a nocebo control	Use a placebo control	Ask, "What 'sugar pill' am I using?"
13. Mushy variables	Using scale responses as surrogates to measure processes and outcomes	Observe real-life processes; create field experiments	Read Ariely (2010) as well as Levitt and List (2007) to stimulate your creativity
14. Outcome description/explanation of behavior-context	Little to none	Rich, nitty-gritty, details	Do "direct research"
15. Outcomes	One dependent/outcome variable	Recipe outcomes	Report on conjunctive outcomes
16. Hypothesis testing	Advocacy hypothesis	Multiple hypothesis	Design/perform critical tests
17. Modeling/forecasting	Create inductively using stepwise regression	A *priori* modeling using theory	Use thought experiments; do not use stepwise regressions
18. Replication of findings	No replication built into study	Replication/extension in the study	Use/test two separate samples; test in multiple contexts

A Profile of Bad Practices Appearing in Most Journal Manuscript Submissions

Most submissions to the *JBR* (and likely other leading journals in the sub-disciplines of business/management) include several to all of the following features:

- A theory construction representable by boxes and arrows that focuses on proposing and testing net effects of 2–20 variables and a few moderating and mediating relationships on a single dependent variable or series of separate dependent variables
- An empirical study focusing exclusively on findings of a survey asking some sample of persons to complete five-point and/or seven-point (verbal response) scales
- Asking one person per unit (e.g., firm, household, near government organization) to complete the survey
- A useable response rate between 5% and 30%
- No presentation of correlations of items in scales and between scales representing variables
- The presentation of multiple regression analysis via stepwise or structural equation models (or a structural equation model, SEM) of findings of significant paths
- A report of findings emphasizing the net effects of terms in one or a few regression models having a few significant plus a few non-significant terms – most models in the study having 5–30 terms in the models
- Fit validation of the model having an adjusted R^2 between .05 and .35
- No report of the predictive validation of models using additional samples of cases
- The mismatch of using variable models to test case-based theories
- Focusing only on main effects, moderating effects, and mediating effects and not modeling cases in the data having contrarian relationships to the hypotheses
- Failure to recognize the relevancy of complexity theory principles in theory and empirical research
- Not showing XY plots of the model as X and the outcome as Y and reporting symmetric test findings and not recognizing the most relationships are asymmetric – 99% of studies in

marketing; failure to recognize the relevancy of Anscombe's
(1973) quartet in business research
- Relying primarily/exclusively on respondents' self-reports for
high accuracy of content/behavior – reporting no or little
direct field observational data.

The following discussions of the details supporting the identification of bad and good practices appearing in Table 1 elaborate
on features in these 13 bullet points. The core propositions put
forth in this chapter include the following points. Bad practices
appear pervasively in most of the leading journals in the business
sub-disciplines. Good practices are available for scholars to use
in place of these bad practices. Journal editors need to recognize
and act on their responsibility to bring bad practices to light and
offer suggestions and examples to cause their demise – what
Fitzsimmons (2008) attempts to do in his editorial in calling for
the "death of dichotomizing." The present chapter expands
Fitzsimmons call by urging the death of bad practices.

Bad Practice: Theory and Analysis Mismatch

Most empirical research in behavioral science and business
research journals present a mismatch theory and data analysis.
Most researchers develop theory from the perspective of the individual firm or consumer but formulate their hypotheses from the
perspective of the net effects influence of individual variables on
a dependent variable (Fiss, 2007; Woodside, 2015). The researchers' shift in thinking is seemingly subtle and likely an unconscious
one. Their prior training in data analyses focuses on how to do
symmetric tests such as analysis of variance, multiple regression
analysis (MRA), and structural equation modeling (SEM); they
apply this training to extract information from their data without
recognizing the transformation in their focus from case (e.g.,
firm, consumer, organization, nation) identification into a symmetrical variable hypotheses (SVH) perspective. Symmetric tests
of variable hypotheses examine two-way directional hypotheses
such as high versus low X (independent) scores associate with
high versus low Y scores. For example, Hofstede's (2003) cultural value theory proposes that each nation is a complex whole

of a combination of distinct cultural values (e.g., collectivism/ individualism, masculinity, uncertainty avoidance, and power distance); a vast number of studies examine Hofstede's theory in many different contexts but almost all of these studies examine the net effects of each cultural value using symmetric tests. Almost none of these studies examine the influence of culture values from the perspective of culture as complex wholes (i.e., recipes), including the studies by Hofstede and colleagues; for exceptions see Hsu, Woodside, and Marshall (2013) and Woodside, Hsu, and Marshall (2011).

Fiss (2007) states the case eloquently for recognizing the nature of the theory-analysis mismatch that pervades the sub-disciplines of business research:

> Configurational approaches to organization are based on the fundamental premise that patterns of attributes will exhibit different features [i.e., antecedent ingredients] and lead to different outcomes depending on how they are arranged [in recipes]. But while theoretical discussions of configurational theory thus stress nonlinearity, synergistic effects, and equifinality, empirical research has so far largely drawn on economic methods that by their very nature tend to imply linearity, additive effects, and uni-finality. For example, the classic linear regression model treats variables as competing in explaining variation in outcomes rather than showing how variables combine to create outcomes. By focusing on the relative importance of rival variables, a correlational approach has difficulty treating cases as configurations and [in] examining combinations of variables. This [mismatch] becomes particularly evident in the fact that regression analysis focuses on the unique contributions of a variable while constant the values of all other variables in the equation. (Fiss, 2007, p. 2007)

Ordanini et al. (2014) build on the work on Fiss (2007, 2011) and others (Ragin, 2000; Rihoux & Ragin, 2009, p. 137, italics in the original article) in applying qualitative comparative analysis (QCA) to perform "a systematic cross-case analysis that models relations among variables in terms of *set membership* and uses Boolean algebra to identify configurations that reflect the *necessary* and *sufficient* conditions for an outcome of interest." QCA builds from complexity theory tenets (Woodside, 2014) including the recognition that the presence of a specific feature or level of a feature in a model can be necessary but is rarely sufficient for a high score in an outcome condition of occur consistently (e.g., almost in all instances). In their study of customer adoption of a new luxury hotel service, Ordanini et al. (2014) conclude from their comparison of multiple regression analysis (MRA) and QCA findings that the QCA findings confirm that the appeal of a new service indeed depends on the combined effects — not the net or additive effects — of its characteristics.

While not identifying the theory-analysis mismatch per se, prior scholars (Bass, Tigert, & Lonsdale, 1968; McClelland, 1998) provide examples of the problems of using symmetric tests (e.g., MRA) in identifying cases (e.g., consumers, executives) having high scores on a study's focal outcome condition (e.g., heavy product users, highly competent executives, and firms fitting a theoretical strategic type). Both Bass, Tigert, and Lonsdale (1968) and McClelland (1998) offer solutions to such problems; these solutions have been ignored widely the fields of marketing and organizational psychology, respectively (Woodside, 2015). McClelland's solution includes using combinations of cases present in all top (bottom) quintiles for 3+ antecedents as screens for identifying highly competent executives. Similar to stock screen construction tools made available by brokerage firms (e.g., Fidelity), McClelland's procedure is viewable correctly as an early version of QCA.

This discussion of theory-analysis mismatch reflects Gigerenzer's (1991, p. 19) wisdom, "Scientists tools are not neutral." Tools drip theory. Such tools-to-theory stances need explicit recognition by scholars rather than the now pervasive implicit shifting between case identification theory construction and symmetric, net effects, focused data analysis. Figure 1 from Sawyer, Laran, and Xu (2008) is an example of the seemingly implicit shift from case identification theory (CIT) to data analysis using symmetric net effects of variables. The title of Sawyer et al.'s (2008) article reflects the focus on CIT: "The Readability of Marketing Journals: Are Award-Winning Articles Better Written?" The focus of the Sawyer et al. (2008) is on identifying the cases of award-winning articles by writing quality — an asymmetric outcome. However, the analysis in Figure 1 focuses on predicting a symmetric outcome — high versus low score on an award versus non-award-winning variable. The comparison between asymmetric versus symmetric outcome appears to be subtle but a full asymmetric analysis would serve to clarify the two unique theory-analysis perspectives.

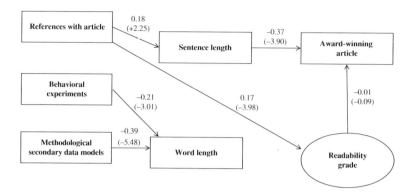

Figure 1. Causal Path of Article Characteristics on Readability Grade. *Source:* Reprinted with permission from *Journal of Marketing*, published by the American Marketing Association, Sawyer et al. (2008, Figure 1, p. 113) (directional sign missing in original for path with β = .17 added). *Notes*: All coefficients are statistically significant at $p < .05$, except for the null relationship between "Readability" and "Award-winning article." Because lower grades indicate better readability, a negative coefficient indicates a positive relationship to readability. For example, longer words and sentences cause higher readability grades (i.e., poorer readability). The top value beside each path is the size of the standardized relationship. The resulting Z-test appear in parentheses.

Designing a screening tool to indicate award-winning cases (i.e., articles winning awards) is an example of an asymmetric tool and CIT perspective. The steps in Figure 2 are an example of such an asymmetric screening tool. This particular three-step screen selects cases in the bottom quintile (i.e., first 20% of the articles in number of references appearing in the article) AND cases reporting a behavioral experiment AND cases in the topic quintile in the number of models in the article using secondary data). In a thought experiment done here as a tutorial tool, Figure 3 shows that 30 among 500 articles pass through this screen successfully.

Figure 3 presents and *XY* plot of the relationship for the model, R•E•S ≤ A. The dictionary for each letter in the model appears in Figure 2. To calculate a case's score for the complex statement, ~R•E•S, the original values of a case for each of the simple conditions (R, E, and S) must first be calibrated. The mid-level tilde, "~", indicates performing negation operation (i.e., calculating the score for 1 minus the positive calibrated score). The mid-level dot, "•", represents the logical "AND" operation of taking the lowest calibrated score for each term in the expression

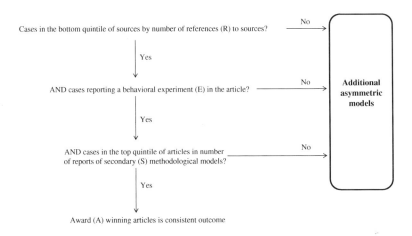

Figure 2. Thought Experiment of a Screening Tool to Identify Award-Winning Articles Assuming 500 Published Articles with 50 Award Winners and 450 Non-Winners. *Note*: Boolean algebra statement of the same model: $\sim R \bullet E \bullet S \leq A$ where "$\sim$" equals the negation of the condition and mid-level dot "$\bullet$" signifies the logical AND operation.

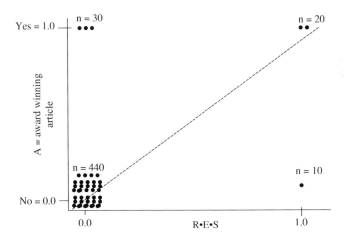

Figure 3. *XY* Plot of an Asymmetric Model Thought Experiment Findings Showing a Model to Modest in Predicting 50 Award-Winning Articles from among 500 Articles Appearing in a Given Set of Journals. *Notes*: Symmetric analysis: each dot represents 10 cases (i.e., articles). In comparing the proportions 20/50 versus 10/440, the *Z*-Score is 10.671, $r = 0.81$. The result is significant at $p < 0.01$. Regression analysis: A = $-1.318 + 0.667$ R$\bullet$E$\bullet$S, adjusted $R^2 = 0.65$. Asymmetric analysis: 66.6% of cases with high scores for the model, R$\bullet$E$\bullet$S, won awards, the model does not indicate high sufficiency for accurately predicting cases winning an award.

to equal the score for the total expression. Calibration scores range from 0.00 to 1.00 (Ragin, 2008; for details). A case's score for ~R•E•S is equal to the Boolean algebra logical "AND" calculation of taking the lowest score for each simple antecedent in the complex condition as the score for the complex statement. Consider the calculation of ~R•E•S for the following three hypothetical cases whereby case number 3 won an award:

Case	~R	E	S	~R•E•S	A
1	1.0	0.0	1.0	0.0	0.0
2	0.4	0.8	0.0	0.0	0.0
3	1.0	1.0	1.0	1.0	1.0

Symmetric tests make use of all available information in the data set. The two symmetric tests (test of difference between two proportions and a regression analysis) at the bottom of Figure 3 indicates a significant net effect of R•E•S calibrated scores on winning awards. An asymmetric test focuses only on cases with high scores for R•E•S; for the symmetric test, all (or nearly all) of the cases with high scores in R•E•S should have high scores in A. From an asymmetric perspective, the findings in Figure 3 do not indicate that high R•E•S scores consistently indicate cases with high A scores (i.e., the researcher would like to achieve a consistency of 80–90% or higher in accurate predictions for a model of a simple or complex antecedent condition). For predictive validation of the models, both the symmetric and asymmetric models should be tested for accuracy using additional samples.

Figure 3 illustrates the equifinality tenet of complexity theory and configural analysis. Being an asymmetric model, R•E•S ≤ A predicts only that high scores on R•E•S indicate high scores on A and does not attempt to tell anything about low scores on R•E•S associating with A. Even if the model is highly predictive of high scores on A, a reasonable large data set will show that low scores on R•E•S will associate with both low and high scores on A. Thus, symmetric analysis is limited in usefulness because symmetric tests are attempts to predict both low and high scores on the outcome within one model. Also, more than one asymmetric model is necessary to predict most of the cases with high scores on the outcome condition (i.e., A in this hypothetical example) — the XY plot shows that 30 award-winning papers have low scores on R•E•S. Additional recipes of complex antecedent conditions other than R•E•S are necessary to identify most to all of the 30 cases with low R•E•S scores.

The use of symmetric tests to identify cases having a specific outcome is bad practice because such tests examine variable relationships; they are not designed to identify specific cases; asymmetric tests are designed to identify cases having specific outcomes. Because of the bad practice in testing findings, Sawyer et al. (2008) do not provide an answer, "are award-winning articles better written?" Rather than this incomplete comparison, the study actually focuses on the question, do well-written articles win awards? The main finding in Sawyer et al. (2008) is that sentence length has a negative association with winning versus not winning an award. No test findings appear in Sawyer et al. (2008) as to what might accurately predict award-winning papers consistently.

A related bad practice in Sawyer et al. (2008) is not including the adjusted R^2 findings for the four regression models in Figure 1 or in the findings section of the article. Mostly likely the explained variances for all four models are very low (e.g., adjusted R^2) due to the asymmetric nature of the relationships between the independent and dependent variables. The failure to test for predictive validity using additional samples is an additional bad practice in Sawyer et al. (2008). The additional sample could have come from splitting the 162 articles in the sample in their study and modeling sub-samples and using the model of the first subsample to predict the scores in the second, and including a correlation and XY plot of the predicted versus actual scores. Then, a cross-validation would be done by performing the opposite procedure. Gigerenzer and Brighton (2009) stress the importance of doing predictive validation using additional samples as well as the pervasive absence in doing so as a bad practice (Armstrong, 2012; McClelland, 1998).

Designing a study to test if better writing associates with winning awards does not indicate good practice in building theory. Theory focusing on substance rather than only writing quality and on article impact rather than winning awards would be a greater contribution than the study by Sawyer et al. Do articles exhibiting good practices indicate articles with high impact? (The number of citations to the article in Web of Science and/or Google.com/scholar would be useful measures of impact.) As Sawyer et al. (2008) review, perceived competence of the author associates negatively with low versus high quality writing (Armstrong, 1980; Hartley, Trueman, & Meadows, 1988) – the worse the writing quality, the higher the perception the reader sees in the author. Thus, the reasonable expectation would be that low versus high writing associates with acceptance versus rejection for publication, high versus low impact, and winning versus not winning awards. However, both from symmetric and asymmetric theory and testing stances, writing quality is likely to play a minor role versus the role played by substance that an article delivers (e.g., Jung and Newton are not known to be authors who wrote using easy-to-read styles). Thus, asking the following question relates to Sawyer et al. (2008) but represents a much more substantive research issue. What configurations (i.e., recipes) of substance with and without high/low quality writing deliver high impact?

Not reporting the correlation matrix table of all variables in Sawyer et al. (2008) is an additional bad practice. In their study, most likely "behavioral experiments" and "methodological secondary data models" associate negatively with "readability grade" (indicating a positive relationship because readability grade is reverse coded). Because multi-collinearity among variables usually occurs among variables in symmetric tests, reporting a correlation matrix of all variables is good practice. (Behavioral experiments and methodological secondary data models are likely to be substantive indicators in recipes for high-impact articles.)

The two main conclusions from reading Sawyer et al. (2008) include the following points. The Sawyer et al. study illustrates the pervasive mismatch between case identity theory and data analysis using symmetric tests. Correcting for the mismatch is possible and might be informative but not a lot. Secondly, Sawyer et al. (2008) focuses on secondary issues for both the principal antecedent condition (i.e., sentence length) and outcome condition (i.e., winning an award). Running a redesigned study focusing on good and bad practices relating to research substance on article impact using asymmetric theory and data analysis is possible and worthwhile for future research.

McClelland (1998) proposes and demonstrates the theoretical and applied/practical benefits of creating screens for identifying particular cases using quintiles – his approach is an example of asymmetric theory/analysis. Ragin's (2008) *Redesigning Social Inquiry: Fuzzy Sets and Beyond* is a more advanced description of asymmetric theory/analysis than McClelland's (1998) approach; Ragin (2008) provides details on how and why to use fuzzy-set qualitative comparative analysis (fsQCA) and he describes the available software (fsQCA.com) for doing so. Ordanini et al. (2014) compare the use of QCA and more conventional approaches such as cluster analysis and latent class analysis; they conclude that QCA provides substantially greater benefits than both conventional approaches. Woodside (2015) discusses the use of QCA versus CHAID (chi-squared automatic interaction detection, see Kass, 1980; Magidson, 1994) and points out that CHAID provides far less capabilities in learning alternative complex antecedent conditions (recipes) in the data that consistently predict high scores in outcome conditions of interest. COMPASSS.ORG is a website and organization dedicated to providing instruction on theory construction using tenets of configural analysis and complexity theory that includes the use of QCA; an excellent source for developing skills in theory construction and data analysis building from complexity theory (Woodside, 2014).

EMBRACING THE COMPLEXITY TURN

In marketing, Kotler (1967, p. 1), famously pronounced, "Marketing decisions must be made in the context of insufficient information about processes that are dynamic, nonlinear, lagged, stochastic, interactive, and downright difficult." Yet the substantial majority of studies in the nearly 50 decades since this pronouncement continue to ignore all the decision features that Kotler describes (Woodside, 2015). Urry's (2005) call for a "complexity turn" echoes Kotler's (1967) perspective. Urry (2005) provides a far-ranging literature review of complexity theory in the natural and social sciences and offers many useful insights. Example insights include the following perspectives, "Relationships between variables can be nonlinear with abrupt switches occurring, so the same 'cause' can, in specific circumstances, produce different effects" (Urry, 2005, p. 4) and "If a system passes a particular threshold with minor changes in the controlling variables, switches occur such that a liquid turns into a gas, a large number of apathetic people suddenly tip into a forceful movement for change (Gladwell, 2002). Such tipping points give rise to unexpected structures and events" (Urry, 2005, p. 5).

Consider the following brief summary of the tenets in the complexity turn (i.e., paradigm shift in theory and research toward asymmetric modeling) that appears in Woodside (2014). T1: A simple antecedent condition may be necessary but a simple antecedent condition is rarely sufficient for predicting a high or low score in an outcome condition. Consequently, regarding the study of articles receiving awards, if a researcher wants to learn what recipes (i.e., configurations of antecedent conditions) indicate receiving an award, a study of net effects of individual antecedent conditions fails to accomplish this objective. T2: A complex antecedent condition of two or more simple conditions is sufficient for a consistently high score in an outcome condition — the recipe principle. Figure 4 shows T2 visually. T3: A model that is sufficient is not necessary for predicting an outcome having a high score accurately and consistently — the equifinality principle. Figure 4 shows two models as alternative routes to receiving an award that also has high impact and appear in an A* ranked journal — an A-star journal in the ABDC (2013) journal rankings. The researcher can expect to uncover 2−5 or more recipes indicting a high score in an outcome of interest in studies where 50−1,000 + recipes are theoretically possible.

T4: Recipes indicating a second outcome (e.g., rejection) are unique and are not the mirror opposites of recipes of a different

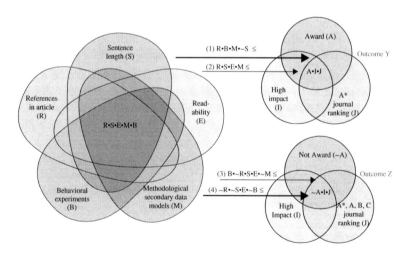

Figure 4. Complex Antecedent Conditions (Recipes) Indicating Two Outcome Recipes. *Notes*: Assume quintiles of cases from very low to high for R, S, E, three levels for M, and two levels for B. Thus, 5X5X5X3X2 possible recipes for 750 possible configurations. Figure 4 includes two possible outcome recipes of interest to the researcher: *Y* and *Z*. Receiving an award or not is the only difference between outcomes *Y* and *Z*. If impact is measured by quintiles and journal ranking are at four levels, then 40 outcomes are possible to study for Award and no award each. A* equals A-star status in the ABDC (2013) journal rankings. Thickness of the arrows is to indicate the number of cases that the specific models are predicted to identify: thick ≥10; thin <10 articles.

outcome (e.g., acceptance) — the causal asymmetry principle. Thus, useful models of recipes indicating failure of an article receiving an award are not the mirror opposites of useful models of recipes indicating receiving an award. Figure 4 reflects T4 by hypothesizing two models for not receiving an award that are asymmetric to the models receiving an award.

T5: An individual feature (attribute or action) in a recipe can contribute positively or negatively to a specific outcome depending on the presence or absence of the other ingredients in the recipes — the contrarian cases tenet. The findings in Figure 5 from a customer service experience evaluation study illustrate T5. Good practice includes recognizing that cases contrary to statistically significant main effects almost always occur in reasonably large data sets. The analyses of responses of 436 customers participating in this service experience evaluation study included creating quintiles as far as possible from very low to very high for both reports of level of effective treatment experiences and overall

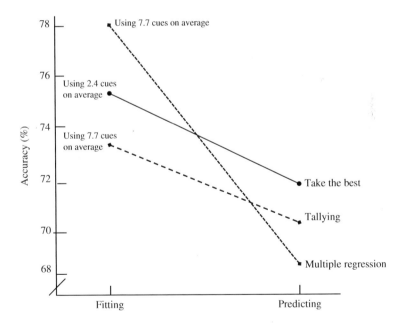

Figure 5. Two Outcomes: Effective Treatment and Service Quality Segments in Beauty Parlor and Health Spa Study. *Source:* Adapted from Wu, Yeh, Huan, and Woodside (Table 5, 2014, p. 1655). *Notes:* The significant main effect relationship indicates a large effect size, phi^2 ≥ .40 (Cohen, 1977). However, negative and positive contrarian cases still occur; the positivistic model does not account for such contrarian cases.

service quality judgments. A variable-level analysis indicates that the main effect is positive and large (phi^2 = .40, $p < .001$). A case-level analysis identifies that contrarian cases occur: 41 of the 436 gave very low to low treatment evaluation and high to very high service quality evaluations and 12 of 436 gave the opposite responses. Researchers using variable-level analysis almost always ignore such contrarian cases; researchers using asymmetric case-level analysis embrace them. Contrarian cases are usually surprising findings and modeling recipes can help to explain their occurrence.

Note in the hypothetical example in Figure 4, model 1 includes sentence length as a positive influence (S) on the outcome, A•I•J while model 2 includes sentence length as a negative influence (~S) on the same outcome. Given that some articles with many long sentences win awards as well as some with short sentences win awards, just reporting that a negative main effect occurs between sentence lengths and winning awards does not provide much information that is in the data. Reporting symmetric variable main and interaction effects only is usually bad practice. The deep issue to report is the circumstances (i.e., the recipes) when a positive impact occurs and when a negative impact occurs.

T6: For high X scores, a useful recipe for identifying high Y would be relevant usually for most but not all cases; thus, coverage is less than 1.00 for any one recipe. A few exceptions occur for high X scores for a given recipe that work well for predicting high Y scores. Note in Figure 3 that the 20 of the 30 cases high in X (i.e., R•E•S) are high in Y (award-winning articles). Case-focused modelers would consider this level of consistency to be low; they set higher consistency levels (e.g., 85–95% of the cases with high scores in the complex antecedent condition (i.e., model on the X-axis) are frequent objectives in case-level modeling).

Bad Practice: Testing for Fit Validity Only; Not Testing for Predictive Validity

Achieving statistically significant findings using multiple regression analysis (MRA) is easy to accomplish. Most reports of MRA findings in articles appearing in A* to C ranked journals (ABDC, 2013) are examples of bad practice. These reports of MRA findings almost always include fit only results and include more than five terms in the models with a few-to-most terms not significant statistically. Armstrong (2012, p. 691) shows how to achieve high fit validity using a table of random numbers as data, "In one of my Tom Swift studies, Tom used standard procedures when starting with 31 observations and 30 potential variables. He used stepwise regression and included only variables where Student's *t* was greater than 2.0. Along the way, he dropped three outliers. The final regression had eight variables and an *R*-square (adjusted for degrees of freedom) of 0.85. Not bad, considering that the data were from Rand's book of random numbers (Armstrong, 1970) ... Studies have continued to find the fit is not a good way to assess predictive ability (e.g., Pant & Starbuck, 1990). The obvious solution is to avoid use of t, p, F, R-squared and the like when using regression."

The usefulness of a model depends on its predictive accuracy using additional samples to test for accuracy. A point that a few iconic studies emphasize (e.g., Armstrong, 2012; Brighton & Gigerenzer, 2015; Gigerenzer & Brighton, 2009; Howard & Morgenroth, 1968; McClelland, 2009; Morgenroth, 1964) but ignored pervasively in most articles using MRA in all journals. Figure 6 illustrates the bad practice of reporting fit validity only as well as how overfitting a model (i.e., using five or more terms in a regression model) generates the false illusion of a good model. The findings in Figure 6 come from Czerlinski, Gigerenzer, and Goldstein (1999) meta-analysis of 20 studies in which both tallying and MRA were tested by cross-validation, correcting for this imbalance. All tasks were paired comparisons; for instance, estimating which of two Chicago high schools will have a higher dropout rate, based on cues such as writing score and proportion of Hispanic students. Ten of the 20 data sets were taken from a textbook on applied MRA (Weisberg, 1985). Averaged across all data sets, tallying achieved a higher predictive accuracy than MRA. Models using MRA tended to overfit the data, as can be seen by the cross-over of lines in Figure 6; MRA models had higher fit than tallying but a lower predictive accuracy when testing the models' usefulness on additional samples (or using cross-validation method of splitting the total sample into two sub-samples and modeling each, then using the model of the first to predict scores in the second and calculating the correlation between the predicted versus actual scores; then, performing the reverse procedure).

Figure 6 shows that the "take-the-best" algorithm uses the least amount of information and provides the highest predictive

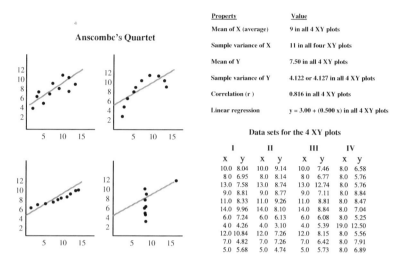

Property	Value
Mean of X (average)	9 in all 4 XY plots
Sample variance of X	11 in all four XY plots
Mean of Y	7.50 in all 4 XY plots
Sample variance of Y	4.122 or 4.127 in all 4 XY plots
Correlation (r)	0.816 in all 4 XY plots
Linear regression	y = 3.00 + (0.500 x) in all 4 XY plots

Data sets for the 4 XY plots

I		II		III		IV	
x	y	x	y	x	y	x	y
10.0	8.04	10.0	9.14	10.0	7.46	8.0	6.58
8.0	6.95	8.0	8.14	8.0	6.77	8.0	5.76
13.0	7.58	13.0	8.74	13.0	12.74	8.0	5.76
9.0	8.81	9.0	8.77	9.0	7.11	8.0	8.84
11.0	8.33	11.0	9.26	11.0	8.81	8.0	8.47
14.0	9.96	14.0	8.10	14.0	8.84	8.0	7.04
6.0	7.24	6.0	6.13	6.0	6.08	8.0	5.25
4.0	4.26	4.0	3.10	4.0	5.39	19.0	12.50
12.0	10.84	12.0	7.26	12.0	8.15	8.0	5.56
7.0	4.82	7.0	7.26	7.0	6.42	8.0	7.91
5.0	5.68	5.0	4.74	5.0	5.73	8.0	6.89

Figure 6. Fit and Predictive Validity. *Source*: Gigerenzer and Brighton (2009, p. 112). *Notes*: Less-is-more effects. Both tallying and take-the-best predict more accurately than multiple regression, despite using less information and computation. Note that multiple regression excels in data fitting ("hindsight"), that is, fitting its parameters to data that are already known, but performs relatively poorly in prediction ("foresight," as in cross-validation). Take-the-best is the most frugal, that is, it looks up, on average, only 2.4 cues when making inferences. In contrast, both multiple regression and tallying look up 7.7 cues on average. The results shown are averaged across 20 studies, including psychological, biological, sociological, and economic inference tasks (Czerlinski et al., 1999). For each of the 20 studies and each of the three strategies, the 95% confidence intervals were ≤4 percentage points.

validity. The take-the-best heuristic is a model of how decision-makers infer which of two objects has a higher value on a criterion, based on binary cue values retrieved from memory. For convenience, the cue value that signals a higher criterion value is 1, and the other cue value is 0. Take-the-best consists of three building blocks: (1) Search rule: Search through cues in order of their validity; (2) Stopping rule: Stop on finding the first cue that discriminates between the objects, (i.e., cue values are 1 and 0); (3) Decision rule: Infer that the object with the positive cue value (1) has the higher criterion value (Gigerenzer & Brighton, 2009, p. 113).

Brighton and Gigerenzer (2015) elaborate on why surprisingly simple models sometimes predict more accurately than more complex, sophisticated models in management, marketing, and finance. They address the question of when and why simple models succeed – or fail – by framing the forecasting problem in terms of the bias–variance dilemma. Controllable error in forecasting consists of two components, the "bias" and the "variance." Using the study of cognitive heuristics, they discuss how to reduce variance by ignoring weights, attributes, and dependencies between attributes, and thus make better decisions.

Articles using MRA in finance, management, and marketing journals often report on controlling for the effects of moderating variables by adding them into the models. Armstrong (2012, p. 691) refers to this practice as the "illusion of control": "Users of regressions assume that by putting variables into the equation they are somehow controlling for these variables. However, this only occurs for experimental data. Adding variables does not mean controlling for them in non-experimental data, because many variables typically co-vary with other predictor variables. The problem becomes worse as more variables are added to the regression. Large sample sizes cannot resolve this problem, so statistics on the numbers of degrees of freedom are misleading." To help reduce this bad practice of attempting to control for the effects of variables besides the independent focal variables of major interest, Armstrong (2012, p. recommends, "do not try to estimate relationships for more than three variables in a regression (the findings of Goldstein & Gigerenzer, 2009, p. 690, are consistent with this rule-of-thumb)." An even better rule-of-thumb might be to report findings for both MRA/SEM (variable-based analysis) and QCA (case-based models) as done by Ordanini et al. (2014) and Woodside (2014) – the MRA/SEM to meet the expectations of most journal reviewers and QCA to offer particularly useful findings. Researchers should take the step of performing and reporting predictive validity using additional samples or cross-validation for their MRA and QCA models – doing so increases the contribution of their studies and likely help increase the likelihood of their manuscripts gaining acceptance for publication. Embracing Armstrong's (2012, p. 693) summary is a worthwhile step away from the pervasive bad practice of presenting MRA models with 5 to 30+ terms (overfitting and having a few/several non-significant terms) along with not reporting predictive validity via additional samples), "In summary, do not use regression to search for causal relationships, and do not try to predict by using variables that were not specified in the *a priori* analysis. Thus, avoid data mining, stepwise regression, and related methods."

Bad Practice: Ignoring Cases with Associations Contrary to Significant Main Effects

Figure 7 is a second example illustrating the substantial presence of the contrarian cases in a set of data. The data are from study by Hosie, Sevastos, and Cooper (2006), *Happy-Performing Managers*. Two hundred middle-managers in 19 Australian firms/organizations in private, public, and third sectors (e.g., NGOs) and their immediate supervisors participated in the study. The 200 middle-managers completed a survey job audit/survey

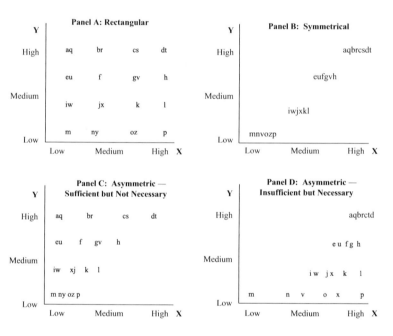

Figure 7. Illustrating the Contrarian Cases among 200 Executives Completing the Positive and Negative Affect Schedule (PANAS): Frequencies of Responses for PA and NA for 200 Managers. *Source*: Data for calculating the cross-tab provided by Peter Hosie from Hosie et al. (2006). *Notes*: (A) Contrarians 1: pa•na = people very happy and very unhappy (bi-polar) (10%); (B) Complements 1: pa•~na = people very happy and not unhappy (16%); (C) Complements 2: ~pa•na = people not happy and very unhappy (sad sacks) (18%); (D) Contrarians 2: ~pa•~na = people not happy and not unhappy (emotionless) (10%). Symmetric findings: phi = .46, *p* <.001.
Example membership (fuzzy-set) scores for PA•NA appear in parenthesis.

that the PANAS – "Positive and Negative Affect Schedule" (Watson, Clark, & Tellegen, 1988) associates with managers' job performances. Positive affect (PA) items in the scale include "enthusiastic," "interested," and "determined." Negative affect (NA) items include "scared," "afraid," "and "upset." Hosie et al. (2006, p. 129) point out that as traits, PA and NA are reflected in individual differences (also referred to as emotionality in the human resources literature).

Consider the following two points about contrarian cases in Figure 7. First, 10% percent of the 200 managers gave high positive responses on PA and high positive responses on NA; these managers support the proposal that contrarian cases occur in the study. The label, "conflicted" might be useful to assign to this first group of cases (i.e., 21 executives). Also, 11% of the 200 managers gave low negative responses on PA and low negative responses on NA; these managers also support the proposal that the study includes contrarian cases. The label, "emotionless" might be useful to assign to this second group of contrarian cases (i.e., executives). Contrarian cases include one in five respondents.

Second, a membership score for all the cases can be constructed for each contrarian case category. For example, one example of computing the membership score for conflicted executives (i.e., PA•NA) appears in parentheses for each cell of Figure 7. The membership scores are then useful as a screening ingredient for predicting an outcome condition or in estimating membership in the expression (e.g., PA•NA) and an outcome condition. Examples of theoretical and practical contributions of studying contrarian cases are available in the relevant literature (Feurer, Baumbach, & Woodside, 2016; Rauch, Deker, & Woodside, 2015). The study of contrarian cases support for idea that greater clarity and deeper understanding follows from learning the conditions cases score highly on a trait (e.g., PA) as well as high on a trait that is seemingly opposite (e.g., NA) to that first trait (as well as the reverse ~PA•~NA group of cases) – and using such scoring for both antecedent and outcome conditions.

Of course, cases much more likely to be expected do occur: high PA•~NA cases and high ~PA•NA cases; one-third of the 200 total managers are represented in one of these two types of expected cases. Doing such steps, quintile cross-tabulations and creating recipe conditions of "pure types" of case complements and contrarian cases, helps to clarify the influences of complex antecedent conditions and memberships in outcome conditions – such work builds on the earlier algorithm constructed work by McClelland (1998) and McClelland, Davis, Kalin, and Wanner (1972).

Bad Practice: Reporting Findings Using t, p, F, r, and R^2

Several independent sources of evidence (Anscombe, 1973; Armstrong, 2012; Soyer & Hogarth, 2012) support the conclusion that symmetric statistical test outputs are misleading even among the world's leading experts in econometrics (Soyer & Hogarth, 2012). Also, such indexes as t, p, F, r, and R^2 fail to answer the most pressing theoretical and practical question: Does a high (or low) score by the model predict accurately consistently outcomes in additional samples?

While shouting out misleading information, symmetric tests only hint at the possibility of useful information. "Anscombe's quartet" of different observable data displays for identical symmetric test findings is highly instructive in reaching this conclusion. Anscombe (1973) created four XY plots of four different data sets having the identical averages, standard deviations, and correlations to illustrate the great usefulness of showing relationships visually – such visual displays should be done before and/or after symmetric as well as asymmetrical testing.

Figure 8 presents Anscombe's quartet. Anscombe's (1973) presentation supports the value of reading Tufte's (2001), *The Visual Display of Quantitative Information*, and insuring use of XY plots in reporting findings from either symmetric or asymmetric tests. "Tufte" pops-up in a Google search for the "Leonardo da Vinci of data." The key point here is that the visual display of data is not only a useful pedagogical tool, visual display is a necessity frequently for accurate interpretation in performing data analysis.

Bad Practice: Focusing on Net Effects in Regression Models

Editors of all the ranked journals are likely to be guilty of accepting articles that focus on reporting net effects only. Such studies often focus on reporting standardized regression coefficients (βs)

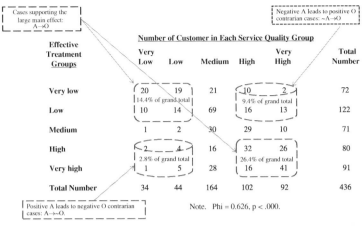

The following describes the data table within the figure:

	Number of Customer in Each Service Quality Group					
Effective Treatment Groups	**Very Low**	**Low**	**Medium**	**High**	**Very High**	**Total Number**
Very low	20	19	21	10	2	72
	14.4% of grand total			9.4% of grand total		
Low	10	14	69	16	13	122
Medium	1	2	30	29	10	71
High	2	4	16	32	26	80
	2.8% of grand total			26.4% of grand total		
Very high	1	5	28	16	41	91
Total Number	34	44	164	102	92	436

Cases supporting the large main effect: A→O

Negative A leads to positive O contrarian cases: ~A→O

Positive A leads to negative O contrarian cases: A→~O.

Note. Phi = 0.626, p < .000.

Key. A = antecedent condition (e.g., effective treatment); O = outcome condition (e.g., service quality).

Figure 8. Anscombe's Quartet of Different *XY* Plots of Four Data Sets Having Identical Averages, Variances, and Correlations. *Source:* Adapted from Anscombe (1973, pp. 19–20).

and describe the relative sizes of these estimates. Frequently these studies report βs for 5 to 30+ variables and claim that their studies control for moderator variables by including them in the regression models. These models frequently have a mix of statistically significant and non-significant ßs in the same models. Nearly all of these studies using regression analysis fail to consider the usefulness (i.e., the predictive accuracy of using an additional sample) such modeling provides. All these practices are bad in ways Armstrong (2012) discusses and this chapter describes earlier. More generally, focusing on net effects is usually a data symmetric analysis mismatch to the asymmetric (i.e., case screening) theory most researchers present earlier in their articles.

Good practice regarding reporting partial standardized regression coefficients (βs) begins with recognizing the these weights of influence can change substantially depending on how many variables appear in the models and the correlations among these variables (i.e., the occurrence of multi-collinearity). Due to multi-collinearity among the independent variables, frequently regression models with several variables can be constructed to show no significant terms (βs) with significant adjusted explained variances (R^2s). Good practices include limiting the number of terms in regression models to three terms as Armstrong (2012) suggests as well as eliminating the theory-analysis mismatch by including asymmetric analysis in the article as Fiss (2007) describes and others illustrate (Ordanini et al., 2014; Woodside, 2013).

Bad Practices: Relying on Verbal Self-Reports Only and Using Five- or Seven-Point Scale Responses to Measure Variables in Mental Processes

While continuing to appear pervasively in relevant journals, substantial evidence supports the general observation by Nisbett and Wilson (1977, p. 231), "... there may be little or no direct introspective access to higher order cognitive processes. Subjects are sometimes (a) unaware of the existence of a stimulus that importantly influenced a response, (b) unaware of the existence of the response, and (c) unaware that the stimulus has affected the response. It is proposed that when people attempt to report on their cognitive processes, that is, on the processes mediating the effects of a stimulus on a response, they do not do so on the basis of any true introspection. Instead, their reports are based on *a priori*, implicit causal theories, or judgments about the extent to which a particular stimulus is a plausible cause of a given response." Reviews (Bargh & Chartrand, 1999; Langer, 1978; Wegner, 2002; Wilson, 2004; Woodside, 2006; Zaltman, 2003) of many empirical studies since Nisbett and Wilson (1977) confirm and extend their general conclusion. Zaltman (2003, p. 9) proposes a great barrier on relying on answers to questions in surveys and generally, "Ninety-five percent of thinking takes place in our unconscious minds – that wonderful, if messy, stew[s] of memories, emotions, thoughts, and other cognitive processes we're not aware of or that we can't articulate."

While asking evaluation (assessment) questions of very recent experiences can provide useful information (e.g., student evaluations of professors and courses; TripAdvisor reports), asking respondents ex post process questions about how they came about making decisions (e.g., use of questioning methods in the "theory of reasoned action" (Ajzen, Albarracín, & Hornik, 2007) and "the theory of planned behavior" (Ajzen, 1991) is ill-advised even though still often done. An especially bad practice is relying on answers from asking one person per organizational unit a set of questions to explain an acceptance/rejection decision–or any other decision. A shift toward high accuracy is likely to occur by using multiple interviews in combination with collecting data independent from asking questions, that is, using unobtrusive and obtrusive data collection methods other than asking questions. Webb et al.'s (2000) lament and call for the use of data collection methods beyond asking questions is highly relevant now:

> Today, the dominant mass of social science research is based on interviews and questionnaires. We lament this overdependence upon a single, fallible method. Interviews and questionnaires intrude as a foreign element into the social setting they would describe, they create as well as measure attitudes, they elicit atypical roles and responses, they are limited to those who are accessible and will cooperate, and the responses obtained are produced in part by dimensions of individual differences irrelevant to the topic at hand. But the principal objection is that they are used alone. No research method is without bias. Interviews and questionnaires must be supplemented by methods testing the same social science variables but having different methodological weaknesses. (Webb, Campbell, Schwartz, & Sechrest, 2000, pp. 1–2)

The strength of using five-, six-, or seven-point scales about processes is that the resulting data are ready for computer analysis. The low substance in the data, the conversion and editing of thoughts to a number by a respondent, and the lack of meaningful information about the context relating to the answers are the telling weaknesses. The lack of depth and substance in reports of means and regressions models based on seven-point scales needs recognition – no wonder no one pays much attention to journal articles that report such findings. Mintzberg (1979) offers the following assessment of five- or seven-point scales in supporting his propositions for doing "direct research":

> [Reporting on thinking to himself] "Hmmmm … what have we here? The amount of control is 4.2, the complexity of environment, 3.6." What does it mean to measure the "amount of control" in an organization, or the "complexity" of its environment? Some of these concepts may be useful in describing organizations in theory, but that

does not mean we can plug them into our research holus bolus as measures. As soon as the researcher insists on forcing the organization into abstract categories — into his terms instead of its own — he is reduced to using perceptual measures, which often distort the reality. The researcher intent on generating a direct measure of amount of control or of complexity of environment can only ask people what they believe, on 7-point scales or the like. He gets answers, all right, ready for the computer; what he does not get is any idea of what he has measured. (What does "amount of control" [or "trust"] mean anyway?) The result is sterile description, of organizations as categories of abstract variables instead of flesh-and-blood processes. And theory building becomes impossible. (Mintzberg, 1979, p. 586)

Process studies by scholars working on "Consumer Culture Theory" (CCT) represent an improved research genre from attempts to use five- to seven-point scales to measure processes. CCT researchers rely on mixed methods to collect data that usually includes direct observations of processes occurring through time in natural contexts. CCT researchers never rely on verbal responses alone to understand and explain interactions of people, completion of tasks done in real-life, or thinking processes. CCT research is an application of contemporary anthropology to the study of buying/using/disposing behavior; go to http://consumerculturetheory.org/ for additional details. The Society of Applied Anthropology is a more general society that includes studies management/business anthropologists; go to http://community.sfaa.net/profiles/blogs/what-is-business-anthropology for additional details. Above all else, move beyond trying to explain and describe processes by using verbal reports only. Get out! Observe processes while they occur in contexts in real life (Woodside, 2011). A review article on why we should do, and how to do "research in a world without questions" is useful reading (Ewing & Pankauskas, 2012); this article is readily available via a Google.com search.

If you do plan on asking questions, first read, "Self-generated validity and other effects of measurement on belief, attitude, intention, and behavior" (Feldman & Lynch, 1988). Feldman and Lynch (1988) describe how respondents provide different answers based on what and how questions are asked and answered in the early parts of surveys. Also, reading Malle's

(2006) "Folk theory of mind" is a very helpful step if you plan on asking questions. Malle's (2006) theory explains and describes how people explain and describe behavior — his focus is **not** on the accuracy of such folk explanations and descriptions; his focus is on theory construction on the antecedents, contents, and outcomes of folk explanations. Both Feldman and Lynch (1988) and Malle (2006) are available by open access by doing a Google.com search.

Bad Practice: Not Studying Behavior Dynamically; Doing Only Cross-Sectional Survey Studies

Many PhD candidates may equate "doing a study" as asking a sample of respondents from a cross-section of a population to complete a questionnaire survey. Such surveys require respondents to interpret the questions asked, search their memories for information to answer, edit the depth and coverage of possible answers, select words to answer, decide to answer, and do this combination of steps in a blend of implicit and explicit thoughts. People's answers to questions about what they did stray frequently from their actual known behaviors even for innocuous behaviors as Nisbett and Wilson (1977) make clear. Woodside and Wilson (2002) report that one in four young, adult, customers buying seeds and plants by home delivery were inaccurate in their reporting their buying and non-buying behavior. Inaccuracy in reporting buying when they did not buy occurred twice as often among these customers versus inaccurately reporting non-buying among buyers. In the Woodside and Wilson study (2002) a brand equity metric toward the brand sponsoring the study was positive significantly among accurate buyers and inaccurate non-buyers but near zero for accurate non-buyers and inaccurate buyers.

Recognize that questionnaire survey-only research is usually bad practice if you wish to learn respondents' beliefs, experiences, and what they would do or have done recently or long ago. Try to take steps to overcome inaccurate answers to questionnaire surveys if you do use questionnaires that people are asked to answer. These steps can include asking the same persons the same and similar questions multiple times during the same and different occasions. Consider interviewing two-to-five persons in the same organization or household separately and then together using the same and similar questions, comparing their answers with them, and asking for clarifications and corrections are steps likely to increase accuracy and deepen explanations. Observing their behavior and asking for respondents to describe their behavior afterwards is likely to increase accuracy in subjective personal introspections in describing and explaining their behaviors. Cox (1967) includes the findings from interviewing two housewives for 18 times — one time each for 18 weeks. These interviews covered the same questions regarding buying in supermarkets and consumer product experiences at home. Both respondents stopped the interviews after 18 weeks not from boredom but from agitation about what they were learning about themselves and their families. If you let people talk long enough, they sometimes do tell you some useful information — a conclusion that echoes the adage, "How do I know what I think [feel] until I hear what I say?"

Bad Practice: Interviewing One Person per Group (Firm, Household, or Organization)

Do different people in the same organization (household) express the same responses to the same questions? Or, do their answers differ substantially? With a reasonably large number of groups, the researcher will be able to segment the groups by level of agreement (confirmation) of answers to questions asked. Then, case and/or variable-based data analysis/modeling can be done separately among group segments having low, medium, and high levels of intra-group answer agreements. The study by Cheng, Chang, and Li (2013) is a rare example of taking these steps in their case-based study of "configural paths to successful product innovation."

Here are the details of segmenting 68 high-tech firms by the level of agreement in responses to questions by Cheng et al. (2013). In order to ensure content validity, researchers collected information about each enterprise from multiple respondents ($n = 3$ per firm), including the R&D manager and other organizational members who were familiar with the product innovation project under study. The individual level responses were aggregated to the firm level by taking the average score within the firm. However, the dispersion of construct measurements (or the level of agreement between each respondent measure and his/her firm's measure on each construct) differed from one enterprise to another. For example, two sample companies report an average score of product innovation performance of 4.0. While the average score of 4.0 for one company may result from individual responses of 3.0 and 5.0, the average score for another one may result from individual responses of 1.0, 4.0, and 7.0. Even though these two companies have the same product innovation scores, the difference in dispersion indicates a reported difference in product innovation performance. The lesson of this example is that one should not treat companies with similar scores but different dispersions the same when examining complex antecedent paths to successful product innovation. To address this issue, the researchers computed standard deviations for firm-level variables to capture the level of agreement across multiple responses for a given firm. Sample companies were then separated into three clusters — high (34 firms), median (28 firms), and low (6 firms) agreement groups — according to the standard deviations of variables by two-stage cluster analysis. The high-agreement group is characterized by the lowest standard deviations for variables than other groups, indicating a higher level of agreement across multiple responses within a firm. Respondents of firms belonging to the low-agreement group had significantly variant perceptions about their firms' innovation efforts and outcomes.

The findings by Cheng et al. (2013) indicate reaching higher levels of consistencies in identifying complex antecedent paths to successful product innovations for the high-agreement answers among firms in comparison to the level of consistencies achieved among firms having medium and low levels of agreement. The Cheng et al. (2013) and the Ordanini et al. (2014) studies represent a substantial step beyond the perspective of "key success factors" (Cooper & Kleinschmidt, 2007) because these two recent studies identify several causal paths, comprising specific combinations of antecedents, to achieve successful product innovation. These findings support the perspective that an individual antecedent provides no guarantee in pursuit of successful product innovation — no one factor is a key to success and while more than one causal recipe or path may be sufficient to achieve successful product innovation, no factor is critical and no one path is necessary to take for success.

Good practice is interviewing two-to-five or more persons separately using the same set of questions. Consider using second and third rounds of asking questions separately of the same respondents to clarify responses and deepen knowledge about answers. Morgenroth (1964) completed 10 rounds of interviews of different persons in the same firm along with completing direct observations and document analyses in his iconic study of how executives in a firm make pricing decisions (Howard & Morgenroth,1968).

The bad practice of interviewing one person per organization/firm/household and relying only on this person's answers is a core ingredient in many research methods appearing in articles in scholarly journals. This bad practice likely has a dominant appearance among articles accumulating fewer than five citations in the ten years following their publications. Most articles in most-to-all business-related scholarly journals are likely to have fewer than five citations in the ten years following their publications. Though no study appears to be available to confirm that bad writing associates with low or high journal article impact, bad or good writing is unlikely to be the principal reason for low impact of journal articles; recipes of bad practices in theory construction, data collection, data analysis, and interpretation of findings are likely to be the causes of low journal article impact. Empirical dis/confirmation of this proposition is possible – doing such studies is the principal implication of this chapter for future research.

Bad Practice: Useable Response Rates Less Than 50% and Measuring Nonresponse Bias

A useable response rate of less than 30% is a modal characteristic for most questionnaire survey studies in business-related journals – a prime indicator of bad practice. Along with relying only on verbal responses to questions, reporting findings of questionnaire studies with response rates of less than 50% represent bad practice. To confirm that the low response rate in their studies do not damage the validity of the findings, the authors of such studies frequently mention using a procedure that Armstrong and Overton (1977) describe: compare the distribution of answers to the questions between waves of respondents in first, second, and/or third attempts to get sampled participants to respond. Invariably, the articles with low response rates (i.e., less than 50%) report that the distributions of demographic characteristics between first and second (and infrequently third) wave respondents do not differ significantly via statistical tests. However, Woodside and Ronkainen (1977) describe substantial differences in product category and brand use behavior among respondents to first, second, and third attempts to each sampled households among 14,000 + households – the focal issue is the impact of non-response bias on behavior with respect to the principal hypotheses of the study and not demographic profiles.

A bad practice useful for gaining low response rates (i.e., <50%) is to identify the brand sponsoring the study to households (firms/organizations) sponsoring the study. Doing so has the benefit of making the study's focal brand look good because the preference and behavior metrics for the focal brand will be higher among the respondents who do respond. Possibly, when reading the request to participate, persons who do respond might think, "I know the focal brand; I have used the focal brand; I will respond to the survey." Non-respondents are likely to include a higher share of people who think, "I may know the focal brand; I have not used the focal brand; I will not respond to the survey." Consequently, sponsor identity bias (i.e., mentioning the brand sponsoring the study in the request to answer the survey) is a bad practice that serves to reduce response rates but increase the favorability of responses toward the sponsoring brand. The findings from a meta-analysis of studies (Woodside & Dubelaar, 2003) which did versus did not identify a focal brand sponsoring the studies supports this conclusion.

Armstrong and Overton's (1977) observations relate to the obtainability of response rates above 50%, "The most commonly recommended protection against nonresponse bias has been the reduction of nonresponse itself. Nonresponse can be kept under 30% in most situations if appropriate procedures are followed" (they provide relevant sources earlier than 1977 supporting this conclusion). Dillman et al. (2014) is an exceptionally useful source for learning how to perform good practices necessary for high response rates. Relying principally on verbal answers to questionnaire surveys with a response rate of less than 50% are bad practices; they are ingredients likely to result in low journal article impact.

Bad Practice: Symmetric (Variable) Only Modeling

Symmetric (variable-focused) only modeling fails to recognize the occurrence of causal asymmetry, that is, the antecedents leading to low scores in an outcome are often not the mirror opposites of the antecedents leading to high scores. For example, the complex antecedent conditions relating to not being a heroin addict tells you little about the complex antecedent conditions of being a heroin addict. Case-based modeling of both outcome conditions is possible. The research should embrace the causal asymmetry tenet as well as the additional tenets of complexity theory (Woodside, 2014).

Symmetric relationships indicate the necessary and sufficient presence of an antecedent condition (a simple variable or a regression model). In real-life, necessary conditions appear in abundance. However, few necessary conditions are sufficient in causing an outcome of interest. A sufficient condition is usually a complex statement indicating the presence of a recipe of antecedent conditions. A sufficient condition is rarely necessary – multiple paths (recipes) occur frequently that lead to the same outcome; this tenet is the "equifinality principle."

Panel B among the four panels in Figure 9 illustrate the expectation for significant findings when testing using regression (symmetric) analysis. Panel C in Figure 9 illustrates the expectation for consistent findings using asymmetric (set-theoretic)

Positive (PA) Quintiles	Negative (NA) quintiles					
	1	2	3	4	5	Total
1 (Very low happy)	5 (.00)	2 (.00)	6 (.00)	10 (.00)	19 (.00)	42
2 (Low)	12 (.00)	2 (.10)	9 (.15)	6(.20)	4 (.30)	33
3 (Medium)	14 (.00)	7 (.15)	12 (.20)	6 (.30)	9 (.60)	48
4 (High)	11 (.00)	5 (.20)	7 (.30)	3 (.60)	1 (.90)	27
5 (Very high happy)	10 (.00)	6 (.30)	17(.60)	13 (.90)	4 (1.00)	50
Total	52	22	51	38	37	200 cases

Figure 9. Hypothetical Relationships Where *X* is a Complex Configural Condition (e.g., G, T, S, ~E) and *Y* is a Service Outcome Condition (e.g., *Y* = Heavy Beer Purchases). *Note*: Consider G = Gender (male =1); T = heavy TV watching; S = sports fan; ~E = less than high school education.

analysis. Panel D in Figure 9 illustrates a necessary but insufficient finding – that is, a high score in X is necessary for a high score in Y to occur but both low and high scores in Y occur with high scores in X. A major shortcoming in symmetric only analysis: explained variance is usually low in regression models because reality is rarely symmetric. A shortcoming in one model asymmetric analysis: one model that works well in identifying high Y scores may apply to only one case – a few asymmetric models are usually necessary to construct and identify a substantial number (to achieve moderate to high coverage) of cases with high Y scores. Asymmetric models provide deeper and richer descriptions and explanations of reality in comparisons with symmetric models; Ordanini et al. (2014) provide several empirical model comparisons supporting this conclusion.

Bad Practice: Using a Void-Treatment Control Group in Experiments; Not Using a Placebo Control Group

The two core requirements for a "true experiment" include a post-test-only two-group design with random assignment of participants to at least one treatment and one control group with the control group receiving a placebo treatment rather than the test treatment that is supposes to have an impact . The "test treatment" is an experience (e.g., taking an amount of a new drug greater than zero) that is expected to achieve a level of an outcome condition different from the members in the control group. In a true experiment the control group receives a placebo treatment, that is, what looks to be the same experience but without the actual substance expected to cause the focal outcome as part of the experience. Consider testing for the efficacy of a drug (e.g., Viagra for erectile dysfunction during sexual encounters). A "double-blind" procedure is typically used in testing the efficacy of a new drug: neither the person administering the drug to the patient nor the patient knows that if the patient is receiving the test treatment or placebo treatment (the placebo treatment is "sugar pill") medication. A "double-blind" procedure is attempting to insure that the participants do not know if they are receiving the experience containing the substance that the researcher believes will result in a specific outcome of interest (i.e. a focal outcome) – neither the participant receiving one of the test or placebo treatments are not permitted to be aware which drug they are receiving/administering.

Random assignment is done to achieve statistical equivalence for all variables for the two groups – especially likely to be achievable when each group has 50+ participants. At least 50 participants is recommended as one step to help build in sufficient statistical power to detect an effect that does exist in the outcomes between to two sets of participants – see Cohen (1977) and Sawyer and Ball (1981) for useful reports on achieving sufficient statistical power). Controlling for administering bias and additional "sources of invalidity" are the rationales for using a placebo and a blind procedure. A source of invalidity is the presence, occurrence, or absence of an occurrence that could have caused the focal outcome other than the treatment condition. Campbell and Stanley (1966) describe twelve sources of invalidity. With human and nonhuman participants a placebo treatment is preferable to administering a void treatment because the responses by both the experimenter and the participants receiving and not receiving a treatment may be due to the process of being measured or not being measured rather than to the treatment administration, that is, measurement reactivity is a possibly explanation of observed differences between the treatment and nocebo groups. A measurement reactivity effect is sometimes referred to as a "Hawthorne effect" (Landsberger, 1958) in reference to a series of lighting experiments during 1924–1932 at the Hawthorne Works (a Western Electric factory outside Chicago); no control group was included in the series of studies at the Wester Electric factory.

A researcher might consider using three groups in a true experiment to include test treatment, placebo control treatment, and void control treatment conditions in order to examine the effects of experiencing the giving/receiving the administration steps that occur in the study versus not experiencing these steps. This three group design could test the hypothesis that the responses by the participants in the group receiving the void treatment were lower than responses of participants in the placebo group which were lower than the responses by participants in the treatment group. Though the practice is widespread, using only a void treatment condition along with a test treatment condition and not using a placebo treatment along with the test treatment in an experiment is a fundamental (fatal to quality) flaw in an experiment.

While a formal study is necessary to support the claim, the bad practice of using a void treatment group rather than a placebo control group in field and laboratory experiments is observable frequently in current volumes of leading business, economics, and psychology journals and studies by highly experienced field experimenters. The following abstract of a recent field experiment by Duflo, Banerjee, Glennerster, and Kinnan (2013, p. 2) illustrates the use of a void treatment control rather than a placebo treatment control group:

This paper reports on the first randomized evaluation of the impact of introducing the standard microcredit group-based lending product in a new market. In 2005, half of 104 slums in Hyderabad, India were randomly selected for opening of a branch of a particular microfinance institution (Spandana) while the remainder were [sic: was] not, although other MFIs were free to enter those slums. Fifteen to 18 months after Spandana began lending in treated areas, households were 8.8 percentage points more likely to have a microcredit loan [than the control areas]. They were no more likely to start any new business, although they were more likely to start several at once, and they invested more in their existing businesses. There was no effect on average monthly expenditure per capita. Expenditure on durable goods increased in treated areas, while expenditures on "temptation goods" declined. Three to four years after the initial expansion (after many of the control slums had started getting credit from Spandana and other MFIs), the probability of borrowing from an MFI in treatment and comparison slums was the same, but on average households in treatment slums had been borrowing for longer and in larger amounts. Consumption was still no different in treatment areas, and the average business was still no more profitable, although we find an increase in profits at the top end. We found no changes in any of the development outcomes that are often believed to be affected by microfinance, including health, education, and women's empowerment. The results of this study are largely consistent with those of four other evaluations of similar programs in different contexts.

An example of a placebo treatment would have been to open Spandana branches in the 52 slums with these additional branches (the placebo control group) providing information only on securing microcredit loans without actually offering loans. Attempting to control for possible spill-over influences by using three treatments with MFIs making loans in 30 slums, an additional 30 placebo MFIs providing information only in 30 additional slums, and 44 slums in a void treatment condition with these void treatment areas first randomly assigned between the two types of MFIs.

The primary recommendation here is to insure that you use random assignment of participants to either a placebo or test treatment condition. If you do test a void treatment to measure for some of the sources of invalidity, you still need to test for experimenter procedure biases using a placebo treatment. A study reporting on the use of void treatment versus placebo treatment in field and laboratory experiments in 10–20 leading journals in business sub-disciplines is a suggestion for future research.

Marketing field experiments focus on the core issue in the discipline: Did the execution of a marketing treatment condition cause an observable impact that would not have occurred if the participants in the study had experienced a placebo treatment condition. The researcher needs to be able to eliminate rival hypotheses of explanations to the observed difference in out-comes between test treatment group and placebo treatment group. Rival hypotheses are explanations other than the partici-pants experiencing the test treatment versus the placebo treat-ment. Famously, Campbell and Stanley (1963) describe seven categories of rival hypotheses:

(1) History: Events, other than the experimental treatments, influence results;
(2) Maturation: during the study, psychological changes occur within subjects;
(3) Testing: exposure to a pretest or intervening assessment influences performance on a posttest; instrumentation;
(4) Testing instruments or conditions are inconsistent; or pret-est and posttest are not equivalent, creating an illusory change in performance;
(5) Statistical regression: scores of subjects that are very high or very low tend to regress towards the mean during retesting;
(6) Selection: systematic differences exist in subjects' character-istics between treatment groups; experimental mortality:

(7) Subject attrition may bias the results;
(8) Diffusion of treatments: implementation of one condition influences subjects in another condition.

Campbell and Stanley (1963) is a must-read book (originally published as a chapter in a handbook on research in education) for improving skills in doing research. In its various published versions, the chapter and book versions of Campbell and Stanley (1963) have received more than 25,000 citations (470 + citations annually) in the behavioral science literature. Campbell and Stanley (1963) continues be read and highly cited because of the profound wisdom and details in the book on how to do true and quasi-experiments well. A true experiment is a study that meets the two requirements of thwarting the seven sources of rival hypotheses: (1) the use of a test treatment condition and a placebo control treatment and (2) random assignment of participants to one of the two conditions before the administration of the conditions. Various quasi-experiments are attempts to measure the impact of test treatment condition in naturally occurring conditions without the ability of using random assignment. Another old but highly readable and useful source on how to do field experiments is the book by Banks (1965). This source is particularly useful for marketing scholars but the worked numerical examples of various true experimental designs makes Banks (1965) highly readable and useful for scholars in all management sub-disciplines.

Work by scholars who do not include placebo treatment conditions with random assignments of participants to conditions suffers from one or more of these rival hypotheses, especially the fourth rival hypothesis. The study by Duflo et al. (2013) includes the presence of one or more rival hypotheses. By using a void treatment condition for the control group, the fourth rival hypothesis that Campbell and Stanley (1963) describe is present in the Duflo et al. (2013). A testing (Hawthorne) effect is present in the study; residents just recognizing (consciously or non-consciously) the presence of a new firm in the slums in the half of the 104 slums in Hyderabad, India that were randomly selected for opening of a branch of a particular microfinance institution (Spandana) versus the remainder was not could be the principal cause of observed differences between the two groups versus the participants taking action to receive loans in the test versus the void treatment conditions.

Bad Practice: Doing Laboratory Experiments Only; Not Doing Field Experiments

Just telling participants to behave in the study as you would behave in your real-life does not substitute for the need to do unobtrusive field experiments (cf. List, 2001). List (2001, p. 1505) observes, "Hypothetical bias' is the difference that we continually see in the way people respond to hypothetical auctions [and lab experiments in general] as compared to real auctions [true field experiments] …" just like the overbidding example that he List (2001) presents. The use of students and other participants with paper-and-pencil instructions in laboratory provides data that relates poorly to field experiments performed real-life contexts; this observation summarizes research and the review by Levitt and List (2007, 2008). Ariely (2008, 2009) and List (201, 2002a, 2002b) are prolific and highly cited scholars in behavioral economics (a sub-discipline that marketing scholars would identify as "marketing experimentation").

Bad Practice: Use of Mushy (Soft, Squishy) Questions to Measure Thinking and Behavior; Failure to Collect/Report Real-Life Contextual Data

By their use of questionnaire surveys, most researchers appear to assume implicitly that respondents can accurately describe what they have done and what they will do – and why. However, the evidence does not support this assumption (Ariely, 2009; Bargh & Chartrand, 1999; Cialdini, 2008; Ewing & Pankauskas, 2012; Nisbett & Wilson, 1977; Webb et al., 2000; Wegner, 2002; Wilson, 2004). Using scaled items measuring importance, trust, anxiety, stress, intentions, plans, reasoned actions, perceptions, beliefs, attitudes, and a host of additional variables alone contributes to the low impact of scholarly research. Cialdini (2010) asks, "Why don't we just cut to the chase? Why do we examine those things that are bridges and links of an imperfect sort to behavior when we can study behavior itself?"

Consider taking a small step toward realism by using "behavioroid" measures rather than scaled responses of intentions. Behavioroid measures ask participants to make a commitment to actions that relates to the study even when the commitments are not going to be actually done. For example, "If we are able to provide free samples to participants, may I send a free sample to your address this month? Yes ( ) No ( ) Other ( ). If yes, please provide your telephone number or mailing address here." Behavioroid measures approximate behavior by assessing a person's commitment to perform a behavior without actually completing the behavior (Kite, 1992).

For the study of actual behavior, at least three routes are available for the taking: contemporary ethnography/anthropology studies such as the studies by members of the "Consumer Culture Theory" (CCT) organization (http://consumerculturetheory.org/) and the management anthropology (Mintzberg, 1975; Van Maanen, 2011; Whyte, 1984); laboratory and field experiments (Ariely, 2008; Harrison & List, 2004; Levitt & List, 2007); and physiological theory and methods including neuroscience tools (Ambler, Brautigam, Stins, Rose, & Swithenby, 2004; Kenning & Plassmann, 2008) and context metrics (Webb et al., 2000).

Consider the following thoughts on breaking away from collecting data using mushy verbal responses to scaled questions. Scholars working as instructors, lecturers, and professors need to solve the conundrum of teaching courses and fulfilling work-related service commitments versus getting into real-life field settings to conduct useful research. Reading brilliant studies using true experiments' performance in natural settings (Ariely, 2008; Cialdini, 2008) and studies by members of CCT are helpful steps in learning the theory and developing the skills necessary to go beyond using only questionnaire surveys.

Regarding contexts and building on Weick's (1979, p. 261) challenge to "complicate yourself," Woodside (2011) advocates, "Get out, get in!" Simon's (1990) scissors' metaphor about thinking and the environment supports the need to collect thick descriptions of real-world contexts. Simon (1990) expresses the occurrence of a loose coupling between mind and world: a pair of scissors whose two blades are the characteristics of the task environment and the computational capabilities of the decision maker shapes bounded rationality. "Here, the mind must fit closely to the environment, but the two are complementary, rather than mirror images" (Todd and Gigerenzer, 2001).

Bad Practice: The Study of One Dependent/Outcome Variable at a Time

Most studies in finance, management, marketing, and additional business sub-disciplines examine one dependent model per regression model. In finance, net income before interest and taxes by sales (ROS) is frequently used as a dependent variable separately from using net income before interest and taxes by assets (ROA). For example, in a study, "Do Buyouts (Still) Create Value?" that constructs advocacy hypotheses and applies symmetric tests, Guo, Hotchkiss, and Song (2011) via a regression model with 14 main terms plus additional dummy variables for years to predict values for ROS and ROA separately with most variables in the regression models being non-significant. Guo et al. (2011) report inaccurately that they control for deal size by including a term for capital (ln capital); the authors focus their analysis on the relative size of the effects of terms in their regression models. However, along with miss matching theory and data analysis, violating Armstrong's (2012) tenet of using a maximum of three terms in regression models, not reporting a correlation matrix of all variables, not consider modeling cases where buyouts destroy value, and believing that moderating variables are controlled by adding terms for additional variables into a regression model, Guo et al. (2011) could have advanced theory and data analysis by constructing conjunctive outcome conditions of ROS and ROA rather than modeling each separately. Such conjunctive construction and testing includes asymmetrical testing of four sets of cases: firms with high ROS and ROA (ROS•ROA), firms with high ROS and low ROA (ROS•~ROA), firms with low ROS and high ROA (~ROS•ROA), and firms low in both ROS and ROA (~ROS•~ROA).

Rather than continuing the current bad practice of modeling single outcomes only, greater use of constructing and testing theories with conjunctive outcomes would advance useful theory. For example, constructing and testing formal complex antecedent conditions of market share and profit outcomes conjoined as a single outcome enables testing of Simon's hypotheses regarding causal recipes explaining "hidden champion" firms — small market share (~MS) firms producing high profits (ROS): ~MS•ROS. Such an approach enables pinpoint modeling and generalizing of causal antecedent paths to explain firms with high market share and high losses (MS•~ROS) as well as additional complex outcome conditions.

Bad Practice: Advocacy Hypothesis Construction and Testing

Reviewing the three plus articles per day submissions to the *JBR* and cursory examinations of the A*, A, B, and C ranked journal (ABDC, 2014) in business-related sub-disciplines supports the observation that the majority of articles consider one theory and make use of advocacy hypothesis. This observation needs confirmation by a formal meta-analysis; however, the findings that Armstrong, Brodie, and Parsons (2001) appear to be accurate now.

> Our review of empirical studies on scientific methodology suggests that the use of a single dominant hypothesis lacks objectivity relative to the use of exploratory and competing hypotheses approaches. We then conducted a publication audit of over 1,700 empirical papers in six leading marketing journals during 1984–1999. Of these, 74% used the dominant hypothesis approach, while 13% used multiple competing hypotheses, and 13% were exploratory. Competing hypotheses were more commonly used for studying methods (25%) than models (17%) and phenomena (7%). Changes in the approach to hypotheses since 1984 have been modest; there was a slight decrease in the percentage of competing hypotheses to 11%, which is explained primarily by an increasing proportion of papers on phenomena. Of the studies based on hypothesis testing, only 11% described the conditions under which the hypotheses would apply, and dominant hypotheses were below competing hypotheses in this regard. (Armstrong et al., 2001, p. 171)

Additional scholars advocate the presentation of alternative theories and the testing of completing hypotheses explicitly and implicitly. Sternthal, Tybout, and Calder (1987) describe testing rival theories, that is, doing a "comparative theory test"; Carlsmith, Ellsworth, and Aronson (1976) describe such steps as performing a "critical test." While not identifying the step explicitly as testing alternative theories, in his famous reversal from negative to positive judgments about the value of case studies, Campbell (1975) calls for comparing the performances of alternative theories by using a "degrees of freedom test" of the relative presence of characteristics of competing theories in a specific case – a generalizing to theory approach to case study research.

Using total citations as a noticing metric, these calls for moving beyond using advocacy hypotheses have received considerable attention; by mid-September 2015, Google.com/scholar citations for Armstrong et al. (2001) was 88 citations; Carlsmith et al. (1976), 273 citations; Sternthal et al. (1987), 83 citations; and Campbell (1975), 1,231 citations. However, a substantial majority of published studies in all four journal rank categories for business-related journals continue to embrace the use of advocacy hypotheses only. Armstrong et al. (2001) present evidence in a survey of marketing scientists indicating a strong preference for the use of testing competing hypotheses versus a dominant hypothesis approach or exploratory testing. Woodside and Baxter (2015) provide an example of a critical test of three competing theories of how interfirm social bonding impacts suppliers' allocations of resources to business customers: imprinting, honeymooning, or maturing.

Bad Practice: Stepwise Regression Analysis

Using stepwise regression analysis suggests that the researcher senses a useful model that may pop-up from the data but that s/he is unsure as to its contents. The researcher implicitly recognizes that a substantial amount of multi-collinearity is likely present among the independent terms especially if s/he is including 5–25 or more terms in the expressing the model. Implicitly as well the focus is on viewing the variables in the model as competing against each other for identification in a place of importance among a final statement of an empirical model. Of course, significantly high correlations will nearly always occur with the inclusion of several variables in a regression model. Because of high levels of multi-collinearity, a seemingly non-significant term in a regression equation can become significant with the removal of a significant term in an equation that has a correlation with the seemingly non-significant term. The net effects of terms in a regression equation often change substantially with the inclusion and removal of other terms in the equation.

Stepwise regression analysis is an exploratory procedure that employs a symmetric search algorithm that fits the purpose well of exploratory research. Armstrong's (2012) direction is worth taking, ("… do not use regression to search for causal relationships, and do not try to predict by using variables that were not specified in the *a priori* analysis. Thus, avoid data mining, stepwise regression, and related methods.") "Also, do not try to estimate relationships for more than three variables in a regression (the findings of Goldstein & Gigerenzer, 2009; are consistent with this rule-of-thumb)" (Armstrong, 2012, p. 690).

The mindless use of software in model construction-testing is possible with fsQCA as well. As with stepwise regression analysis, the analysis software command in fsQCA brings forth all possible models which offer high consistency in accurately identifying high membership scores in an outcome (*Y*) condition with few to no low scores for *Y* occurring when these complex antecedent conditions have high scores. The researcher should carefully specify *a priori* at least some of the complex models which should have such high consistencies for *Y* and for ~*Y*.

Bad Practice: Failure to Plan to Include a Replication in the Study or to Invite Other Scholars to Attempt to Replicate Findings

While "vital" is a word overused, independent replications of significant and non-significant findings are vital for confirming the consistency of earlier findings. Are the original findings reproducible? The tendency for a community of scholars is to reject radically new findings (Armstrong & Collopy, 1996; Gigerenzer & Brighton, 2009) without a fair hearing — performing and reporting replications is the best procedure for holding a fair hearing. Hubbard and Armstrong (1994) provide the following useful definitions. A "replication" is defined as a duplication of a previously published empirical study that is concerned with assessing whether similar findings can be obtained upon repeating the study. Likewise, a "replication with extension" is a duplication of a previously published empirical research project that serves to investigate the ability to generalize earlier research findings.

Findings exciting or otherwise can be one-off events for a variety and combination of reasons: random surprising events sometimes appear to be as systematic information; the failure of analytical tools to measure accurately; the lack of skill and inability of the researcher to use measurement tools accurately, and dishonesty and lying. A macro review of three meta-analyses of comparisons of findings from original and independent replicated studies indicates that failure to confirm original core findings occurred partially/fully in the majority of studies (Evanschitzky, Baumgarth, Hubbard, & Armstrong, 2007). Where major conflicts between original and new studies occur, attempting to replicate is fertile ground for future research.

While Evanschitzky et al. (2007, p. 412) identify the *JBR* as performing best among five marketing-related journals in terms of publishing replication studies, the number of such studies in the *JBR* is still a meager meal, "A comparatively brighter picture emerged when analyzing the incidence of replications featured in the *Journal of Business Research*, whose editorial policy is sympathetic toward such work. Of the 861 empirical articles published in JBR between 1990 and 2004, 2.8% were replications with extensions, a figure marginally higher than H&A's (Hubbard & Armstrong, 1994) 2.4% (Table 1)." Evanschitzky et al. (2007) offer several useful suggestions for nurturing the growth of replications; taking time to read and apply these suggestions is worth the effort by authors and editors. Authors encouraging replication studies to their original works is one way of nurturing impact of the original study; such encouraging steps include making the data and codes of the original study available to all and inviting other scholars to ask for such information (Evanschitzky et al., 2007; Gleditsch, Petter, & Strand, 2003). However, authors of original studies are more prone not to provide data when asked (Hubbard & Little, 1997) possibly out of fear of being made to look bad if other authors find major flaws in theory, data analysis, and/or fail to replicate the findings in the original studies. Being ignored and achieving scant impact are dangers infrequently.

The contribution of a study increases when the authors build in their own replications. Such built-in self-replications are useful though not sufficient as substitutes for replications performed independently. Testing theory and specific hypotheses with additional samples provides the means for cross-validating the usefulness of MRA or fsQCA models. Unfortunately, cursory examinations of ranked journals in business-related sub-disciplines indicates the inclusion of cross-validation evidence occur rarely.

Bad Practice: Including Non-Significant Terms in Regression Models

Most researchers report MRA models that include non-significant terms to show that "control variables" do or do not reduce the influence of the main independent variables (MDVs) that are the focus of their studies. The practice is bad. First, if a term is non-significant in a regression model, its lack of influence on the dependent variable (DV) may be due to the distributions of values among the other terms in the model and not due to the linear or other proposed relationships among the independent variables. Second, only true experiments (random assignment and the use of treatment and placebo control groups control for the effects of control variables (Armstrong, 2012). If a researcher reports an MRA model with lots of terms, a frequent outcome is none of the terms have significant betas (standardized partial regression coefficients) and yet the model explains a significant amount of total variance in the DV. A better practice: create quintiles of the DV and 2–5 independent variables. Create and tests theories that focus on building and testing algorithms or test the theory asymmetrically via fsQCA.

Bad Practice: Using Median Splits

McClelland (1998) calls for thinking in quintiles and creating theory building from algorithms based on the top/bottom 20% of cases for continuous variables. McClelland's (1998) reasoning: data are noisy; cases closer to the ends of distributions often clarify tests of theories. Also, the near pervasive occurrence of contrarian cases become visible if the researcher creates and cross-tabulates variables by quintiles. The necessity of modeling contrarian cases has yet to become revealed to most researchers (i.e., to defenders of using median splits, e.g., Iacobucci, Posovac, Kardes, Schneider, & Popovich, 2015) and even among researchers who recognize that "death to dichotomizing" is correct (McClelland, Lynch, Jr., Irwin, Spiller, & Fitzsimmons, 2015; Rucker, McShane, and Preacher, 2015). Rucker et al.'s (2015, p. 666) conclusion and recommendation are dead wrong, "We show that dichotomizing a continuous variable via the median split procedure or otherwise and analyzing the resulting data via ANOVA involves a large number of costs that can be avoided by preserving the continuous nature of the variable and analyzing the data via linear regression. As a consequence, we recommend that regression remain the normative procedure both when the statistical assumptions explored by Iacobucci et al. hold and more generally in research involving continuous variables." Do think algorithms, doe discretize continuous variables or use fussy-set calibrations, do not use median splits. A researcher can substantially increase the quality of theory and information extracted from data by discretizing continuous variables and constructing algorithm models of outcomes that support and are contrarian to simple main effects hypotheses.

Researchers usually state "main effect" hypotheses in directional (symmetrical) formats; for example, X has a positive relationship with Y in that low X associates with low Y and high X associates with high Y. With reasonably large sample sizes ($n \geq 100$), discretizing both X and Y into quintiles (lowest 20%, low 20%, medium 20%, high 20%, and highest 20% of values) and cross-tabulating the X and Y quintiles results in cases appearing in all 25 cells in the cross-tab for almost all X and Y variables — even when the correlation for the two continuous variables is high (e.g., $r^2 \geq .30$. Figures 5 and 7 in this chapter illustrate this point. Thus, most data display four principal X-Y relationships: $\sim X \bullet \sim Y$, $\sim X \bullet Y$, $X \bullet \sim Y$, and $X \bullet Y$. Theoretical and empirical examinations of all four relationships are possible and valuable to do rather focuses only on the symmetric perspective of the first ($\sim X \bullet \sim Y$) and fourth ($X \bullet Y$) relationships.

Conclusion

Most articles in likely all of the scholarly journals in business-related sub-disciplines achieve scant impact. Most articles in business-related journal articles are ignored by scholars in these disciplines, the business press, and the wider general public. The underlying premise of this chapter is that the presence of one to a dozen or more recognizable bad practices are present in each of most articles in these leading journals and the presence of these bad practices contribute to their lack of impact. Many of these bad practices are well-known but they are still practiced widely.

Certain partially formal organizations of scholars rebel against the use of certain bad practices — such as CCT members direct observations of behavior in real-world contexts and rarely using verbal scaled responses as well as behavioral economists' use of true experiments performed in real-life field contexts as their preferred method for data collection. The evidence is overwhelming that verbal reports of human processes and behavioral outcomes is frequently inaccurate and unreliable; while relatively easy to collect via questionnaire surveys, scaled responses to describing such processes to measure the associations among beliefs, attitudes, intentions, and behavior are useful for developing a folk theory of mind (Malle, 2006) but for purposes of reporting on real-life processes, such studies are closer to rubbish rather than accurate indicators of real-life behavior. This conclusion may be recognized implicitly by readers of article in business-related journals. Readers know that accurate information on what happened and the actual antecedents of what happened, or the thinking processes at the time of the event, are not going to found by reading these articles.

While Bargh and Chartrand (2000) do not cite Nisbett and Wilson's (1977) iconic earlier study on the same topic, the title of Bargh and Chartrand's (2000) essay, "the unbearable automaticity of being," comes close to matching perfectly with Nisbett and Wilson's (1977, p. 257) closing sentence, "It is frightening to believe that one has no more certain knowledge of the workings of one's own mind than would an outsider with intimate knowledge of one's history and of the stimuli present at the time the cognitive process occurred." An additional bad practice is the failure to identify iconic studies relevant to your more recent work; for example, even though Nisbett and Wilson's essay (1977) has achieved 9,200 + citations and the essay is on the same topic and offers similar conclusions as that of Bargh and Chartrand's (2000) essay (3,200 + citations), discussion of Nisbett and Wilson (1977) is missing in the Bargh and Chartrand (200) essay.

The objective of the present chapter is not to name names or blame individuals but to propose that (1) bad practices are pervasive in journal articles in business-related sub-disciplines and that (2) these bad practices contribute to the lack of impact of most articles in these journals. If anyone is to blame, the blame should rest with thesis supervisors, PhD dissertation chairs, and journal editors for not nurturing good practices among postgraduate students and early career colleagues. Also, the proposal here is that good practices are available and recognizable. For doing useful research and achieving impact, the time has come to recognize and reject the use of bad practices and embrace the use of good practices.

References

ABDC. (2013). *Australian business deans council journal quality list 2013*. Retrieved from http://www.abdc.edu.au/pages/abdc-journal-quality-list-2013.html. Accessed on September 18, 2016.

ABDC. (2014). *Australian business Deans' council*. Retrieved from http://www.abdc.edu.au/

Ajzen, I. (1991). The theory of planned behavior. *Organizational Behavior and Human Decision Processes*, 50(2), 179–211.

Ajzen, I., Albarracín, D., & Hornik, R. (2007). *Prediction and change of health behavior: Applying the theory of reasoned action approach*. Mahwah, NJ: Lawrence Erlbaum.

Ambler, T., Brautigam, S., Stins, J., Rose, S., & Swithenby, S. (2004). Salience and choice: Neural correlates of shopping decisions. *Psychology & Marketing*, 21, 247–261.

Anscombe, F. J. (1973). Graphs in statistical analysis. *American Statistician*, 27, 17–21.

Ariely, D. (2008). *Predictably irrational: The hidden forces that shape our decisions*. New York, NY: HarperCollins.

Ariely, D. (2009). *Are we in control of our own decisions?* TED Conference. Retrieved from http://www.ted.com/talks/dan_ariely_asks_are_we_in_control_of_our_own_decisions?language=en. Accessed on September 14, 2015.

Ariely, D. (2010). *Predictable irrationality*. New York, NY: Harper Perennial.

Armstrong, J. S. (1970). How to avoid exploratory research. *Journal of Advertising Research*, 10(4), 27–30.

Armstrong, J. S. (1980). Unintelligible management research and academic prestige. *Interfaces*, 10, 80–86.

Armstrong, J. S. (2012). Illusions in regression analysis. *International Journal of Forecasting*, 28, 689–694.

Armstrong, J. S., Brodie, R. J., & Parsons, A. G. (2001). Hypotheses in marketing science: Literature review and publication audit. *Marketing Letters*, 12, 171–187.

Armstrong, J. S., & Collopy, F. (1996). Competitor orientation: Effects of objectives and information on managerial decisions and profitability. *Journal of Marketing Research*, 23, 188–199.

Armstrong, J. S., & Overton, T. S. (1977). Estimating nonresponse bias in mail surveys. *Journal of Marketing Research*, 14, 396–402.

Banks, S. (1965). *Marketing experimentation*. New York, NY: McGraw-Hill.

Bargh, J. A., & Chartrand, T. L. (1999). The unbearable automaticity of being. *American Psychologist*, *54*, 462–479.

Bargh, J., & Chartrand, T. (2000). The unbearable automaticity of being. *American Psychologist*, *54*, 462–479.

Bass, F. M., Tigert, D. J., & Lonsdale, R. T. (1968). Market segmentation: Group versus individual behavior. *Journal Marketing Research*, *5*, 264–270.

Brighton, H., & Gigerenzer, G. (2015). The bias bias. *Journal of Business Research*, *68*, 1772–1784.

Campbell, D. T. (1975). Degrees of freedom in the case study. *Comparative Political Studies*, *8*, 178–193.

Campbell, D. T., & Stanley, J. C. (1963). Experimental and quasi-experimental designs for research on teaching. In N. L. Gage (Ed.), *Handbook of research on teaching* (pp. 171–246). Chicago, IL: Rand McNally. Also published as a separate, Experimental and quasi-experimental designs for research, Chicago, IL: Rand McNally, 1966. Retrieved from http://moodle.technion.ac.il/pluginfile.php/367640/mod_resource/content/1/Donald_T._%28Donald_T._Campbell%29_Campbell,_Julian_Stanley-Experimental_and_Quasi-Experimental_Designs_for_Research-Wadsworth_Publishing%281963%29%20%281%29.pdf

Campbell, D. T., & Stanley, J. C. (1966). *Experimental and quasi-experimental designs for research*. Boston, MA: Houghton Mifflin. Retrieved from http://moodle.technion.ac.il/pluginfile.php/219643/mod_resource/content/0/Campbell_and_Stanley_1963.pdf

Carlsmith, J. M., Ellsworth, P. C., & Aronson, E. (1976). *Methods of research in social psychology*. Reading, MA: Addison-Wesley.

Cheng, C.-F., Chang, M.-L., & Li, C.-S. (2013). Configural paths to successful product innovation. *Journal of Business Research*, *66*, 2561–2573.

Cialdini, R. B. (2008). *Influence: Science and practice*. Boston, MA: Allyn and Bacon.

Cialdini, R. B. (2010). *Quote in the business of choice*. M. Willcox (Vol. 2015, p. 3). Upper Saddle, NJ: Pearson.

Cohen, J. (1977). *Statistical power analysis for the behavioral sciences*. NewYork, NY: Academic Press.

Cooper, R. G., & Kleinschmidt, E. J. (2007). *Winning businesses in product development: The critical success factors*. Research-Technology Management. Retrieved from http://www.proddev.com/downloads/working%20papers/wp_6.pdf. Accessed on May 6, 2012.

Cox, D. F. (1967). Risk handling in consumer behavior-an intensive study of two cases. In D. F. Cox (Ed.), *Risk taking & information handling in consumer behavior* (pp. 34–81). Boston, MA: Harvard University Press.

Czerlinski, J., Gigerenzer, G., & Goldstein, D. G. (1999). How good are simple heuristics? In G. Gigerenzer, P. M. Todd, & the ABC Research Group (Eds.), *Simple heuristics that make us smart* (pp. 97–118). New York, NY: Oxford University Press.

Dillman, D. A., Smyth, J. D., & Christian, L. M. (2014). *Internet, phone, mail, and mixed-mode surveys: The tailored design method*. New York, NY: Wiley.

Duflo, E., Banerjee, A., Glennerster, R., & Kinnan, C. G. (2013). *The miracle of microfinance? Evidence from a randomized evaluation.* Working Paper No. 18950. Retrieved from http://www.nber.org/papers/w18950

Eskin, G. J., & Baron, P. H. (1977). Effects of price and advertising in test-market experiments. *Journal of Marketing Research, 14,* 499–508.

Evanschitzky, H., Baumgarth, C., Hubbard, R., & Armstrong, J. S. (2007). Replication research's disturbing trend. *Journal of Business Research, 60*(4), 411–415.

Ewing, T., & Pankauskas, B. (2012). *Research in a world without questions.* ESOMAR Congress presentation. Retrieved from http://media.brainjuicer.com/media/files/ESOMAR_Congress_2012_Research_in_a_World_Without_Questions_1.pdf

Feldman, J. M., & Lynch, J. G., Jr. (1988). Self-generated validity and other effects of measurement on belief, attitude, intention, and behavior. *Journal of Applied Psychology, 73,* 421–435.

Feurer, S., Baumbach, E., & Woodside, A. G. (2016). Applying configurational theory to build a typology of ethnocentric consumers. *International Marketing Review, 33,* 351–375.

Fiss, P. (2011). Building better causal theories: A fuzzy set approach to typologies in organization research. *Academy of Management Journal, 54,* 393–420.

Fiss, P. C. (2007). A set-theoretic approach to organizational configurations. *The Academy of Management Review, 32,* 1180–1198.

Fitzsimmons, G. J. (2008). Editorial: A death to dichotomizing. *Journal of Consumer Research, 35,* 5–8.

Gigerenzer, G. (1991). From tools to theories: A heuristic of discovery in cognitive psychology. *Psychological Review, 98,* 254–267.

Gigerenzer, G., & Brighton, H. (2009). Homo heuristics: Why biased minds make better inferences. *Topic in Cognitive Science, 1,* 107–143.

Gladwell, M. (2002). *The tipping point: How little things can make a big difference.* Boston, MA: Back Bay Books.

Gleditsch, N., Petter, M., & Strand, H. C. (2003). Posting your data: Will you be scooped or will you be famous? *International Studies Perspectives, 4,* 89–97.

Golder, P. N. (2000). Historical method in marketing research with new evidence on long-term market share stability. *Journal of Marketing Research, 37,* 156–172.

Goldstein, D. G., & Gigerenzer, G. (2009). Fast and frugal forecasting. *International Journal of Forecasting, 25,* 760–772.

Guo, S., Hotchkiss, E. S., & Song, W. (2011). Do buyouts (still) create value? *The Journal of Finance, 66,* 479–517.

Harrison, G. W., & List, J. A. (2004). Field experiments. *Journal of Economic Literature, 42,* 1009–1055.

Hartley, J., Trueman, M., & Meadows, A. J. (1988). Readability and prestige in scientific journals. *Journal of Information Science, 14,* 69–75.

Hofstede (2003). *Cultures' consequences.* Thousand Oaks, CA: Sage.

Hosie, P. J., Sevastos, P. P., & Cooper, C. L. (2006). *Happy-performing managers.* Cheltenham: Edward Elgar.

Howard, J. A., & Morgenroth, W. M. (1968). Information processing model of executive decision. *Management Science, 14*, 416–428.

Hsu, S.-Y., Woodside, A. G., & Marshall, R. (2013). Critical tests of multiple theories of cultures' consequences: Comparing the usefulness of models by Hofstede, Inglehart and Baker, Schwartz, Steenkamp, as well as GDP and distance for explaining overseas tourism behavior. *Journal of Travel Research, 52*, 679–704.

Hubbard, R., & Armstrong, J. S. (1994). Replications and extensions in marketing: Rarely published but quite contrary. *International Journal of Research in Marketing, 11*, 233–248.

Hubbard, R., & Little, E. L. (1997). Share and share alike? A review of empirical evidence concerning information sharing among researchers. *Manage Research News, 20*, 41–49.

Iacobucci, D., Posavac, S. S., Kardes, F. R., Schneider, M. J., & Popovich, D. L. (2015). Toward a more nuanced understanding of the statistical properties of a median split. *Journal of Consumer Psychology, 25*(1), 652–665

Inman, J. J. (2012). *Presidential address: The elephant not in the room—The need for useful, actionable insights in behavioral research* (Vol. 40, pp. 1–4). Vancouver, Canada: Association for Consumer Research. Advances in Consumer Research.

Kass, G. V. (1980). An exploratory technique for investigating large quantities of categorical data. *Applied Statistics, 29*, 119–127.

Kenning, P. H., & Plassmann, H. (2008). How neuroscience can inform consumer research. *IEEE Transactions on Neural Systems and Rehabilitation Engineering, 16*, 532–537.

Kite, M. E. (1992). Individual differences in males' reactions to gay males and lesbians. *Journal of Applied Social Psychology, 22*, 1222–1239.

Kotler, P. (1967). *Marketing management: Analysis, planning, and control.* Englewood Cliffs, NJ: Prentice-Hall.

Landsberger, H. A. (1958). *Hawthorne revisited, Cornell studies in industrial and labor relations* (Vol. IX). Ithaca, NY: Cornell University Press.

Langer, E. J. (1978). Rethinking the role of thought in social interaction. In J. H. Harvey, W. Ickes, & R. F. Kidd (Eds.), *New directions in attribution research* (Vol. 2, pp. 35–58). Hillsdale, NJ: Erlbaum.

Levitt, S. D., & List, H. A. (2007). What do laboratory experiments measuring social preferences reveal about the real world? *The Journal of Economic Perspectives, 21*, 153–174.

Levitt, S. D., & List, J. A. (2008). *Field experiments in economics: The past, the present, and the future.* Working Paper No. 14356. Cambridge, MA: National Bureau of Economic Research. Retrieved from http://www.nber.org/papers/w14356

List, J. A. (2001). Do explicit warnings eliminate the hypothetical bias in elicitation procedures? Evidence from field auctions for sportscards. *American Economic Review, 91*(5), 1498–1507.

List, J. A. (2002a). Preference reversals of a different kind: The more is less phenomenon. *American Economic Review, 92*(5), 1636–1643.

List, J. A. (2002b). Testing neoclassical competitive market theory in the field. *Proceedings of the National Academy of Science, 99*(24), 15827–15830.

Lutz, R. L. (1991). Editorial. *Journal of Consumer Research*, 17(4), i–iv.

Magidson, J. (1994). The CHAID approach to segmentation modeling: Chi-squared automatic interaction detection. In R. P. Bagozzi (Ed.), *Advanced methods of marketing research* (pp. 118–159). Oxford: Blackwell.

Malle, B. F. (2006). *How the mind explains behavior: Folk explanations, meaning, and social interaction*. London: Bradford Books.

McClelland, D. C. (1998). Identifying competencies with behavioral-event interviews. *Psychological Science*, 9, 331–339.

McClelland, D. C., Davis, W. N., Kalin, R., & Wanner, E. (1972). *The drinking man*. New York, NY: The Free Press.

McClelland, G. H., Lynch, J. G., Jr., Irwin, J. R., Spiller, S. A., & Fitzsimmons, G. J. (2015). Median splits, Type II errors, and false-positive consumer psychology: Don't fight the power. *Journal of Consumer Psychology*, 25, 679–689.

McClelland, J. L. (2009). The place of modeling in cognitive science. *Topics in Cognitive Science*, 1, 11–38.

Mick, D. G. (2006). Presidential address: Meaning and mattering through transformative consumer research. In C. Pechmann & L. Price (Eds.), *NA—Advances in consumer research* (Vol. 33, pp. 1–4). Provo, UT: Association for Consumer Research.

Mintzberg, H. (1975). The manager's job: Folklore and fact. *Harvard Business Review*, 53, 49–61.

Mintzberg, H. (1979). An emerging strategy of "direct" research. *Administrative Science Quarterly*, 24(4), 582–589.

Morgenroth, W. M. (1964). A method for understanding price determinants. *Journal of Marketing Research*, 1, 17–26.

Nisbett, R. E., & Wilson, T. D. (1977). Telling more than we can know: Verbal reports on mental processes. *Psychological Review*, 84, 231–259. Retrieved from http://people.virginia.edu/~tdw/nisbett&wilson.pdf

Ordanini, A., Parasuraman, A., & Rubera, G. (2014). When the recipe is more important than the ingredients: A qualitative comparative analysis (QCA) of service innovation configurations. *Journal of Service Research*, 17, 134–149.

Pant, P. N., & Starbuck, W. H. (1990). Innocents in the forest: Forecasting and research methods. *Journal of Management*, 16, 433–446.

Pham, M. T. (2013). The seven sins of consumer psychology. *Journal of Consumer Psychology*, 23(4), 411–423.

Ragin, C. C. (2000). *Fuzzy-set social science*. Chicago, IL: University of Chicago Press.

Ragin, C. C. (2008). *Redesigning social inquiry: Fuzzy-sets and beyond*. Chicago, IL: University of Chicago Press.

Rauch, A., Deker, J. S., & Woodside, A. G. (2015). Consuming alone: Broadening Putnam's "bowling alone" thesis. *Psychology & Marketing*, 32, 967–976.

Rihoux, B., & Ragin, C. C. (2009). *Configurational comparative methods*. Thousand Oaks, CA: Sage.

Rucker, D., McShane, B. B., & Preacher, K. J. (2015). A researcher's guide to regression, discretization, and median splits of continuous variables. *Journal of Consumer Psychology*, 25, 666–678.

Sawyer, A. G., & Ball, A. (1981). Statistical power and effect size in marketing research. *Journal of Marketing Research*, *18*, 275–290.

Sawyer, A. G., Laran, J., & Xu, J. (2008). The readability of marketing journals: Are award-winning articles better written? *Journal of Marketing*, *72*, 108–117.

Shadish, W. R., Cook, & Campbell, D. T. (2002). *Experimental and quasi-experimental designs for generalized causal inference*. Boston, MA: Houghton Mifflin. Retrieved from https://depts.washington.edu/methods/readings/Shadish.pdf

Sheth, J. N. (1982). Consumer behavior: Surpluses and shortages. In *Advances in consumer research* (Vol. 9, pp. 13–16). Provo, UT: Association for Consumer Research.

Simon, H. A. (1990). Invariants of human behavior. *Annual Review of Psychology*, *41*, 1–19.

Soyer, E., & Hogarth, R. (2012). The illusion of predictability: How regression statistics mislead experts. *International Journal of Forecasting*, *28*, 695–711.

Sternthal, B., Tybout, A M., & Calder, B. J. (1987). Confirmatory versus comparative approaches to judging theory tests. *Journal of Consumer Research*, *14*, 114–125.

Todd, P. M., & Gigerenzer, G. (2001). Shepherd's mirrors or Simon's scissors? *Behavioral and Brain Sciences*, *24*, 704–705.

Tufte, E. R. (2001). *The visual display of quantitative information* (2nd ed.). Cheshire, CT: Graphics Press.

Urry, J. (2005). The complexity turn. *Theory, Culture & Society*, *22*, 1–14.

Van Maanen, J. (2011). *Tales of the field: On writing ethnography*. Chicago, IL: Chicago University Press.

Watson, D., Clark, D. A., & Tellegen, A. (1988). Development and validation of brief measures of positive and negative affect: The PANAS scale. *Journal of Personality and Social Psychology*, *54*, 1063–1070.

Webb, E. J., Campbell, D. T., Schwartz, R. D., & Sechrest, L. (2000). *Unobtrusive measures* (Rev. ed.). Thousand Oaks, CA: Sage.

Wegner, D. M. (2002). *The illusion of conscious will*. Cambridge, MA: Bradford Books, MIT Press.

Weick, K. (1979). *The social psychology of organizing* (2nd ed.). New York, NY: McGraw Hill.

Weisberg, S. (1985). *Applied linear regression*. New York, NY: Wiley.

Wells, W. D. (1993). Discovery-oriented consumer research. *Journal of Consumer Research*, *19*, 489–504.

Whyte, W. F. (1984). *Learning from the field*. Thousand Oaks, CA: Sage.

Wilson, T. D. (2004). *Strangers to ourselves: Discovering the adaptive unconscious*. Boston, MA: Belknap.

Woodside, A. G. (2006). Overcoming the illusion of will and self-fabrication: Going beyond naïve subjective personal introspection to an unconscious/conscious theory of behavior explanation. *Psychology & Marketing*, *23*, 257–272.

Woodside, A. G. (2011). Responding to the severe limitations of cross-sectional surveys: Commenting on Rong and Wilkinson's perspectives. *Australasian Marketing Journal*, *19*, 153–156.

Woodside, A. G. (2013). Moving beyond multiple regression analysis to algorithms: Calling for a paradigm shift from symmetric to asymmetric thinking in data analysis, and crafting theory. *Journal of Business Research*, 66, 463–472.

Woodside, A. G. (2014). Embrace•perform•model: Complexity theory, contrarian case analysis, and multiple realities. *Journal of Business Research*, 67, 2495–2503.

Woodside, A. G. (2015). Visualizing·matching·generalizing: Case identification hypotheses and case-level data analysis. *Australasian Marketing Journal*, 23, 246–258.

Woodside, A. G., & Baxter, R. (2015). Imprinting, honeymooning, or maturing: Testing three theories of how interfirm social bonding impacts suppliers' allocations of resources to business customers. *Australasian Marketing Journal*, 23, 96–106.

Woodside, A. G., & Dubelaar, C. (2003). Increasing quality in measuring advertising effectiveness: A meta-analysis of question framing in conversion studies. *Journal of Advertising Research*, 43, 78–85.

Woodside, A. G., Hsu, S.-Y., & Marshall, R. (2011). General theory of cultures' consequences on international tourism behavior. *Journal of Business Research*, 64, 785–799.

Woodside, A. G., & Ronkainen, I. A. (1977). How serious is non-response bias in advertising conversion research. *Journal of Travel Research*, 22, 34–37.

Woodside, A. G., & Wilson, E. J. (2002). Respondent inaccuracy. *Journal of Advertising Research*, 42, 7–18.

Wu, P.-L., Yeh, S.-S., Huan, & Woodside, A. G. (2014). Applying complexity theory to deepen service dominant logic: Configural analysis of customer experience-and-outcome assessments of professional services for personal transformations. *Journal of Business Research*, 67, 1647–1670.

Zaltman, G. (2003). *How customers think*. Boston, MA: Harvard Business School Press.

Embrace Complexity Theory, Perform Contrarian Case Analysis, and Model Multiple Realities

Arch G. Woodside

ABSTRACT

This chapter describes tenets of complexity theory including the precept that within the same set of data X relates to Y positively, negatively, and not at all. A consequence to this first precept is that reporting how X relates positively to Y with and without additional terms in multiple regression models ignores important information available in a data set. Performing contrarian case analysis indicates that cases having low X with high Y and high X with low Y occur even when the relationship between X and Y is positive and the effect size of the relationship is large. Findings from contrarian case analysis support the necessity of modeling multiple realities using complex antecedent configurations. Complex antecedent configurations (i.e., 2−7 features per recipe) can show that high X is an indicator of high Y when high X combines with certain additional antecedent conditions (e.g., high A, high B, and low C) − *and* low X is an indicator of *high Y as well* when low X combines in other recipes (e.g., high A, low R, and high S), where A, B, C, R, and S are additional antecedent conditions. Thus, modeling multiple realities — configural analysis — is necessary, to learn the configurations of multiple indicators for high Y outcomes and the negation of high Y. For a number of X antecedent conditions, a high X may be necessary for high Y to occur but high X alone is almost never sufficient for a high Y outcome.

Keywords: Antecedent; configuration; contrarian case; fsQCA; model

For every complex problem, there is a solution that is simple, neat, and wrong.

H. L. Mencken

Introduction: Beyond Rote Applications of Regression Analysis

This chapter elaborates on the perspective that the current symmetric-based dominant logic in research in the management sub-disciplines is less informative and less theoretically useful than the alternative logic of asymmetric testing (McClelland, 1998; Woodside, 2013a, 2013b). The contribution here provides details of why and how to use this relatively new theoretical stance and analytics in the management sub-disciplines.

The dominant logic in research in papers submitted to leading journals in the fields of marketing, management, finance, and international business includes question-and-answer surveys using five- and seven-point scales and analyses of the resulting data using structural equation modeling; for example, about 7–10 submissions to the *Journal of Business Research* employ these features. The use of structural equation modeling (SEM) became popular in the 1980s and has grown to become central in the dominant logic in crafting and testing models well into the 21st century. SEM combines and extends factor analysis and multiple regression analysis (MRA). SEM and MRA are symmetric tests that report on the "net effects" of variables on a dependent variable with a set of independent variables.

Along with using SEM/MRA and structured scale measures, the current dominant logic includes the following features: collecting survey data via scaled responses from one person per organization with the respondent answering the questions one-time only; useable response rates less than 20% of the surveys sent to potential respondents; presentation of the fit validities of one-to-five sets of empirical models with no testing for predictive validity with holdout samples (Gigerenzer & Brighton, 2009 for a review of problems associating with not testing for predictive validity with holdout samples and how to do so); reporting of empirical models that include both significant and non-significant terms; no testing or reporting of contrarian cases in these papers — no recognition that the direction of impacts is the opposite of that found in the models reported for some of the respondents; and thus, no recognition of why the resulting models (empirical findings) explain little of the variance in the dependent variable (adjusted R^2s most frequently less than 0.20).

Even though SEM reports are usually elegant to contemplate, the limitations of employing the current dominant logic in the management sub-disciplines are tellingly severe. The limitations include requiring respondents transform their beliefs and evaluations to five- or seven-point scales, the operational step of collecting answers from one person per organization or household rather than seeking confirmatory/negative answers from two or more respondents in the same organization (for an exception, see Cheng, Chang, & Li, 2013), modeling using net effects symmetric tools such as MRA or SEM when patterns of relationships in the data are asymmetric, and testing only for fit validity and not testing for predictive validity. However, describing such limitations is insufficient to achieve useful innovations to theory construction and testing. Proposing and showing useful research analytic innovations are necessary steps for achieving change — especially in moving early-career academic researchers away from using MRA and SEM only and to embrace the use of asymmetric theory construction and testing.

Question surveying from a distance severely limits the collection of contextual information; context is one of the two blades in Herbert Simon's metaphor of human decision making. "Human rational behavior is shaped by a scissors whose blades are the structure of task environments and the computational capabilities of the actor (Simon, 1990, p. 1). Simon's scissors metaphor supports calls for "direct research" (Mintzberg & Campbell, 1979) — to include the study of context as well as to craft isomorphic models of real-life thinking processes in these contexts (Woodside, 2011, 2013b). Asking questions alone to describe and explain decision processes requires a respondent to interpret the question, retrieve relevant information usually from long-term memory, edit the retrieved information for relevancy and self-protection, and report in a format and style usually to appear sane and accurate to some degree; responses following these steps quite often have little relationship to reality (Bargh & Chartrand, 1999; Nesbitt & Wilson, 1977). Verbal responses in answering questions require subjective personal introspections (SPI); SPI's frequently include accurate information only to a modest degree (Woodside, 2006) and frequently both attitudes and beliefs expressed following SPIs serve as poor predictors of future behavior.

The theoretical and practical value of asking respondents to convert their SPI thinking into five- or seven-point scales joins with the lack of contextual data collection to result data of highly questionable value. As Mintzberg and Campbell (1979) ruminants aloud to himself and to us:

> "Hmmmm ... what have we here? The amount of control is 4.2, the complexity of environment, 3.6." What does it mean to measure the "amount of control" in an organization, or the "complexity" of its environment? Some of these concepts may be useful in describing organizations in theory, but that does not mean we can plug them into our research holus-bolus as measures. As soon as the researcher insists on forcing the organization into abstract categories — into his terms instead of its own — he is reduced to using perceptual measures, which often distort the reality. The researcher intent on generating a direct measure of amount of control or of complexity of environment can only ask people what they believe, on 7-point scales or the like. He gets answers, all right, ready for the computer; what he does not get is any idea of what he has measured. (What does "amount of control" [or "trust"] mean anyway?) The result is sterile description, of organizations as categories of abstract variables instead of flesh-and-blood processes. And theory building becomes impossible. (Mintzberg & Campbell, 1979, p. 586)

Woodside (2013a) compares and contrasts the use of symmetric (e.g., MRA and SEM) versus asymmetric (e.g., analysis by quintiles and by fuzzy set qualitative comparative analysis) whereby symmetric tests consider the accuracy in high values of X (an antecedent condition) indicating high values of Y (an outcome condition) and low values of X indicting low values of Y where asymmetric tests consider the accuracy of high values of X indicating high values of Y without predicting how low values of X relates to values of Y. Might not seem that different but symmetric tests rarely match well with reality except for testing the association of two or more items to measure the same construct (coefficient alpha is a symmetric test and researchers seek high coefficient alphas (e.g., $r > 0.70$). Asymmetric tests reflect realities well given that the causes of high Y scores usually differ substantially from the causes of low Y scores (i.e., the principle of causal asymmetry, see Fiss, 2011); examples of this tenet appear later in this chapter.

Following this introduction, this treatise includes three complementary parts. First, tenets in complexity theory provides useful foundation for analyzing data — the nearly rote statements of main effects and rote applications of multiple regression analysis (MRA) appearing in most academic studies in management-related sub-disciplines ignore the complexities inherent in realities and apparent (with a little digging) in the data sets of academic studies. Second, contrarian case analyses confirm that substantial numbers of cases occur which display relationships that are counter to a negative (or positive) main effect between X and Y — even when the effect size is large of the reported X-Y relationship. For example, when X associates positively with Y with a correlation of 0.60 ($p < .001$), the same data set includes cases of high X and low Y and cases of low X and high Y; researchers ignore these contrarian cases in most reports even though examining such cases is highly informative. Third, using configural analysis of complex antecedent conditions, modeling of the multiple realities is possible and insightful — modeling the existence of a net effect of X for different numbers of additional independent variables offers a meager portion of the meal-of-information extractable by drilling deeper.

The study here is valuable in describing how complexity theory serves as a useful foundation for building and testing theory beyond the now dominant logic of applying MRA perspectives of net effects main and interaction terms. Embracing a complexity theory perspective (CTP) provides vision for explicit consideration of hypotheses counter to the dominant logic of presenting one theory per study. Thus, a CTP expands on Armstrong, Brodie, and Parsons' (2001) observation that advocating of a single dominant hypothesis lacks objectivity relative to the use of exploratory and competing hypotheses approaches — even though their "publication audit" of over 1,700 empirical papers in six leading marketing journals during 1984–1999 indicates that three of every four studies use only the single, dominant, hypothesis perspective.

The study here is valuable in describing how contrarian case analysis is useful in probing complexity theory tenets and building and testing new theory by developing compound outcome statements — descriptions and examples of such statements appear in the section "Contrarian Case Analysis." The study here is valuable in bridging configural analysis using fuzzy set qualitative comparative analysis (fsQCA) with complexity theory in sub-disciplines of management (e.g., finance, marketing, organization science, and strategic management); such bridging expands on the contributions of Ragin (2008) in sociological methods, Fiss (2007, 2011) and Meier and Donzé (2012) in organization science, and Woodside and colleagues (Woodside, Muniz, & Sood, 2013a; Woodside, Sood, & Muniz, 2013b; Chung and Woodside, 2011; Schuhmacher, von Janda, & Woodside, 2013; Woodside & Zhang, 2013) in marketing.

Following this introduction, the section "Complexity Theory Tenets" presents tenets in complexity theory. The section "Contrarian Case Analysis" describes how contrarian case analysis and findings show that cases occur contrarian to main effects having large effects sizes — most researchers usually ignore such contrarian cases both in formulating theory, examining data, and in predicting fit validity. The section "Modeling Multiple Realities" reports on models of the multiple realities that occur within each of several data sets. The section "Conclusion" concludes with the call to recognize the need to perform and report multiple models showing how high X associates with high Y in more than one model/path (being done to some extent now using MRA), how *low* X also associates with high Y in more than one model (rarely being done), and how models of the negation of Y are not the mirror opposites of models of high Y — "causal asymmetry" (Fiss, 2011; Fiss, Marx, & Cambré, 2013) occurs whereby complex antecedent conditions indicate the negation of Y are not simply the opposites of the recipe of simple conditions in the complex antecedent statements indicating high Y.

Complexity Theory Tenets

The literature on complexity theory is expansive and heads in several discernable directions. Anderson (1999) provides advances in theory and research on complexity theory relevant to organization science. Several useful studies expand on the insights of Anderson's (1999) and prior work (e.g., March & Simon, 1958) especially in the advancing complexity theory of organizational behavior through simulation methods (e.g., Davis, Eisenhardt, & Bingham, 2007; Huff & Huff, 2000). Urry (2005) provides a far-ranging literature review of complexity theory in the natural and social sciences and offers many useful insights. Example insights include the following perspectives, "Relationships between variables can be nonlinear with abrupt switches occurring, so the same 'cause' can, in specific circumstances, produce different effects" (Urry, 2005, p. 4); "If a system passes a particular threshold with minor changes in the controlling variables, switches occur such that a liquid turns into a gas, a large number of apathetic people suddenly tip into a forceful movement for change (Gladwell, 2002). Such tipping points give rise to unexpected structures and events" (Urry, 2005, p. 5). Reporting on findings that include reversals in causal effects (e.g., positive to negative for the same antecedent with the same outcome) and reporting on tipping-point patterns in phenomena are primary foci in the present chapter.

Simon's (1962) presentation of "the architecture of complexity" focuses on confirming and expanding on the tenet that complexity takes the form of hierarchy – the complex system being composed of subsystems that, in turn, have their own subsystems, and so on. Related to the central task of science relating to complexity and in general, in his essay, "Science seeks parsimony, not simplicity: searching for pattern in phenomena," Simon (1967) provides the following dictum, "The primordial acts of science are to observe phenomena, to seek patterns (redundancy) in them, and to redescribe them in terms of the discovered patterns, thereby removing redundancy. The simplicity that is sought and found beautiful is the simplicity of parsimony, which rests, in turn, on the exploitation of redundancy." Simon's working definition of parsimony is "pattern in the phenomena." The core focus of the present chapter is to advocate formulating parsimonious theories – descriptions, explanations, and predictions of patterns in phenomena — and to show research method fundamentals for testing such theories. Implemented decision rules by firms are parsimonious patterns which are operational algorithms (Howard & Morgenroth, 1968; Morgenroth, 1964); related to consumer research profiles of buyers are examples of parsimonious patterns.

In marketing, famously, Kotler (1967, p. 1) pronounced, "Marketing decisions must he made in the context of insufficient information about processes that are dynamic, nonlinear, lagged, stochastic, interactive, and downright difficult." Yet the substantial majority of studies in the nearly 50 decades since this pronouncement continue to ignore all the decision features that Kotler describes. Gummesson (2008) urges marketing scholars and educators to accept the complexity of marketing and develop a network-based stakeholder approach — balanced centricity — epitomized by the concept of many-to-many marketing. Gummesson (2008) calls for a rejuvenation of marketing.

> Reality is complex whether we like it or not. This is where network theory comes in. Its basics are simple; a network is made up of nodes (such as people or organizations) and relationships and interaction between those. Network theory is part of "complexity theory," recognizing that numerous variables interact, that the number of unique situation is unlimited, that change is a natural state of affairs, and that processes are iterative rather than linear .... But is balanced centricity a realistic objective or is it yet another professorial whim? I do not have the answer but I am convinced that if we keep fragmenting marketing and other business functions and duck complexity, context and dynamics, we will not move ahead. A change requires that we reconsider marketing basics and abandon mainstream methodological rigidity and move toward a more pragmatic and holistic research agenda. (Gummesson, 2008, p. 16, 17)

Scholars before Gummesson (2008) describe the need to reconsider mainstream methodological rigidity and move toward more pragmatic and holistic (i.e., patterns or systems) research agenda. Bass, Tigert, and Lonsdale (1968) offer evidence that the contention that the low R^2s obtained in regression analysis leads to false conclusions about the ability of socioeconomic variables as well as attitudinal measures to substantially explain variance in dependent variables since R^2

is a measure of a model's ability to predict individual rather than group behavior. McClelland (1998) goes further in stressing that most researchers do not really want to explain variance in dependent variables; what they want to do is to describe, explain, and accurately predict high scores in an outcome condition (i.e., create algorithms — decision rules — that work almost all the time in providing an effective decision and avoiding bad decisions). Without likely being aware of McClelland's (1998) contributions to asymmetric thinking, research methods, and parsimony, Ragin (2000, 2006, 2008) relies on Boolean algebra rather than the dominating use of matrix algebra-based statistical methods to offer parallel insights and methods in sociological research and beyond.

Three additional points need stressing that relate to complexity theory's focus on patterns in phenomena. First, "Scientists' tools are not neutral" (Gigerenzer, 1991). Research methods and instruments shape the way we think and test theories. Thus, reviewers' question whether a given paper is trying to make a contribution to theory or method sometimes misses the point that a research paper tries to do both — as is the case here. Second, reports of model confirmation relying only on fit validity need to stop; reports that partial regression coefficients in an MRA model are significant are insufficient findings and of limited usefulness. Analysts assume that models with a better fit provide more accurate forecasts. This view ignores the extensive research showing that fit bears little relationship to ex ante forecast accuracy, especially for time series. Typically, fit improves as complexity increases, while ex ante forecast accuracy decreases as complexity increases, a conclusion that Zellner (2001) traces back to Sir Harold Jeffreys in the 1930s (Armstrong, 2012). Gigerenzer and Brighton provides substantial empirical evidence supporting the focus for accuracy and theory advancement via predictive validity and not just fit validity.

Third, "Developing the full potential of complexity theory, especially in the social sciences, requires more rigorous theory development and fewer popular articles extolling the virtues of the 'new paradigm', more studies testing the new theories and fewer anecdotal claims of efficacy, greater development of tools tailored for particular contexts, and fewer claims of universality. Without such rigor, social scientists face the danger that, despite its high potential, 'complexity theory' will soon be discarded, perhaps prematurely, as yet another unfortunate case of physics envy" (Sterman & Wittenberg, 1999, p. 338). The following tenets (Ti) and sections are steps to contribute rigor in response to Sterman and Wittenberg's (1999) call to do so.

A SIMPLE ANTECEDENT CONDITION MAY BE NECESSARY BUT A SIMPLE ANTECEDENT CONDITION IS RARELY SUFFICIENT FOR PREDICTING A HIGH OR LOW SCORE IN AN OUTCOME CONDITION

$$X \rightarrow Y \tag{1}$$

For example, being male may be a necessity condition to play in the U.S. National Football League (NFL) but being male is insufficient in describing or predicting membership in the NFL. Such modeling of complex antecedent conditions frequently ignores simple conditions and outcome associations that are nearly always true (e.g., males as a necessary condition for NFL membership).

A high score of a simple antecedent condition is insufficient in describing, explaining, or predicting a high score for most outcome conditions. The configurations in Figure 1 provide examples of this tenet. Figure 1 is a summary map of decision rules representing the decisions of a professional supermarket

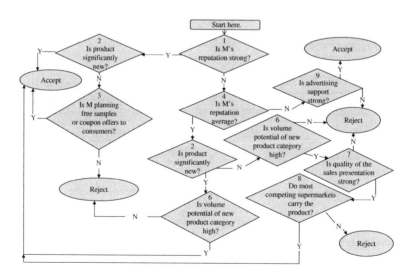

Figure 1. An Ethnographic Decision Process Model of Supermarket Committee Buying Decisions of a Manufacturer's (M's) New Product Offering. *Source*: Adapted from Montgomery (1975).

buying committee's process of accepting and rejecting new product offerings from manufacturers. The first question asked about a new product under consideration, "Does the manufacturer have a strong reputation?" If the answer is yes, this answer is not sufficient for the committee to accept the new product for the supermarket stores. The product under consideration has to pass a second hurdle, "Is the product significantly new?" If yes, the product is accepted by the selection committee. This one configuration describes one of several accept configurations in Figure 1.

The first sufficiency model in Figure 1 describes a recipe consistency of two features – a strong manufacturer's reputation (R) and a new grocery product offered by this manufacturer that the committee judges to be significantly new (N). An offering having high membership in both conditions ($R \bullet N$) indicates that the supermarket buying committee will accept (i.e., agree to buy) the new offering (i.e., $R \bullet N \rightarrow$ Accept). The mid-level dot, " $\bullet$ ", indicates the logical "and" condition in Boolean algebra, that is, $R \bullet N$ is equal to the lowest score for the recipe, $R \bullet N$. Thus, if $R = .05$ and $N = .99$, then $R \bullet N = .05$. Both R and N must be high for this recipe to indicate an "Accept" outcome. Figure 2 shows that high $R \bullet N$ is sufficient for "Accept" but not necessary – additional models (paths) appear in Figure 1 for reaching the "Accept" decision.

A key point here is that the objective of building and examining configurations is not to explain variance but to describe and explain combinations of features which accurately indicate a high score in an outcome condition. The outcome condition could be a "Yes" decision by a supermarket buying committee to take-on a manufacturer's new product offering or the negation of doing so, "No," or other outcomes in different problems (e.g., a hiring decision; an employee promotion decision; a decision as to which university to apply to enter; to accept or reject a proposal to go to a movie or a marriage proposal; to select a vehicle to test drive and/ or to buy). A sideways tilde ("~") indicates the negation score of a simple condition; thus, "~R" represents the negation of the reputation score in the supermarket buying committee example.

A COMPLEX ANTECEDENT CONDITION OF TWO OR MORE SIMPLE CONDITIONS IS SUFFICIENT FOR A CONSISTENTLY HIGH SCORE IN AN OUTCOME CONDITION – THE RECIPE PRINCIPLE

Both nodes must have high scores in the first configuration in Figure 1 for an accept outcome (A) to occur: reputation (R) must

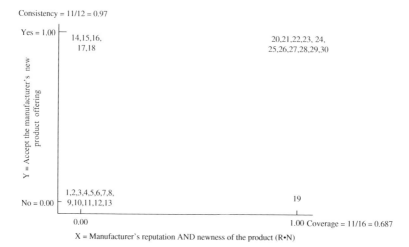

Figure 2. Thought Experiment for 30 Decisions ($n = 30$) of a Complex Antecedent Condition and a Simple Outcome Condition: Supplier Reputation and Newness of Grocery Product Association with Decision to Carry the Product. *Notes*: In this example, each number is a case identification and represents the plot of one decision. Note that the high $R \bullet N$ scores has high consistency with "Yes" (accept) but consistency is not 100%. Also note the relationship is asymmetric; low scores on $R \bullet N$ associate with both low and high scores on the outcome condition — more than one recipe is available to get to an accept condition. As in real-life, most outcomes are to reject the new product proposals.

be high and significantly new (N) must be high. If both R and N are high, then $A = 1.0$ is the outcome predicted to occur. Model 2 represents this one configuration of a complete decision rule for the supermarket buying committee.

$$R \bullet N \to A \qquad (2)$$

A configuration score of 1.00 is the highest score possible for all configurations using Boolean algebra and calibrated scores. Calibrating scores is converting original values to a scale of 0.00–1.00. Ragin (2008) provides details on how and why scores are calibrated in creating and testing asymmetric theory using Boolean algebra versus doing so via matrix algebra and symmetrical tests (i.e., statistical hypothesis testing). Additional details on calibration appear below.

Note that calibrated scores can be dummy codes of 0.00 and 1.00 or calibrated scores can range between 0.00 and 1.00. From the information in Figure 1, consider a manufacturer's reputation includes three levels: weak/low, average, and strong/high. These three levels can be calibrated to equal 0.00, 0.50, and 1.00. The benefits of calibrating scores and using Boolean algebra include the ability to plot complicated statement on the X-axis to test the consistency of asymmetric relationships between X and Y. For example, is the statement accurate that all decisions where $R \bullet N$ = 1.00 indicate that Y = 1.00? Consider the simulated findings from a thought experiment of 30 supermarket buying decisions testing the $R \bullet N$ complex antecedent conditions in the XY plot in Figure 2 — a buying committee made decisions one day on 30 new products being offered by 30 different manufacturers.

Note that the X-axis in Figure 2 displays $R \bullet N$ and not R or N. $R \bullet N$ is a combinatory statement. For this introduction, $R \bullet N$ can take on two membership scores (0.0, 1.0). Note that when $R \bullet N$ = 1.0, nearly all cases are accepted consistently — 11 of 12 cases or .0.97 of the $R \bullet N$ cases are accepted. The coverage by all the accepted cases by this model is high as well; this model ($R \bullet N$) represents 11 of the 16 accept cases (coverage = 11/16 = 0.69). The two indexes, consistency and coverage, indicate the usefulness of a model in explaining high outcome scores. Consistency is an asymmetric metric analogous to the symmetric correlation metric; coverage is an asymmetric metric analogous to the symmetric "coefficient of determination" (i.e., r^2). Table 1 shows the calculations for consistency and coverage for the $R \bullet N$ model in the thought experiment.

A useful rule of thumb to apply: for a model to be predictive of high scores for an outcome condition, consistency should greater than 0.80 and coverage should be greater than .01 (cf. Ragin, 2008). A model with high consistency and very low coverage score indicates a rare bird — a model for a rare case among the cases of data — whereby this rare case associates with a high outcome score. Doug Flutie (retired American NFL and Canadian league football player) is one such rare bird: a quarterback "too short to play quarterback and win" who consistently won games. Flutie would have a high score for short (S) and in the NFL draft for quarterbacks, not short ($\sim S$ = 1.00) is a requirement in all NFL teams' selection models. Thus, Flutie was almost not selected by any NFL team in the draft year he was available even though he was a Heisman Trophy winner the year of his draft (i.e., Flutie was selected as the best college football player

Table 1: Calculating Consistency and Coverage for a Complex
Antecedent Condition and an Outcome Condition.

Case	$R \bullet N$	A	Minimum $(R \bullet N_i, A_i)$
1	0.0	0.0	0.0
2	0.0	0.0	0.0
3	0.0	0.0	0.0
4	0.0	0.0	0.0
5	0.0	0.0	0.0
6	0.0	0.0	0.0
7	0.0	0.0	0.0
8	0.0	0.0	0.0
9	0.0	0.0	0.0
10	0.0	0.0	0.0
11	0.0	0.0	0.0
12	0.0	0.0	0.0
13	0.0	0.0	0.0
14	0.0	1.0	0.0
15	0.0	1.0	0.0
16	0.0	1.0	0.0
17	0.0	1.0	0.0
18	0.0	1.0	0.0
19	1.0	0.0	0.0
20	1.0	1.0	1.0
21	1.0	1.0	1.0
22	1.0	1.0	1.0
23	1.0	1.0	1.0
24	1.0	1.0	1.0
25	1.0	1.0	1.0
26	1.0	1.0	1.0
27	1.0	1.0	1.0
28	1.0	1.0	1.0
29	1.0	1.0	1.0
30	1.0	1.0	1.0
Σ	12.0	16.0	11.0

Consistency $(R \bullet N_i \le A_i) = \sum(\min (R \bullet N_i, A_i)/ \sum(R \bullet N_i) = 11.0/12.0 = 0.96667$
Coverage $(R \bullet N_i \le A_i) = \sum(\min (R \bullet N_i, A_i)/ \sum(A_i) = 11.0/16.0 = 0.6875$

Note: R = manufacturer's reputation; N = product newness; A = accept the
product.

nationally). Flutie is short; his height is less than 5′10″ (1.778 meters) when almost all NFL quarterbacks are tall (≥6.0′).

A MODEL THAT IS SUFFICIENT IS NOT NECESSARY FOR AN OUTCOME HAVING A HIGH SCORE TO OCCUR — THE EQUIFINALITY PRINCIPLE

Additional paths occur for reaching an accept decision in Figure 1. Table 2 summarizes six paths appearing in Figure 1 leading to an accept decision and six paths leading to a reject decision. Equifinality is the principle that multiple paths occur which lead to the same outcome. The occurrences of different paths usually do not occur with the same frequency among the set of paths. Complexity theory informs that the equifinality

Table 2: Management Decision Paths Leading to Supermarket Buying Committee Adopting versus Rejecting Manufacturers' New Product Proposals.

Path	Boolean Expression	Key
1. 1-2	$R \bullet N \to A$	R = Reputation; N = New; A = Accept
2. 1-2-3 (a)	$R \bullet \sim N \bullet F \to A$	F = Free samples
3. 1-2-3 (b)	$R \bullet \sim N \bullet \sim F \to R$	$\sim$ = Not; R = Reject
4. 1-4-9	$\sim R \bullet \sim RA \bullet S \to A$	RA = Reputation average; S = ad support
5. 1-4-9 (b)	$\sim R \bullet \sim RA \bullet \sim S \to R$	
6. 1-4-2-6 (a)	$\sim R \bullet RA \bullet N \bullet V \to A$	V = Volume potential
7. 1-4-9-6 (b)	$\sim R \bullet RA \bullet N \bullet \sim V \to R$	
8. 1-4-2-6 (b)	$\sim R \bullet RA \bullet \sim N \bullet \sim V \to R$	
9. 1-4-2-6-7	$\sim R \bullet RA \bullet \sim N \bullet V \bullet \sim Q \to R$	
10. 1-4-2-6-7-8	$\sim R \bullet RA \bullet \sim N \bullet V \bullet Q \bullet C \to A$	Q = quality of sales presentation
		C = Competitors' carry new product
11. 1-4-2-6-7-8 (a)	$\sim R \bullet RA \bullet \sim N \bullet V \bullet Q \bullet C \to A$	
12. 1-4-2-6-7-8 (b)	$\sim R \bullet RA \bullet \sim N \bullet V \bullet Q \bullet \sim C \to R$	

Note: Mid-level dot ("•") indicates the conjunctive "and." The horizontal arrow ("→") points to an accept or reject outcome.

principle that the occurrences of anyone feature may not be necessary for reaching a given outcome. For example, a high manufacturer's reputation is not necessary as an antecedent for all accept decisions to occur.

RECIPES INDICATING A SECOND OUTCOME (E.G., REJECTION) ARE UNIQUE AND NOT THE MIRROR OPPOSITES OF RECIPES OF A DIFFERENT OUTCOME (E.G., ACCEPTANCE) — THE CAUSAL ASYMMETRY PRINCIPLE

The causal asymmetry principle indicates that the study of the causes of acceptance often tells us very little about the causes of failure. Consequently, separate asymmetric models of failure (or other outcomes besides the original focus of a study on success or other positive condition) are necessary if a researcher seeks to describe and explain success versus failure, promotion versus dismissal, hiring versus rejection, and so on. The causal asymmetry principle serves as a foundation principle of complexity theory in research on "highly reliable organizations" (HROs) (Weick & Sutcliffe, 2001, 2007; Weick, Sutcliffe, & Obstfeld, 1999). Weick and Sutcliffe (2001) identify five characteristics of HROs as responsible for the "mindfulness" that keeps them working well when facing unexpected situations: preoccupation with failure; reluctance to simplify interpretations; sensitivity to operations; commitment to resilience; and deference to expertise.

The causal asymmetry principle and the recipe principle support the suggestions that the study of "key success factors" (KSFs) (Cooper, 1993; Di Benedetto, 1999) using a net effects approach (Cooper, 1993; Di Benedetto, 1999) to explain and describe success is misleading and insufficient. No one factor is sufficient or likely necessary for success and research focusing only on success is unlikely to be very informative about the causes of failure. The literature on KSFs suggests the certain activities consistently associate with success and never with failure (e.g., submitting products to customers for in-use testing, Di Benedetto, 1999), while the literature focusing on recipes proposes and finds that the same attribute can either foster or inhibit new service adoption, depending on how it is configured with other attributes (Ordanini, Parasuraman, & Rubera, 2014; Prado & Woodside, 2014). This finding and prior findings that an attribute can contribute positively and negatively to the same outcome depending upon the other ingredients specific recipes follows from the fifth principle of complexity theory.

AN INDIVIDUAL FEATURE (ATTRIBUTE OR ACTION) IN A RECIPE CAN CONTRIBUTE POSITIVELY OR NEGATIVELY TO A SPECIFIC OUTCOME DEPENDING ON THE PRESENCE OR ABSENCE OF THE OTHER INGREDIENTS IN THE RECIPES

The findings in Figure 3 illustrate this fifth complexity principle. The findings are from a study of customer evaluations of services received from a beauty parlor and health spa (Wu, Yeh, Huan, & Woodside, 2014). Four recipe models appear in Figure 3 for customer evaluations of quality of the work by the service professional experienced by the customer. Notice that the absence of a companion visiting the beauty parlor and health spa contributes positively in the first three models but negatively in the fourth model appearing at the top of Figure 3. The first three models include youthful customers and the fourth model includes older customers in the recipes. Rather than making blanket statements that older or younger customers rate the work of service professionals highly positively with or without being accompanied by a companion, each of the four recipes include a unique blend of ingredients to indicate that high scores on these recipes associated with high scores on the same outcome.

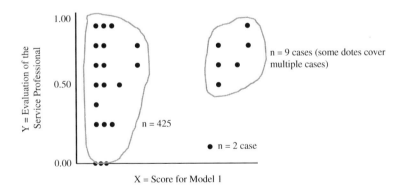

Figure 3.   *XY* Plot for Model 1. *Source*: Table 7 in Wu et al. (2014, p. 1657) covering demographics, companion present/absent, and customer expenditure level on beauty/salon visits — algorithm model predicting high quality of service provider (service professional evaluation). *Notes*: For example, model 1 states that a case (customer) with a high score for the configuration of no companion, not a service worker, a housekeeper, female, with low education, and young will give a high score for service professional evaluations. The presence of a companion contributes either positively or negatively to the outcome (high score for service professional evaluation) depending on the additional ingredients in each particular model.

FOR HIGH *Y* SCORES, A GIVEN RECIPE IS RELEVANT FOR
SOME BUT NOT ALL CASES; COVERAGE IS LESS THAN 1.00 FOR
ANY ONE RECIPE

A few exceptions occur for high *X* scores for a given recipe that works
well for predicting high *Y* scores

Note in Figure 3 that for 9 of the 11 cases with high X scores
also have high Y scores for model 1 in the XY plot. For the two
cases having low Y scores with high recipe (X) scores, some additional ingredient would need to be identified to shift these two
cases to the left without also shifting the other nine cases high in
X. Such theory to analysis to theory to analysis pondering is a
central aspect for improving on the informativeness of recipes.

Contrarian Case Analysis

From a study of employees' evaluations of their work environments including their overall happiness with their jobs, Table 3
illustrates the occurrence of contrarian cases that run counter to
a large main effect. This study merges two data files; the first file
includes the employees' job evaluations and the second file
includes their supervisors' evaluations of the work performances
of these same employees.

Table 3: Hospitality Employees' Happiness and Managers'
Evaluations of Employees' In-Role Performances.

			In-Role Performance Quality (IRP)					
			Very Low				Very High	Total Count
			1	2	3	4	5	
Happiness	Very low	1	14	8	13	10	4	49
Quintiles for	Low	2	12	14	10	11	13	60
Hospitality								
Employees	Medium	3	10	9	9	4	7	39
	High	4	9	10	14	6	11	50
	Very high	5	7	6	10	12	14	49
	Total count		52	47	56	43	49	247

Notes: Total sample: 9 = .259; p < .413; ($p2$ = .07 (very small effect size). Q1 and
Q5 happiness and five quintiles for IRP: 9 = .299, p < .068; 92 = .09 (medium
effect size). Comparing Q1 and Q5 for both happiness and IRP: 9 = .478, 92 = .228
(medium-to-large effect size). Italic values: Possibly surprising findings: cases do
occur of very unhappy employees with very high IRP scores and vice versa.

Table 3 reports a quintile analysis of hospitality employee happiness and their managers' in-role performance (IRP) evaluations (Hsiao, Chyi Jaw, Huan, & Woodside, 2015). A quintile analysis includes dividing the respondent cases from the lowest to highest quintile for each measured construct and examining the relationships among two or more constructs (McClelland, 1998). Even though the findings for the total sample are not significant statistically, note the modest positive relationship – 14 versus 4 employees very low in happiness are very low versus very high in employees' in-role performances (IRP), respectively. The distribution of the 49 very happy employees includes 14 with very high IRP scores and only 7 with very low IRP scores. The key point here relates to the occurrence of employees unhappy to very unhappy who have high to very high IRPs (10 + 4 + 11 + 13 = 38 cases or 38/247 or 15.4% of the total cases) as well as employees happy to very happy having low to very low IRPs (9 + 10 + 7 + 6 = 32 or 32/247 or 13.0% of the total cases. Thus, more than one-fourth of the total cases in the study exhibit two relationships counter to the symmetric relationship that happy employees are productive employees and unhappy employees are unproductive employees.

Hsiao et al. (2015) were able to offer asymmetric empirical models via qualitative comparative analysis for all four sets of relationships: unhappy and highly unproductive employees, unhappy and highly productive employees, happy and highly unproductive employees, and happy and highly productive employees. The state of happiness alone was not sufficient or necessary in their study for low or high IRP. However, employees' high IRP was sufficient for predicting high "Customer-Directed Extra Role Performances" (CDERP) – that is, "going beyond the call of duty" and doing extra actions to insure high customer happiness.

The Hsiao et al. (2015) findings on contrarian case responses are illustrative of usual occurrences among large data sets ($n \geq 100$). Even when an effect size is large between two variables, cases exist in almost all large data sets that run counter to the main effects relationship. Hypothesizing main effects and moderating effects only without examining and explaining such contrarian cases represents over simplistic theorizing and handing of a data set.

Modeling Multiple Realities

Examples of modeling multiple realities here appear in the Wu et al. (2014) study of customer evaluations of beauty parlor and health club visits. Table 4 provides examples of additional models of equifinal solutions whereby high scores on these models (i.e., complex X recipes) indicate high scores on the outcome conditions. Note in Table 4 that models include indicators of high scores for arouse pleasure, delivered service quality, effective treatment, and high value for the money. Each set of models includes different ingredients for gender; separate models include female and ~female (i.e., male). This finding illustrates the point that reporting a main effect for gender is an inadequate representation of the impact of gender on high scores for any of the four outcome conditions. Similar conclusions are supportable for the other ingredients in the four sets of models. However, high education is a necessary condition for the effective treatment outcome condition in Table 4 — both of the two useful models for this outcome condition include education as an ingredient.

Figure 4 presents Venn diagrams as a way of illustrating the possibilities of the presence and absence of ingredients in complex antecedent conditions (i.e., recipes) indicating high scores in an outcome condition. For example, for demographics 16 configurations are possible visually in Figure 4.

Table 4: Four Sets of Models for Customer Evaluations of Experiencing Four Service Facets.

	Raw Coverage	Unique Coverage	Consistency
A. Models for Arouse Pleasure			
1. educ • servicew • ~housek • ~female	0.016	0.008	0.968
2. edu • age • servicew • ~housek	0.011	0.098	0.905
3. ~edu • ~age • ~servicew • ~female	0.021	0.021	0.895
B. Models for Delivered Service Quality			
4. educ • servciew • ~housek • ~female	0.015	0.008	0.972
5. educ • age • servicew • ~housek	0.102	0.094	0.916
C. Models for Effective Treatment			
6. educ • servicew • ~housek • ~female	0.020	0.020	0.072
7. educ • ~age • ~servicew • housek • female	0.036	0.036	0.866
D. Models for High Value for the Money			
8. edu • servicew • ~housek • ~female	0.017	0.017	0.919
9. ~age • ~servicew • housek • female	0.053	0.053	0.863

Source: Table 11a in Wu et al. (2014, p. 1664).

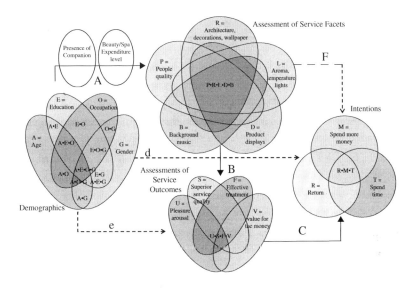

Figure 4. Modeling Multiple Realities. *Source*: Figure 2, Wu et al. (2014, p. 1650). *Note*: Thick arrows indicate propositions regarding effective algorithms; thin and dotted arrows indicate predictions of low accuracy.

Actually 81 combinations are possible if you consider any one of the features having three possible impacts within a recipe: high score (e.g., old age or *A*), low score (e.g., young age or ~*A*) and age not an ingredient in the recipe). Both theory and the mechanics of the software program (available for free at fsQCA. com) are useful bases for interacting with data for information on relevant recipes. Such analyses provide a useful match among the tenets of complexity theory and the inherent complexity of relationships in data.

Conclusion

Prior studies (e.g., Armstrong, 2012; Bass et al., 1968; McClelland, 1998; Montgomery, 1975) identify serious problems with the near total reliance by most researchers on symmetric statistical tests and difficulties in achieving theory advances relying on such tools (Gigerenzer, 1991). Gigerenzer (1991) and McClelland (1998) call attention and demonstrate the value of using asymmetric tests to both advance theory as well as provide useful empirical models of the occurrence of multiple realities.

Ragin (2008) has been the principal advocate in the behavioral sciences along with Gigerenzer (1991) and Armstrong (2012) on advancing new competencies in the theory and research relevant for advancing theory-crafting and analytical skills of academic researchers in the sub-disciplines of management. Because the body of work and rigorous tools relating to complexity theory applications and fsQCA is growing in the management sub-disciplines, the present dominant logic of MRA/SEM and survey research features described in this chapter will end during the second decade of the 21st century. At least this prediction is what this chapter advocates and attempts to show how to accomplish.

Acknowledgment

The author gratefully acknowledges permission granted by the publisher, Elsevier, to reuse content in this chapter originally appearing in Woodside (2014).

References

Anderson, P. (1999). Complexity theory and organization science. *Organization Science*, *10*, 216–232.

Armstrong, J. S. (2012). Illusions in regression analysis. *International Journal of Forecasting*, *28*, 689–694.

Armstrong, J. S., Brodie, R. J., & Parsons, A. G. (2001). Hypotheses in marketing science: Literature review and publication audit. *Marketing Letters*, *12*, 171–187.

Bargh, J. A., & Chartrand, T. L. (1999). The unbearable automaticity of being. *American Psychologist*, *54*, 462–479.

Bass, F. M., Tigert, D. J., & Lonsdale, R. T. (1968). Market segmentation: Group versus individual behavior. *Journal of Marketing Research*, *5*(3), 264–270.

Cheng, C.-F., Chang, M.-L., & Li, C.-L. (2013). Configural paths to successful product innovation. *Journal of Business Research*, *66*, 2561–2573.

Chung, M., & Woodside, A. G. (2011). Causal recipes sufficient for identifying market gurus versus mavens. In A. Meier & L. Donzé (Eds.), *Fuzzy methods for customer relationship management and marketing: Applications and classification* (pp. 312–331). Hershey, PA: IGI Global.

Cooper, R. G. (1993). *Winning at new products: Accelerating the process from idea to launch*. Reading, MA: Addison-Wesley.

Davis, J. P., Eisenhardt, J. P., & Bingham, C. B. (2007). Developing theory through simulation methods. *Academy of Management Review*, *32*, 490–499.

Di Benedetto, C. A. (1999). Identifying the key success factors in new product launch. *Journal of Product Innovation Management, 16*, 530–544.

Fiss, P. C. (2007). A set-theoretic approach to organizational configurations. *The Academy of Management Review, 32*(2), 1180–1198.

Fiss, P. C. (2011). Building better casual theories: A fuzzy set approach to typologies in organizational research. *Academy of Management Journal, 54*(2), 393–420.

Fiss, P. C., Marx, A., & Cambré, B. (2013). Configurational theory and methods in organizational research: Introduction. In P. C. Fiss, B. Cambré, & A. Marx (Eds.), *Configurational theory and methods in organizational research* (Vol. 38, pp. 1–22. Research in the Sociology of Organizations). Bingley, UK: Emerald Group Publishing Limited.

Gigerenzer, G. (1991). From tools to theories: A heuristic of discovery in cognitive psychology. *Psychological Review, 98*, 254–267.

Gigerenzer, G., & Brighton, H. (2009). Homo heuristics: Why biased minds make better inferences. *Topics in Cognitive Science, 1*, 107–143.

Gladwell, M. (2002). *Tipping points: How little things can make a big difference*. Boston, MA: Little, Brown.

Gummesson, E. (2008). Extending the service-dominant logic: From customer centricity to balanced centricity. *Journal of the Academy of Marketing Science, 36*, 15–17.

Howard, J. A., & Morgenroth, W. M. (1968). Information processing model of executive decision. *Management Science, 14*, 416–428.

Hsiao, J. P.-H., Chyi Jaw, C., Huan, T. C., & Woodside, A. G. (2015). Applying complexity theory to solve hospitality contrarian case conundrums: Illuminating happy-low and unhappy-high performing frontline service employees. *International Journal of Contemporary Hospitality Management, 27*, 608–647.

Huff, A. S., & Huff, J. O. (2000). *When firms change direction*. Oxford: Oxford University Press.

Kotler, P. (1967). *Marketing management: Analysis, planning, and control*. Englewood Cliffs, NJ: Prentice-Hall.

March, J. G., & Simon, H. (1958). *Organizations*. New York, NY: Wiley.

McClelland, D. C. (1998). Identifying competencies with behavioral-event interviews. *Psychological Science, 9*, 331–3339.

Meier, A., & Donzé, L. (Eds.). (2012). *Fuzzy methods for customer relationship management and marketing: Applications and classification* (pp. 312–331). Hershey, PA: IGI Global.

Mintzberg, H., & Campbell, C. G. (1979). An emerging strategy of direct research. *Administrative Science Quarterly, 24*, 582–589.

Montgomery, D. B. (1975). New product distribution: An analysis of supermarket buyer decisions. *Journal of Marketing Research, 12*(August), 255–264.

Morgenroth, W. M. (1964). A method for understanding price determinants. *Journal of Marketing Research, 1*(3), 17–26.

Nesbitt, R. E., & Wilson, T. D. (1977). Telling more than we can know: Verbal reports on mental processes. *Psychological Review, 84*, 231–259.

Ordanini, A., Parasuraman, A., & Rubera, G. (2014). When the recipe is more important than the ingredients: A qualitative comparative analysis (QCA) of service innovation configurations. *Journal of Service Research*, 17, 134–149.

Prado, A. M., & Woodside, A. G. (2014). Deepening understanding of certification adoption and non-adoption of international-supplier ethical standards. *Journal of Business Ethics*, 132, 105–125.

Ragin, C. C. (2000). *Fuzzy set social science*. Chicago, IL: Chicago University Press.

Ragin, C. C. (2006). Turning the tables: How case-oriented research challenges variable-oriented research. *Comparative Social Research*, 16, 27–42.

Ragin, C. C. (2008). *Redesigning social inquiry: Fuzzy sets and beyond*. Chicago, IL: Chicago University Press.

Schuhmacher, M. C., von Janda, S., & Woodside, A. G. (2013). Configural theory of why people shop for clothes: Personal-attribute explanations of four stalwart segments. *Journal of Global Fashion Marketing*, 4, 1–25.

Simon, H. A. (1962). The architecture of complexity. *Proceedings of the American Philosophical Society*, 106, 467–482.

Simon, H. A. (1990). Invariants of human behavior. *Annual Review of Psychology*, 41, 1–19.

Sterman, J. D., & Wittenberg, J. (1999). Path dependence, competition, and succession in the dynamics of scientific revolution. *Organization Science*, 10, 322–341.

Urry, J. (2005). The complexity turn. *Theory, Culture & Society*, 22, 1–14.

Weick, K. E., & Sutcliffe, K. M. (2001). *Managing the unexpected: Assuring high performance in an age of complexity*. San Francisco, CA: Jossey-Bass.

Weick, K. E., & Sutcliffe, K. M. (2007). *Managing the unexpected: Resilient performance in an age of uncertainty*. San Francisco, CA: Jossey-Bass.

Weick, K. E., Sutcliffe, K. M., & Obstfeld, D. (1999). Organizing for high reliability: Processes of collective mindfulness. In B. M. Staw & L. L. Cummings (Eds.), *Research in organizational behavior* (Vol. 21, pp. 81–123). Greenwich, CT: JAI Press, Inc.

Woodside, A. G. (2006). Overcoming the illusion of will and self-fabrication: Going beyond naïve subjective personal introspection to an unconscious/conscious theory of behavior explanation. *Psychology & Marketing*, 23, 257–272.

Woodside, A. G. (2011). Responding to the severe limitations of cross-sectional surveys: Commenting on Rong and Wilkinson's perspectives. *Australasian Marketing Journal*, 19, 153–156.

Woodside, A. G. (2013a). Moving beyond multiple regression analysis to algorithms: Calling for a paradigm shift from symmetric to asymmetric thinking in data analysis, and crafting theory. *Journal of Business Research*, 66, 463–472.

Woodside, A. G. (2013b). Proposing a new logic for data analysis in marketing and consumer behavior: Case study research of large-N survey data for estimating algorithms that accurately profile X (extremely high-use) consumers. *Journal of Global Scholars of Marketing Science*, 22(4), 277–289.

Woodside, A. G. (2014). Embrace perform model: Complexity theory, contrarian case analysis, and multiple realities. *Journal of Business Research*, 67, 2495–2503.

Woodside, A. G., Muniz, K., & Sood, S. (2013). Archetype enactments in travelers' stories about places: Theory and advances in positivistic and qualitative methods. In S. McCabe (Ed.), *Routledge handbook of tourism marketing* (pp. 221–239). Abingdon, Oxford: Tayler & Francis.

Woodside, A. G., Sood, S., & Muniz, K. M. (2013). Creating and interpreting visual storytelling art in extending thematic apperception tests and Jung's method of interpreting dreams. In E. Ko & A. G. Woodside (Eds.), *Luxury fashion and culture* (Vol. 7, pp. 15–45). Advances in Culture, Tourism and Hospitality Research. Bingley, UK: Emerald Group Publishing Limited.

Woodside, A. G., & Zhang, M. (2013). Cultural diversity and marketing transactions: Are market integration, large community size, and world religions necessary for fairness in ephemeral exchanges. *Psychology & Marketing*, *30*, 263–276.

Wu, P.-L., Yeh, S. S., Huan, T. C., & Woodside, A. G. (2014). Applying complexity theory to deepen service dominant logic: Configural analysis of customer experience-and-outcome assessments of professional services for personal transformations. *Journal of Business Research*, *67*, 1647–1670.

Zellner, A. (2001). Keep it sophisticatedly simple. In H. Keuzenkamp & M. McAleer (Eds.), *Simplicity, inference, and modeling: Keeping it sophisticatedly simple*. Cambridge: Cambridge University Press.

Moving beyond Multiple Regression Analysis and Symmetric Tests to Algorithms and Asymmetric Tests

Arch G. Woodside

ABSTRACT

This chapter proposes moving beyond relying on the dominant logic of multiple regression analysis (MRA) toward thinking and using algorithms in advancing and testing theory in accounting, consumer research, finance, management, and marketing. The chapter includes an example of testing an MRA model for fit and predictive validity. The same data used for the MRA is used to conduct a fuzzy-set qualitative comparative analysis (fsQCA). The chapter reviews a number of insights by prominent scholars including Gerd Gigerenzer's treatise that "Scientists' tools are not neutral." Tools impact thinking and theory crafting as well theory testing. The discussion may be helpful for early career scholars unfamiliar with David C. McClelland's brilliance in data analysis and in introducing business research scholars to fsQCA as an alternative tool for theory development and data analysis.

Keywords: Algorithm; causal recipe; configuration; consistency; coverage

Introduction: Tools-to-Theory Perspective

MRA is more than just a statistical tool — the method shapes thinking and theory crafting. "Scientists' tools are not neutral" (Gigerenzer, 1991, p. 19). This chapter is an echo and an application of Gigerenzer's (1991) general thesis that scientific tools (both methods and instruments) suggest new theoretical metaphors and theoretical concepts once they are entrenched in scientific practice; familiarity with the tools within a scientific community also lays the foundation for the general acceptance of the theoretical concepts and metaphors inspired by the tools. This chapter is not to suggest that researchers should always avoid using MRA.

Most MRA applications in business research and JBR submissions are done badly and that researchers should think and craft algorithms for building and testing theory much more often they do now. The comments and recommendations concerning MRA apply to structural equation modeling (SEM) as well. Additional comments on the severe limitations of MRA and SEM research using fixed-point five- and seven-point self-report scales to learn cognitive processes appear elsewhere (Woodside, 2011). The limitations of using one-shot, one-person-per-firm, or one-person-per household, self-reports as valid indicators of causal relationships of actual processes are so severe that academics should do more than think twice before using such surveys as the main method for collecting data — if scholars seek to understand and describe actual thinking processes additional methods are necessary for data collection. The relevant literature includes several gems of exceptionally high quality, validity, and usefulness in the study of actual processes; reading these studies are a useful step toward reducing the reliance on one-shot self-report surveys (Woodside, 2011; describes some of these exceptionally high-quality studies).

A Call to Move beyond MRA

Several tenets support this call to move beyond MRA to crafting and testing theory using algorithms. First, researchers using MRA focus on estimating whether or not the influence (i.e., the effect size) of each hypothesized independent variable associates significantly with a dependent variable after separating out the influence of other independent variables in an equation involving two or more independent variables – a "net effects" estimation approach to research. Frequently, such research reports include comparisons of models with specific independent variables having significant versus insignificant net effects depending on the presence or absence of other independent variables in the models.

Given that multicollinearity (i.e., significant correlations among the independent variables) always occurs with a high number of variables in a model (e.g., 10 variables), a researcher may show that none of the independent variables has a significant net effect while at the same time the model explains a substantial share of the variance in the dependent variable or that a given variable of high interest (e.g., private-equity ownership) shifts from significant to nonsignificant status in influencing a dependent variable (e.g., loan default) depending upon what other variables the researcher includes in the models (Hotchkiss, Smith, & Strömberg, 2013; Tables 6 – 9; Mauro, 2001, "Table 6").

The focus on net effects is misleading for several reasons and more useful perspectives on theory and method are available. Reasons not to rely on MRA exclusively include the point that cases counter to the observed net effects nearly always occur – not all the cases in the data support a negative or positive relationship between the independent and dependent variable. Rather than showing a limited number of models in which X has a positive (or negative) net influence on Y, the researcher can increase the contribution of the study by showing the combinatory conditions for which X is a positive influence on Y as well as the combinatory conditions when X is a negative influence on Y. For example, in an award-winning paper on adoption of industry certification standards in the cut flower industry in Colombia and Ecuador, Prado (2010) shows that a dummy country variable (with Colombia equals 1 and Ecuador equals zero) results in a consistent negative net-effect influence on adoption. Yet, many firms in Colombia adopt the industry standards. Prado (2010) does not address the issue of how the seemingly negative country influence is overcome to achieve the outcome of adoption – what combination of influences of antecedent conditions in Colombia leads to industry certification adoption?

Second, reality usually includes more than one combination of conditions that lead to high values in an outcome condition (i.e., high values in a dependent variable); thus, reality usually indicates any insightful combination of conditions has an asymmetrical relationship with an outcome condition and not a symmetrical relationship. MRA tests the extent to which the relationship between a causal statement (i.e., statement X) involving one and more weighted variables and an outcome variable Y is symmetrical. In symmetrical relationships, low values of (a single or complex statement of) X associate with low values of Y and high values of X associate with high values of Y.

Figure 1a shows a symmetric relationship for a causal statement and a dependent variable. Figure 1b shows an asymmetric relationship for a causal statement and a dependent variable. A symmetric relationship indicates that high values of X are both necessary and sufficient for high values of Y to occur and that

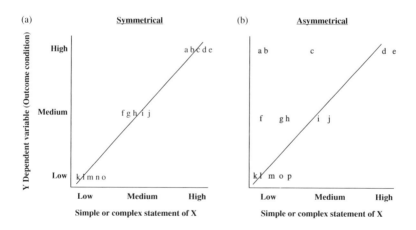

Figure 1.   Symmetrical and Asymmetrical Relationships between X and Y for 15 Cases of Synthetic Data.

low values of Y occur with low values of X. The asymmetric relationship in Figure 1b indicates that high values of X are sufficient for high values of Y to occur but high values of X are not necessary for high values of Y to occur; high values of Y occur when values of X are low, indicating that additional "causal recipes" (i.e., simply and complex X statements) associate with high values of Y. "Causal recipes" (Ragin, 2008) are combinatory statements of two or more simple antecedent conditions, for example the combination statement of "old, wealthy, and divorced male" is a conjunctive statement of four antecedent conditions – a possible causal recipe with high values on this statement associating with a high score on buying a Lexus convertible automobile.

Significant correlations above .80 indicate symmetric relationships; significant correlations in the range of .30−.70 indicate asymmetric relationships. Except for findings of tests for reliability of items in a measurement scale, significant correlations between unique variables usually fall below .70 because different combinations of independent variables associate with high values of Y, and any given X statement that relates substantially with Y has both low as well as high values that relate to high values for Y.

Table 1 includes data that matches with Figure 1. In Table 1 the correlation for the data in Figure 1a equals 0.98 – indicating a symmetric relationship. In the second data set in Table 1 the correlation for the data for Figure 1b equals 0.49 – indicating an asymmetric relationship. Using the software program for fuzzy-set qualitative comparative analysis (available at fsQCA.com), the first two data sets are transformed to "calibrated" scores in the third and fourth parts of Table 1. For the calibrated scores, Table 1 reports "consistency" and "coverage" indices.

The consistency index is analogous to a correlation and the coverage index is analogous to the "coefficient of determination" (i.e., r^2). Details appear below on calculating consistency and coverage; the point for now is that whether or not a relationship between X and Y is symmetrical or asymmetrical has little impact on consistency scores. Note that the consistency scores equal 0.98 and 0.95 for the symmetric and asymmetric data sets in Figure 1. Unlike correlation analysis, consistency is a test for sufficiency and not a test for sufficiency and necessity. While correlation and multiple regression analysis are matrix algebra

Table 1:   Correlation and QCA Tests of Symmetric and
Asymmetric Relationships.

Symmetrical Data			Asymmetric Data		Calibrated Symmetric Data		Calibrated Asymmetric	
Case	X	Y	Xx	yy	X	Y	xx	yy
A	2.6	3	1	3	0.9	0.98	0.02	0.98
B	2.7	3	1.1	3	0.93	0.98	0.03	0.98
C	2.8	3	1.7	3	0.95	0.98	0.25	0.98
D	2.9	3	2.9	3	0.97	0.98	0.97	0.98
E	3	3	3	3	0.98	0.98	0.98	0.98
F	1.7	2	1	2	0.25	0.5	0.02	0.5
g	1.8	2	1.3	2	0.32	0.5	0.07	0.5
h	1.9	2	1.4	2	0.41	0.5	0.1	0.5
i	2	2	1.8	2	0.5	0.5	0.32	0.5
j	2.1	2	1.9	2	0.59	0.5	0.41	0.5
k	0.8	1	1	1	0.01	0.02	0.02	0.02
l	0.9	1	1.1	1	0.02	0.02	0.03	0.02
m	1	1	1.2	1	0.02	0.02	0.05	0.02
n	1.1	1	1.3	1	0.03	0.02	0.07	0.02
o	1.2	1	1.4	1	0.05	0.02	0.1	0.02
	$r = .98$		$r = .49$		Consistency	0.98	Consistency	0.95
					Coverage	0.91	Coverage	0.44

applications, consistency and coverage are Boolean algebra applications. Appendix A shows the formula with example calculations for consistency and coverage.

For most contexts in reality no one simple or one complex statement of an independent variable (X) is necessary for high values of a dependent variable (Y). The dominant-logic approach to theory proposals of one given model that leads eventually to a principal dependent variable needs replacing to account for the reality of multiple combinations (i.e., causal recipes, alternative routes) resulting in high values in the dependent variable.

Consider the findings of Cooper and Kleinschmidt (2007) — authors of a series of highly cited studies on the effects of key success factors (KSFs) and profitability (numbers in parentheses are correlations of the KSFs with profitability). The study uses five-point Likert scales to measure each item. In one of their studies, the correlations below of 161 firms engaging in new product development indicate that the presence versus absence of a factor is not sufficient for high profitability:

- A high-quality new product process (.416)
- A defined new product strategy for the business unit (.228)
- Adequate resources-people and money-for new products (.244)
- R&D spending on new products (as % of the business's sales) (ns = not significant)
- High-quality new product development teams (.196)
- Senior management commitment to new products (.268)
- An innovative climate and culture in the business unit (.243)
- The use of cross-functional teams for product development (.230)
- Senior management accountability for new product results (.228).

The use of the expressions, "key success factors" and "critical success factors," are misleading in that none of the correlations indicate necessary or sufficiency for high profitability. The effect size of these correlations indicate that while some of these actions may be useful in combinations with other actions, none alone are sufficient for high profitability. None of the factors are necessary or sufficient for a highly successful product development.

If these nine dimensions represent somewhat unique KSFs, what combinations of high versus low values among the 9 KSFs lead to high profitability? Any one firm among firms with a highly profitable new product is unlikely to achieve level 5 (highest) evaluations for all nine dimensions. Using a property-space approach (Lazarsfeld, 1937), considering three levels for each dimension – low, moderate, high – a total of 19,683 combinations are possible (p. 39). A few of these paths are likely to result in highly profitable new product outcomes – possibly 10% of the paths or about 200 paths. About 30% of the paths are likely to result in substantial losses – about 600 paths. The remaining paths are likely to be untried and most may represent non-implementable decision recipes. Multiple "key success paths" (KSPs) relate to high scores for product innovation success rather than KSFs.

Third, referring to success and competencies, McClelland (1998) stresses that many relationships among a dependent variable and independent variables are not linear and not well described by correlation coefficients. Instead, such relationships are describable as "tipping points" (Gladwell, 1996). What sociologists often observe in changes in a societal variable making little difference until the changes reach a certain level is likely to occur in business research contexts as well.

McClelland (1998) illustrates this tenet for the relationship of competency frequencies and levels to success as an executive. For example, Figure 2 shows that for "Impact and Influence," the T (i.e., typical executives) group is more likely than the O (i.e., outstanding executives) group to have a frequency score anywhere from 0 to 7; the O group is more numerous than the T group only when the frequency score reaches 8–10; further, this O versus T difference does not change at higher frequency scores, above 10. So it would be a misrepresentation of the relationship to describe it in terms of a linear correlation coefficient. For the data graphed in Figure 1, for example, the biserial r is .22, $p < .10$, between O versus T status and frequency of the competency "Impact and Influence," but this statistic understates the significance of the relationship (55% of the O executives vs. 20% of the T executives had frequencies of 8 or more, $p < .001$) and misrepresents its nature for frequencies below 8.

Thirteen studies of managers were examined to see whether the O group satisfied the following algorithm: mean frequency or maximum-levels core significantly higher than that of the T (T = typical) managers (a) on at least one of the initiative and one of the organizational competencies and (b) on a total of five competencies drawn from the list in McClelland's Table 1

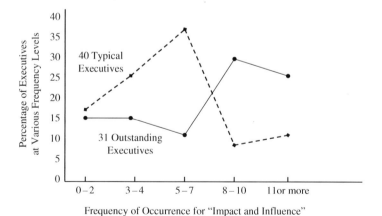

Figure 2. Percentages of Outstanding and Typical Executives Showing Different Frequencies of the Competency "Impact and Influence." *Source:* McClelland (1998).

(McClelland's Table 1 includes 12 competencies from "Achievement Orientation" to "Team Leadership"). The O groups in 11 (85%) of the studies satisfied this algorithm, compared with only 1 out of 8 (13%) studies of individual contributors, that is, technical and professional personnel such as geologists, consultants, and insurance raters ($p < .01$ for the difference in proportions).

Thus, in McClelland's (1998) study competency algorithms that associate with success in various types of executive positions are observable by using the principle of substitutability; that is, a variety of different but functionally equivalent alternative predictor variables may relate to an outcome criterion. To some extent, therefore, different competencies can substitute for each other.

In a seminal paper, Mauro (1995) makes the same point about substitutability in his research on the impact of country-level corruption, red tape, and institution inefficiency on total investment as well as GDP growth. Mauro's (1995) data set consists of the Business International (BI) indices on corruption, red tape, and the inefficiency of the judicial systems for 1980–1983. The indices are based on standard questionnaires filled in by BI's correspondents stationed in about 70 countries. He restricts his analysis to nine indicators; each averaged over four years – "a less noisy indicator of institutional variables, which we may expect to change only slowly" (Mauro, 1995, p. 684).

The BI indices are integers between 0 and 10 and a high value of the index means that the country in question has "good" institutions. In his "Section III" and the first five columns after "nation" in Appendix B to this chapter, each indicator is the simple average for the country in question for the period 1980–1983. Mauro grouped together each of the nine indicators into one of five summary indicators based on "closely related on a prior grounds, the indices that I choose to group together are more strongly correlated with each other" (Mauro, 1995, p. 686).

Mauro (1995) observes that all BI indices are positively and significantly correlated before and after controlling for gross domestic product (GDP) per capita. "A number of mechanisms may contribute to explaining the positive correlation[s] among all categories of institutional efficiency. Corruption may be expected to be more widespread in counties where red tape slows down bureaucratic procedures .... At the same time this multicollinearity makes it difficult to tell which of the several institutional factors examined is crucial for investment and growth. As a consequence, it may be desirable to combine groups of variables into composite indices" (Mauro, 1995, pp. 685–686).

The difficulty is overcome if the researcher moves beyond thinking in terms of which of the several institutional factors are crucial; none are crucial but a few combinations of these variables are likely to associate with high levels of investment and high levels of growth. Rather than developing theory and thinking in terms of relative impacts of independent variables, thinking in terms of alternative mechanisms (i.e., algorithms) indicates that several causal recipes relate to high economic growth.

The following additional point has profound theoretically and practical importance. For one or more cases a **low** score on anyone antecedent condition (such as "Achievement Orientation" in McClelland's study or corruption in Mauro's study) may combine with other antecedents to result in a **high** score on the outcome condition. With medium-to-large sample sizes, cases occur with seemingly unusual scores on any one simple antecedent condition ("independent variable") that are counter to the primary influence (the "main effect") of the simple condition and the outcome.

While in Mauro's (1995) study the BI indices all correlate positively, at the case level combinations occur that run counter to this finding – as Mauro reports in "Table II" in his paper. While some countries have relatively high or low scores in all five indices relating to corruption, red tape, and efficiency, other countries have surprising combination of low, medium, and high scores. For example, consider Zimbabwe's scores in Appendix B for 1980–1983; the scores include high calibrated values for judicial efficiency, red tape (indicating low red tape), corruption (indicating low corruption), and bureaucracy efficiency – and a low calibrated score for political stability (indicating high instability). Does such a country causal recipe associate with high economic growth? In the case of Zimbabwe, the answer is no – calibrated growth is zero.

As McClelland (1998) and others (Gigerenzer & Brighton, 2009) stress, the critical question is whether or not a model (e.g., an empirical multiple regression model or an algorithm) predicts a dependent variable in additional samples – holdout samples that are separate data sets from the data sets used to test the fit of data to a theory. Gigerenzer and Brighton (2009, p. 118) confirm "that achieving a good fit to observations does not necessarily mean we have found a good model, and choosing the model with the best fit is likely to result in poor predictions. Despite this,

Roberts and Pashler (2000) estimated that, in psychology alone, the number of articles relying on a good fit as the only indication of a good model runs into the thousands." Currently, this bad practice occurs for most submissions to the JBR and likely for most submissions and published articles in all business-related journals.

Gigerenzer and Brighton's (2009) study explains in-depth why high model fit results in low predictive validity. Their observation and conclusions are central to the purpose of the present chapter. Their Figure 1 (Figure 3 here) is profound in illustrating Armstrong's (2012) observations about MRA.

Analysts assume that models with a better fit provide more accurate forecasts. This ignores the research

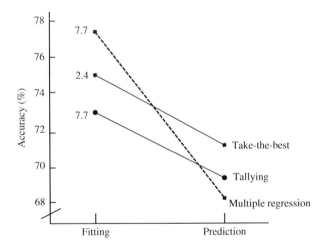

Figure 3. Moving beyond Fit to Prediction Validity *Notes*: Figure 1: Less is more effects. Both tallying and take-the-best predict more accurately than multiple regression, despite using less information and computation. Note that multiple regression excels in data fitting ("hindsight"), that is, fitting its parameters to data that are already known, but performs relatively poorly in prediction ("foresight," as in cross-validation. Take-the-best is the most frugal, that is, it looks up on average, only 2.4 cues when making inferences. In contrast, both multiple regression analysis and tallying look up 7.7 cues on average. The results shown are averaged across 20 studies, including psychological, biological, sociological, and economic inference tasks (Czerlinski, Gigerenzer, & Goldstein, 1999). For each of the 20 studies and each of the three strategies, the 95% confidence intervals were ≤4 percentage points. *Source*: Gigerenzer and Brighton (2009, Figure 1, p. 112).

showing that fit bears little relationship to ex ante forecast accuracy, especially for time series. Typically, fit
improves as complexity increases, while ex ante forecast
accuracy decreases – a conclusion that Zellner (2001)
traced back to Sir Harold Jeffreys in the 1930s. In addition, analysts use statistics to improve the fit of the model
to the data. In one of my Tom Swift studies, Tom used
standard procedures when starting with 31 observations
and 30 potential variables. He used stepwise regression
and included only variables where t was greater than 2.0.
Along the way, he dropped three outliers. The final
regression had eight variables and an R-square (adjusted
for degrees of freedom) of 0.85. Not bad, considering
that the data were from Rand's book of random numbers
(Armstrong, 1970). I traced studies on this illusion back
to at least 1956 in an early review of the research on fit
and accuracy (Armstrong, 1985). Studies have continued
to find the fit is not a good way to assess predictive ability (e.g., Pant & Starbuck, 1990). The obvious solution is
to avoid use of t, p, F, R-squared and the like when using
regression. (Armstrong, 2012, p. 690)

Armstrong's (2012) observations are valuable for referencing
in particular when looking at an MRA table with six-to-twenty
independent terms in the attempt to control for influences beyond
the focal independent variables. "Users of regression assume that
by putting variables into the equation they are somehow controlling for these variables. This only occurs for experimental data.
Adding variables does not mean controlling for variables in non-
experimental data because many variables typically co-vary with
other predictor variables. The problem becomes worse as variables are added to the regression. Large sample sizes cannot
resolve this problem, so statistics on the number of degrees of
freedom are misleading" (Armstrong, 2012, p. 691).

Armstrong (2012) recommends against estimating relationships for more than three variables in a regression – findings
from Goldstein and Gigerenzer (2002) are consistent with this
rule-of-thumb. A complementary recommendation is not to
report MRA findings without also reporting findings from using
simple algorithms and never report findings for fit validity
only – always report predictive validity findings from tests of
models with holdout samples.

Illustrating MRA and Algorithms

Appendix B includes "gdpgro" that represents data for average annual GDP (in purchasing power parity USD, PPP) per capita for 2006–2011 – hereafter GDP growth. These data are available from the annual Central Intelligence Agency (CIA) World Factbook. The CIA World Factbook publications are available online, for example, CIA World Factbook (2012). The study here examines the issue of whether or not Mauro's data on corruption, red tape, and efficiency for 1980–1983 relates to average GDP growth for 2006–2011. Given that all variables usually change slowly, the study is likely to support the hypothesis that the corruption, red tape, and inefficiency reduce growth.

For the total available sample of 66 nations, the MRA findings in Table 2 do not support the hypothesis. Significant partial regression (b) coefficients do not occur from entering all five variables (or anyone variable – not shown) into a regression equation to predict GDP growth. A correlation matrix (Table 3) shows that all five indexes for corruption, red tape, and efficiencies relate to each other significantly and none relate to 2006–2011 GDP growth.

Figure 4a shows findings from using two of the variables and an interaction term for these variables in examining the data for a randomly created subsample of nations from the total data set. These findings provide modest support of the hypothesis that judicial inefficiency and corruption affects GDP growth, if a model includes these two variables with an interaction term (adjusted R^2 = .133, p < .083). The impact of both variables meets expectations that less corruption and more efficiency serve to increase GDP growth – both variables have b coefficients with t values greater than 2.00.

Figure 4b shows the findings for the remaining data in the random split of the data for testing the same model. These results are similar to the other model though the b coefficient for only judiciary efficiency is significant statistically (t = 2.267, p < .030).

However, testing for predictive validity of the first model on the second holdout sample indicates that the model does not have acceptable predictive validity. The correlation appears at the bottom of Figure 4a and b for the comparison of predicted and actual scores, r = 0.67 (p < .698). Using the estimated model from the second sample to predict the scores of the first sample

Table 2: Multiple Regression Analysis for Entire Sample of 66 Nations Model Summary.

Model Summary

Model	R	R^2	Adjusted R^2	Std. Error of the Estimate
1	.223[a]	.050	−.029	.06819

ANOVA[b]

Model	Sum of Squares	df	Mean Square	F	Sig.
1 Regression	.015	5	.003	.630	.678[c]
Residual	.279	60	.005		
Total	.294	65			

Coefficients[d]

Model	Unstandardized Coefficients		Standardized Coefficients	t	Sig.
	B	Std. Error	Beta		
1 (Constant)	−.001	.050		−.025	.980
judiciary	.015	.012	.475	1.266	.210
redtape	.006	.011	.197	.521	.605
corruption	.018	.014	.659	1.261	.212
polstability	.009	.009	.180	.989	.327
bureu_eff	−.041	.032	−1.302	−1.277	.206

[a]Predictors: (Constant), bureu_eff, poistability, redtape, judiciary, corruption.
[b]Dependent Variable: gdp_grow_06_11_ave.
[c]Predictors: (Constant), bureu_eff, polstability, redtape, judiciary, corruption.
[d]Dependent Variable: gdp_grow_06_11_ave.

leads to the same conclusion; the model provides more noise than information.

Table 4 follows from taking an additional look at the data to test the hypothesis the countries scoring the highest in judicial inefficiency in combination with highest scores in corruption had lower GDP growth in comparison to the countries with low scores in judicial inefficiency. Nine countries had extremely high scores for both of these two variables — that is, scores of 1.0 for each variable (recall that 10.0 is equal to excellent performance and 1.0 is extremely low performance). For these nine countries, average GDP growth is equal to −0.0042 with a standard error of the mean equal to 0.0195 while average GDP growth is

Table 3: Correlations of Measures for Inefficiency and Corruption and GDP Average Annual Growth per Capita in PPP Correlations.

Correlations		Judiciary	Redtape	Corruption	Polstability	Bureu_eff	Gdp_grow_06_11_ave
judiciary	Pearson Correlation	1	.747**	.751**	.675**	.891**	.080
	Sig. (2-tailed)		.000	.000	.000	.000	.522
	N	66	66	66	66	66	66
redtape	Pearson Correlation	.747**	1	.749**	.633**	.891**	.000
	Sig. (2-tailed)	.000		.000	.000	.000	.999
	N	66	66	66	66	66	66
corruption	Pearson Correlation	.751**	.749**	1	.494**	.929**	.043
	Sig. (2-tailed)	.000	.000		.030	.000	.730
	N	66	66	66	66	66	66
polstability	Pearson Correlation	.675**	.633**	.494**	1	.653**	.102
	Sig. (2-tailed)	.000	.000	.000		.000	.413
	N	66	66	66	66	66	66
bureu_eff	Pearson Correlation	.891**	.891**	.929**	.653**	1	.027
	Sig. (2-tailed)	.000	.000	.000	.000		.830
	N	66	66	66	66	66	66
gdp_grow_06_11_ave	Pearson Correlation	.080	.000	.043	.102	.027	1
	Sig. (2-tailed)	.522	.999	.730	.413	.830	
	N	66	66	66	66	66	66

**Correlation is significant at the 0.01 level (2-tailed).

substantially higher for countries with lower scores on the combination of judiciary inefficiency and corruption. Details in Table 4 include a large effect size ($\eta^2 = .155$).

Note that the findings in Table 4 indicate that high GDP growth associate with many nations with relative high, but not the highest, levels of corruption, red tape, and inefficiency. The mean findings are suggestive that some interesting patterns among the five efficiency indices are likely to occur in regards to influencing GDP growth.

To further explore the possibility that causal recipes of two or more variables of corruption, red tape, and government inefficiencies may influence GDP growth, each of the variables in the original data were calibrated using the computer software subroutine in the fsQCA software program. The procedure is analogous to performing a z-scale transformation of original data; see Ragin (2008) for details. The researcher needs to specify three values for calibrating an original scale into a fuzzy-set scale: the original value covering 5% of the data values, 50% of the values, and 95% of the values. Table 5 provides the original values for these three points for each of the five independent variables and GDP growth.

In fsQCA, configural statements proposed by theory as well as all possible configural statements are testable using the fsQCA software. The program tests "logical and" statements of the possible combinations of the independent (simple to complex) antecedent expressions. The score for a "logical and" statement is equal to the lowest value of the simple antecedents in a statement containing two or more antecedent conditions. For example, Algeria appears in the first row of Appendix B; the score for Algeria for the conjunctive statement judic_cal AND redtape_cal AND corrupt_cal is equal to 0.08. The score 0.08 is the lowest value among the three scores for Algeria for the respective simple antecedent conditions of judic_cal (0.63), redtape_cal (0.08), and corrupt_cal (0.23).

Using the software for fsQCA to test for the occurrence of different conjunctive statements (i.e., Mauro's "mechanisms"), six conjunctive statements (causal recipes) associate with high growth. In fsQCA, a researcher usually concludes that a model is informative when consistency is above 0.74 and coverage is between .25 and .65 (Ragin, 2008).

Table 6 describes these six complex antecedent conditions. The first complex statement is the combination of high judicial inefficiency (indicated by the negation symbol, "~" for judicial

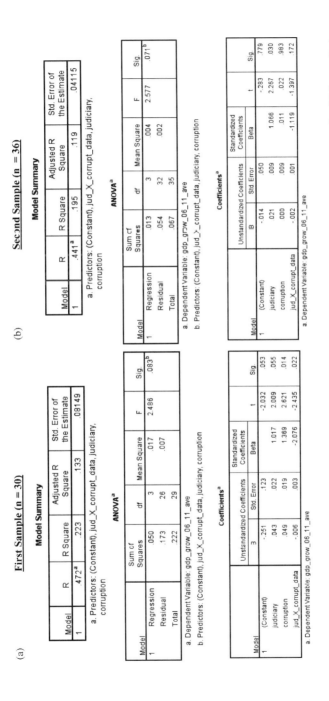

Figure 4. Multiple Regression Analysis for Two Random Samples of Nations. *Notes:* Using first sample model to predict GDP growth for first sample data: $r = 0.067$, $p < .698$, $n = 36$. Using second sample model to predict GDP growth for second sample data: $r = 0.004$, $p < .984$, $n = 30$.

Table 4: Analysis of the Joint Lagged Impact of Judicial
Inefficiency and Corruption on GDP Growth.

Report

gdp_grow_06_11_ave

Judicial by Corruption 4 Grps	Mean	N	Std. Error of Mean
Highest	−.0042	9	.01951
High	.0723	31	.01184
Low	.0750	9	.03096
Lowest	.0471	17	.00885
Total	.0558	66	.00827

ANOVA Table

			Sum of Squares	df	Mean Square	F	Sig.
gdp_grow_06_11_ave * Judicial by corruption 4 grps	Between groups	(Combined)	.045	3	.015	3.781	.015
		Linearity	.001	1	.001	.139	.711
		Deviation from linearity	.045	2	.022	5.603	.006
	Within groups		.248	62	.0004		
	Total		.294	65			

Measures of Association

	R	R^2	Eta	Eta Squared
gdp_grow_06_11_ave * Judicial by corruption 4 Grps	.043	.002	.393	.155

efficiency, AND low corruption, AND high political instability. Negation scores in fsQCA are equal to 1 minus the original calibrated score. For example, for Algeria in Appendix B, the negation score for the nation's judicial score equal to 0.63 is equal to 0.37.

Figure 5 is an XY plot for the first complex antecedent condition in Table 6 (representing not judicial efficiency AND low corruption AND not political stability) and GDP growth using calibrated scores. The bottom right quarter of the plot is nearly empty – indicating high sufficiency but not necessary condition for high GDP growth. South Africa has a relatively high score for the conjunctive statement but low GDP growth – this nation fails to support the conclusion that high GDP growth always occurs among nations with scores above 0.5 for the first complex antecedent condition. The research would want to study South Africa

Table 5: Summary Data for Country Efficiency, Corruption, Political Stabil.ty, and GDP Growth Study Statistics.

		Judiciary	Redtape	Corruption	Polstability	Bureu_eff	gdp_grow_06_11_ave
N	Valid	66	66	66	66	66	66
	Missing	0	0	0	0	0	0
Mean		7.0970	6.1562	6.8920	7.5305	6.6974	.0558
Std. error of mean		.26634	.28159	.30673	.16792	.26437	.00827
Median		6.8750	6.0000	7.0000	7.6900	6.4200	.0433
Std. deviation		2.16376	2.28762	2.49192	1.36421	2.14772	.06721
Minimum		2.00	1.25	1.50	3.25	2.00	−.09
Maximum		10.00	10.00	10.00	10.00	10.00	.27
Notes: Calibration values at:							
95%		9.00	9.00	9.00	9.00	9.00	.2200
50%		6.875	6.000	7.000	7.690	6.42	.0433
5%		2.50	1.75	2.00	3.75	2.50	.0000

Table 6:   Findings from fsQCA for Efficiency, Corruption, Red Tape, an GDP Growth.

—COMPLEX SOLUTION—

Frequency cutoff: 1.000000

Consistency cutoff: 0.758904

	Raw Coverage	Unique Coverage	Consistency
~judic_cal*corrupt_cal*~polstab_cal	0.328338	0.047343	0.778047
judic_cal*~redtape_cal*~corrupt_cal*~bureau_cal	0.370232	0.053815	0.778096
~judic_cal*redtape_cal*~corrupt_cal*~bureau_cal	0.331403	0.029292	0.819023
judic_cal*~redtape_cal*polstab_cal*~bureau_cal	0.361035	0.030995	0.761494
redtape_cal*corrupt_cal*~polstab_cal*bureau_cal	0.349796	0.076976	0.743664
~judic_cal*redtape_cal*polstab_cal*bureau_cal	0.314033	0.019755	0.763877

solution coverage: 0.655313

solution consistency: 0.723853

Cases with greater than 0.5 membership in term ~judic_cal*corrupt_cal*~polstab_cal: angola (0.88,0.97), iraq (0.65, 0.72), nicaragua (0.65, 0.53), s_africa (0.65, 0.01), peru (0.52, 0.69).

Cases with greater than 0.5 membership in term judic_cal*~redtape_cal*~corrupt_cal*~bureau_cal: india (0.67, 0.09), jamaica (0.66, 0.88), algeria (0.63, 0.09), colomiba (0.63, 0.65), nigeria (0.63, 0.94), trinidad (0.55, 0.84), greece (0.54, 0.57).

Cases with greater than 0.5 membership in term ~judic_cal*redtape_cal*~corrupt_cal*~bureau_cal: egypt (0.56, 0.65), korea_s (0.56, 0.65), panama (0.52, 0.81).

Cases with greater than 0.5 membership in term ~judic_cal*~redtape_cal*polstab_cal*~bureau_cal: israel (0.75, 0.57), chile (0.72, 0.61), Zimbabwe (0.71,0) s_africa (0.66, 0.01).

Cases with greater than 0.5 membership in term ~judic_cal*redtape_cal*polstab_cal*bureau_cal: austria (0.78, 0.44), argentina (0.52, 0.17), taiwan (0.52, 0.57).

further to learn why this complex causal statement does not relate to high GDP growth for the country.

The findings in Table 6 indicate that high corruption may associate with high GDP growth and low corruption may associate with high GDP growth depending on other simple antecedents forming conjunctive statements with high and low corruption – the same conclusion applies for judicial efficiency and political stability. Understanding how corruption, red tape, and government inefficiencies affect GDP growth requires going beyond examining simple main effects and two-way interaction effects. Thinking and advancing theory using causal recipes are useful in particular in business research, as well as the study of chronic (i.e., measured) variables or a mix of chronic and manipulated (i.e., active or "experimental") variables.

The country identifications in findings for high GDP growth in Table 6 indicate that countries with consistently high calibrated scores across all five simple antecedent conditions do not have high calibrated scores for GDP growth – though they do have growth rates above the a separate group of nations with zero GDP growth rates. The conclusion is that nations low in corruption and high in all forms of government efficiencies do

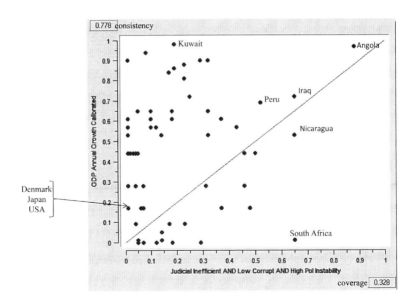

Figure 5.   Example fsQCA Findings for Efficiency, Corruption, Red Tape, and GDP Growth.

not appear to experience very high GDP growth rates and also avoid the bottom level of GDP growth rates. Very high growth rates may extend to a few years with a recipe that includes a high corruption while maintaining low inefficiencies or the reverse recipe – Iceland and Greece during 2002–2007 would be examples of such antecedent combinations and high GDP growth.

Consider the substantial benefit from studying the case findings in Figure 4 and Table 6. In fsQCA the researcher is able to generalize beyond the individual case but still identify individual cases in specific models relevant to her investigation.

The following observation by Ragin (2006, p. 7) relates to comparing the examination of conjunctive statements using MRA versus fsQCA: "The search for patterns of multiple conjunctural causation[s], a common concern of case-oriented researchers, poses serious practical problems for variable-oriented research." To investigate this type of causation with statistical techniques, it is necessary to examine high-level interactions (e.g., three-way interactions in the causal argument just described).

> However, these sophisticated techniques are very rarely used by variable-oriented researchers. When they are, they require at least two essential ingredients: (1) a very large number of diverse cases, and (2) an investigator willing to contend with a difficult mass of multi-collinearity. These techniques are simply not feasible in investigations with small or even moderate Ns, the usual situation in comparative social science. When Ns are small to moderate, causal complexity is more apparent, more salient, and easier to identify and interpret; yet it is also much less amenable to statistical analysis. (Ragin, 2006, pp. 7–8)

Conclusion

Tools shape theory as well as how a researcher goes about analyzing data. Taking time to read Gigerenzer's (1991) brilliant review on this perspective is worthwhile. Researchers need to embrace Armstrong's (2012) recommendations on testing for predictive validity and not just fit validity and not attempting to control the effects of other variables by simply adding them to produce regression equations with many terms. Adopt McClelland (1998) approach in moving beyond the use of MRA and crafting and testing algorithms. Embrace Ragin's (2008) thinking and modeling in terms of conjunctive statements — think and test algorithms — rather than thinking only in net effects of variables on a dependent variable.

Acknowledgment

The author gratefully acknowledges permission granted by the publisher, Elsevier, to reuse content appearing in this chapter from Woodside (2013).

References

Armstrong, J. S. (1970). How to avoid exploratory research. *Journal of Advertising Research*, *10*(4), 27–30.

Armstrong, J. S. (1985). *Long-range forecasting*. New York, NY: Wiley.

Armstrong, J. S. (2012). Illusions in regression analysis. *International Journal of Forecasting*, *28*, 689–694.

CIA World Factbook. (2012). Retrieved from https://www.cia.gov/library/publications/the-world-factbook/index.html

Cooper, R. G., & Kleinschmidt, E. J. (2007). Winning businesses in product development: The critical success factors. *Research-Technology Management*, *50*, 52–66. Retrieved from http://www.proddev.com/downloads/working_papers/wp_6.pdf

Czerlinski, J., Gigerenzer, G., & Goldstein, D. G. (1999). How good are simple heuristics? In G. Gigerenzer, P. M. Todd, & the ABC Research Group (Eds.), *Simple heuristics that make us smart* (pp. 97–118). New York, NY: Oxford University Press.

Gigerenzer, G. (1991). From tools to theories: A heuristic of discovery in cognitive psychology. *Psychological Review*, *98*, 254–267.

Gigerenzer, G., & Brighton, H. (2009). Homo heuristicus: Why biased minds make better inferences. *Topics in Cognitive Science*, *1*, 107–143.

Gladwell, M. (1996). The tipping point. *The New Yorker*, *72*, 32–39.

Goldstein, D. G., & Gigerenzer, G. (2002). Models of ecological rationality: The recognition heuristic. *Pyschological Review*, *109*, 75–90.

Hotchkiss, E., Smith, D. C., & Strömberg, P. (2013). Private equity and the resolution of financial distress. *Journal of Finance*, *64*, 1549–1582.

Lazarsfeld, P. F. (1937). Some remarks on the typological procedures in social research. *Zeitschrift fur Sozialforschung*, *6*, 119–139.

Mauro, P. (1995). Corruption and growth. *The Quarterly Journal of Economics*, *110*(3), 681–712. doi:10.2307/2946696.

McClelland, D. C. (1998). Identifying competencies with behavioral-event interviews. *Psychological Science*, *9*, 331–3339.

Pant, P. N., & Starbuck, W. H. (1990). Innocents in the forest: Forecasting and research methods. *Journal of Management, 16*(2), 433–460.

Prado, A. (2010). *Choosing among competing environmental and labor standards: An exploratory analysis of producer adoption.* Working Paper. November 15, 2010. Stern School, New York University, New York, NY. Retrieved from http://www. hec.fr/var/fre/storage/original/application/2077b49afc2915a82b50d9675729f99f.pdf

Ragin, C. (2006). Turning the tables: How case-oriented research challenges variable-oriented research. *Comparative Social Research, 16*, 27–42.

Ragin, C. (2008). *Redesigning social inquiry: Fuzzy sets and beyond.* Chicago, IL: Chicago University Press.

Roberts, S., & Pashler, H. (2000). How persuasive is a good fit? A comment on theory testing. *Psychological Review, 107*, 358–367.

Woodside, A. G. (2011). Responding to the severe limitations of cross-sectional surveys: Commenting on Rong and Wilkinson's perspectives. *Australasian Marketing Journal, 19*, 153–156.

Woodside, A. G. (2013). Moving beyond multiple regression analysis to algorithms: Calling for adoption of a paradigm shift from symmetric to asymmetric thinking in data analysis and crafting theory. *Journal of Business Research, 66*, 463–472.

Woodside, A. G. (2013). Proposing a new logic for data analysis in marketing and consumer behavior: Case study research of large-N survey data for estimating algorithms that accurately profile X (extremely high-use) consumers. *Journal of Global Scholars of Marketing Science, 22*, 277–289.

Zellner, A. (2001). Keep it sophisticatedly simple. In H. Keuzenkamp & M. McAleer (Eds.), *Simplicity, inference, and modeling: Keeping it sophisticatedly simple.* Cambridge: Cambridge University Press.

Appendix A

Table A1: Computing Consistency and Coverage in Fuzzy-Set Qualitative Comparative Analysis.

x_Calibrated	y_Calibrated	Minimum (X_i, Y_i)
0.02	0.98	0.02
0.03	0.98	0.03
0.25	0.98	0.25
0.97	0.98	0.97
0.98	0.98	0.98
0.02	0.5	0.02
0.07	0.5	0.05
0.1	0.5	0.05
0.32	0.5	0.32
0.41	0.5	0.41
0.02	0.02	0.02
0.03	0.02	0.02
0.05	0.02	0.02
0.07	0.02	0.02
0.1	0.02	0.02
$\Sigma = 3.44$	7.5	3.2
Consistency $(X_i \leq Y_i) =$	$\Sigma[\min(X_i, Y_i)]/\Sigma(X_i)$	3.2/3.44 = 0.93
Coverage $(X_i \leq Y_i) =$	$\Sigma[\min(X_i, Y_i)]/\Sigma(\ Y_i)$	3.2/7.5 = 0.43

Notes: Data are same as the final two columns in Table 1. The small differences in the consistency and coverage indexes in Table 2 and Figure 1b are due to rounding.

Appendix B

Table B1:   Efficiency, Corruption, Red Tape, and GDP Growth Data, Countries A through M.

Nation	Judic	Redtape	Corrpupt	Polstab	Burea	Gdpgro	Judi c_ca l	Redtape_c	Aclorrupt_c	Pl olstab_c	Bl ureau_ca	Lgpd_gro_cal
Algeria	7.25	2.5	5	7.71	4.92	0.01	0.63	0.08	0.23	0.51	0.24	0.39
Angola	4	6.33	8.66	4.61	6	0.24	0.12	0.58	0.92	0.09	0.42	0.97
Argentina	6	6.66	7.66	7.72	6.77	0.02	0.35	0.66	0.73	0.52	0.6	0.17
Australia	10	9.25	10	8.5	9.75	0.05	0.99	0.96	0.99	0.86	0.98	0.53
Austria	5	7.25	8	9.04	8.25	0.04	0.22	0.78	0.82	0.96	0.89	0.44
Bangladesh	6	4	4	6.5	4.67	-0.02	0.35	0.2	0.14	0.29	0.21	0.01
Belgium	9.5	8	9.76	8	9.08	0.04	0.98	0.88	0.98	0.67	0.96	0.44
Brazil	5.75	4	5.75	7.54	5.17	0.05	0.32	0.2	0.32	0.47	0.28	0.53
Cameroon	7	6	7	8.5	6.67	0.05	0.54	0.5	0.5	0.86	0.57	0.53
Canada	9.25	9.5	10	9	9.58	0.04	0.97	0.97	0.99	0.95	0.98	0.44
Chile	7.25	9.25	9.25	6.46	8.58	0.07	0.63	0.96	0.97	0.28	0.92	0.61
Colomiba	7.25	4.5	4.5	6	5.42	0.08	0.63	0.26	0.18	0.22	0.32	0.65
Denmark	10	9.5	9.25	8.5	9.58	0.02	0.99	0.97	0.97	0.86	0.98	0.17
DominiCa	6.75	6	6.5	7.58	6.42	0.06	0.48	0.5	0.43	0.48	0.5	0.57
Ecuador	6.25	6	5.5	6.63	5.58	0.17	0.39	0.5	0.29	0.31	0.34	0.9
Egypt	6.5	8	3.25	8.67	4.25	0.08	0.44	0.88	0.1	0.9	0.16	0.65
Finland	10	8.5	9.5	8.79	9.33	0.03	0.99	0.92	0.98	0.93	0.97	0.28
France	8	6.75	10	8.92	8.25	0.02	0.83	0.68	0.99	0.94	0.89	0.17

Ge rmany	9	7.5	9.5	8.21	8.67	0.04	0.95	0.82	0.98	0.77	0.93	0.44
Ghana	4.66	2.33	3.66	5	3.55	−0.04	0.18	0.07	0.12	0.11	0.1	0
Greece	7	4	6.25	8.63	5.76	0.06	0.54	0.2	0.39	0.9	0.38	0.57
Haiti	2	2	2	6.67	2	−0.04	0.03	0.06	0.05	0.32	0.03	0
Hongkong	10	9.75	8	9.5	9.26	0.04	0.99	0.98	0.82	0.98	0.96	0.44
India	8	3.25	5.25	7	5.5	0.01	0.83	0.13	0.26	0.37	0.33	0.09
Indonesia	2.5	2.75	1.5	7.46	2.25	0.03	0.05	0.09	0.04	0.46	0.04	0.28
Irand	2	1.25	3.25	3.25	2.17	0.08	0.03	0.03	0.1	0.03	0.04	0.65
Iraq	6	3	10	5.72	6.33	0.1	0.35	0.11	0.99	0.18	0.48	0.72
Ireland	8.75	7.5	9.75	7.67	8.67	0.03	0.93	0.82	0.98	0.5	0.93	0.28
Israel	10	7.5	9.25	6.25	8.92	0.06	0.99	0.82	0.97	0.25	0.95	0.57
Italy	6.75	4.75	7.5	7.92	6.33	0.02	0.48	0.29	0.68	0.63	0.48	0.17
Jamaica	7.33	4	5	7.5	5.44	0.16	0.66	0.2	0.23	0.46	0.32	0.88
Japan	10	8.5	8.75	9.42	9.08	0.02	0.99	0.92	0.93	0.98	0.96	0.17
Jordan	8.66	6.33	8.33	7.78	7.77	0.02	0.93	0.58	0.88	0.55	0.83	0.17
Kenya	5.75	6	4.5	6.96	5.08	0.07	0.32	0.5	0.18	0.36	0.26	0.61
Korea_s	6	6.5	5.75	7.5	6.08	0.08	0.35	0.62	0.32	0.46	0.44	0.65
Kuwait	7.5	6.25	7.75	8.33	7.17	0.27	0.71	0.56	0.75	0.81	0.71	0.98
Liberia	3.33	5	2.66	5	3.66	−0.09	0.08	0.33	0.07	0.11	0.11	0
Malaysia	9	6	6	8.42	7	0.08	0.95	0.5	0.35	0.84	0.66	0.65
Mexico	6	5.25	3.25	6.88	4.83	0.07	0.35	0.37	0.1	0.35	0.23	0.61
Morocco	6.66	5.33	5.66	7.11	5.88	0.03	0.46	0.38	0.31	0.39	0.4	0.28

Table B2: Efficiency, Corruption, Red Tape, and GDP Growth Data, Countries N through Z.

Nation	Judic	Redtape	Corrupt	Polstab	Burea	Gdpgro	JUDIC_cal	Redtape_cal	Corrupt_cal	Polstab_cal	Bureau_cal	Gdp_gro_cal
The Netherlands	10	10	10	8.83	10	0.06	0.99	0.98	0.99	0.93	0.98	0.57
New Zealand	10	10	10	8.5	10	0.03	0.99	0.98	0.99	0.86	0.98	0.28
Nicaragua	6	4	8.75	5.5	6.25	0.05	0.35	0.2	0.93	0.16	0.47	0.53
Nigeria	7.25	2.75	3	7.29	4.33	0.21	0.63	0.09	0.08	0.42	0.17	0.94
Norway	10	9	10	9.5	9.67	0.07	0.99	0.95	0.99	0.98	0.98	0.61
Pakistan	5	4	4	5.33	4.33	0	0.22	0.2	0.14	0.14	0.17	0.05
Panama	6.75	7.25	5	7.54	6.33	0.13	0.48	0.78	0.23	0.47	0.48	0.81
Peru	6.75	5.75	7.25	6.04	6.58	0.09	0.48	0.46	0.59	0.22	0.55	0.69
Philippines	4.76	5	4.5	6.08	4.75	−0.06	0.19	0.33	0.18	0.23	0.22	0
Portugal	5.5	4.5	6.75	7.54	5.58	0.04	0.28	0.26	0.46	0.47	0.34	0.44
Saudi Arabia	6	5.25	4.75	8.33	5.33	0.15	0.35	0.37	0.21	0.81	0.3	0.86
Singapore	10	10	10	10	10	0.17	0.99	0.98	0.99	0.99	0.98	0.9
South Africa	6	7	8	6.5	7	−0.02	0.35	0.73	0.82	0.29	0.66	0.01
Spain	6.25	6	7	6.67	6.42	0.04	0.39	0.5	0.5	0.32	0.5	0.44
Sri Lanka	7	6	7	7.22	6.67	0.03	0.54	0.5	0.5	0.41	0.57	0.28
Sweden	10	8.5	9.23	9	9.25	0.06	0.99	0.92	0.97	0.95	0.96	0.57
Switzerland	10	10	10	9.25	10	0.04	0.99	0.98	0.99	0.97	0.98	0.44
Taiwan	6.75	7.25	6.75	8.58	6.92	0.06	0.48	0.78	0.46	0.88	0.64	0.57
Thailand	3.25	3.25	1.5	5.63	2.67	0.01	0.08	0.13	0.04	0.17	0.05	0.09

Trinidad	8	4	6.5	7.79	6.17	0.14	0.83	0.2	0.43	0.56	0.45	0.84
Turkey	4	5.33	6	8.17	5.11	0.1	0.12	0.38	0.35	0.75	0.27	0.72
The United Kingdom	10	7.75	9.25	8.33	9	0.03	0.99	0.85	0.97	0.81	0.95	0.28
The United States	10	9.25	10	9.33	9.75	0.02	0.99	0.96	0.99	0.98	0.98	0.17
Urugray	6.5	6	8	9	6.83	−0.02	0.44	0.5	0.82	0.95	0.62	0.01
Venezuela	6.5	4	5.75	7.71	5.42	0.17	0.44	0.2	0.32	0.51	0.32	0.9
Zimbabwe	7.5	7.75	8.75	6.5	8	−0.07	0.71	0.85	0.93	0.29	0.86	0

Case-Based Modeling of Business—Business Relationships

Arch G. Woodside and Roger Baxter

ABSTRACT

This chapter points out that the use of a wide range of theoretical paradigms in marketing research requires researchers to use a broad range of methodologies. As an aid in doing so, the chapter argues for the use of case study research (CSR), defines CSR, and describes several CSR theories and methods that are useful for describing, explaining, and forecasting processes occurring in business-to-business (B2B) contexts. The discussion includes summaries of six B2B case studies spanning more than 60 years of research. This chapter advocates embracing the view that learning and reporting objective realities of B2B processes is possible using CSR methods. CSR methods in the chapter include using multiple interviews (2 +) separately of multiple persons participating in B2B processes, direct research and participant observation, decision systems analysis, degrees-of-freedom analysis, ethnographic-decision-tree-modeling, content analysis, and fuzzy-set qualitative comparative analysis (fs/QCA.com). The discussion advocates rejecting the dominant logic of attempting to describe and explain B2B processes by arms-length fixed-point surveys that usually involve responses from one executive per firm with no data-matching of firms in specific B2B relationships — such surveys lack details and accuracy necessary for understanding, describing, and forecasting B2B processes.

Keywords: Business-to-business relationship; case study research; direct research; participant observation; ethnographic decision tree model

Introduction

This chapter points out how marketing researchers can strengthen both the theoretical and the analytical basis of their research by broadening their range of research techniques to include case study research (CSR). As Hult (2011) points out, marketing researchers, including business-to-business (B2B) researchers, use an eclectic mix of theoretical bases for the understanding of phenomena. These theories include general-level theories of marketing, such as Hult's proposal of a marketing organization (MOR) theory and the Vargo & Lusch service-dominant logic (2004) proposal; general theories from other disciplines such as the work of economist Penrose (1959), and midlevel bridging theories such as the contemporary marketing practices (Brodie, Saren, & Pels, 2011).

Because marketing researchers are likely to continue to use a broad range of theoretical bases they need a broader range of epistemologies and methodologies in future in order to investigate marketing phenomena in full depth using these theories (Nicholson, Lindgreen, & Kitchen, 2009). The application of Giddens' (1979) structuration theory is an example. Researchers have applied structuration concepts to marketing problems (Vallaster & de Chernatony, 2006). Nicholson et al. (2009) propose such research for wide applications in relationship marketing to encompass multiple ontological paradigms and to cope with issues of time and space in longitudinal research. Structuration can also help account for both human agency and social structure, which would be beneficial at a fine-grained level of research (Hult, 2011) into the activities of the single human actor in a relationship (Baxter & Olesen, 2008).

Different general-level theories, whether scholars use them individually or in blended forms that incorporate more than one theory or paradigm, can potentially inform marketing research in different ways. However, ontological and epistemological tensions may occur in adopting theories, particularly when they embrace a wide range of paradigms. For example, studies that use structuration often apply it with an interpretivist approach such as the work of Orlikowski (1992) that recognizes multiple realities, whereas marketing tends to look for "one reality," with realism as the predominant ontology (Healy & Perry, 2000). Nicholson et al. (2009) argue that structuration can cope with multiple paradigms. However, there is much debate about this in the literature (DeSanctis & Poole, 1994; Sarason, Dean, & Dillard, 2006). The use of structuration may involve a conflict of paradigms and thus involve epistemological and hence methodological conflict.

These issues of possible incommensurability of paradigms may or may not present problems, but marketing researchers do need to consider them. They need to do so particularly when they blend theories and paradigms because of the potential problems that blending brings (Okhuysen & Bonardi, 2011). Researchers certainly need to understand how these epistemological issues affect the best choice of methodologies to deal with differing paradigms, which is relevant to the focus of this chapter. Although an orientation towards the more positivist, objectivist, and quantitative approaches may have served marketing researchers well in the past, researchers will continue to need a wider range of techniques.

This chapter addresses some of these methodological issues and provides techniques to deal with them. Even if researchers take the approach to research that there is "one imperfectly apprehensible reality" (Healy & Perry, 2000, p. 118), researchers benefit from recognizing and modeling multiple perspectives within that approach. Such recognition requires at least a multiple-respondent approach if not a multiple-technique approach, with triangulation of data sources. CSR can help to apply these approaches.

Before moving on to discussion of CSR foundations and specific techniques in more depth, the chapter now discusses what CSR is. In doing so, the chapter principally takes realism's one-reality multiple-perspective view. Although this discussion will not address the deeper ontological and epistemological issues that the use of new and blended theories and lenses potentially brings, it does provide a rationale for moving to a wider range of methodologies and analysis techniques and a basis for doing so.

Nature of Case Study Research

CSR is an inquiry that focuses on describing, understanding, predicting, and/or controlling the individual (i.e., process, animal, person, household, organization, group, industry, culture, or nationality) (Woodside, 2010). This definition is intentionally broader than the definition that Yin (1994, p. 13) proposes, "A *case study* is an empirical inquiry that investigates a contemporary phenomenon within its real-life context, especially when the boundaries between phenomenon and context are not clearly evident."

For a given study, focusing the research issues, theory, and/or empirical inquiry on the individual ($n = 1$) is the central feature of CSR. As Skinner notes (1966, p. 21), "… instead of studying a thousand rats for one hour each, or a hundred rats for ten hours each, the investigator is likely to study one rat for a thousand hours." This view is not intended to imply that CSR is limited to a sample of $n = 1$. Reports of multiple case studies are available in organization science (Nutt, 1993, 1994) involving business-to-business contexts. In the marketing literature, Howard and Morgenroth (1968) illustrate transforming the research context in one supply chain from $n = 1$ to $n > 30$ by examining alternative thought/action routes taken in separate, but seemingly similar, decisions that include five principal parties in the corporate context: a senior decision-maker, a regional manager, a local distributor, and two sets of competitors.

This chapter's objectives include achieving four outcomes. First, the chapter serves to inform the reader of core assumptions about B2B relationships that serve as rationales for conducting case study research in business-to-business (B2B) contexts. These rationales highlight the need for a range of methodological approaches that cope better with temporal and spatial transferability of results. Cross-sectional research findings, in particular, have the problem that they "offer weak transferability from one contextual setting to another" (Nicholson et al., 2009), whereas CSR, as explained below, has the potential to overcome that problem.

Second, the chapter provides brief summaries of exemplar methods in the literature of B2B CSR studies. Third, the review of these studies provides principles for advancing a behavioral theory of the firm (cf. Cyert & March, 1963). Fourth, the chapter provides examples of useful strategy implications that result from CSR reports.

CORE ASSUMPTIONS SERVING AS RATIONALES FOR CSR

This section of the chapter outlines several assumptions that provide the rationale for the use of CSR. A number precedes each of the core assumptions about B2B relationships that follow and that support the rationale for in-depth CSR. The first two assumptions are about the challenges that the environment poses in B2B research. Assumption (1) notes the concern that in B2B research, there are multiple perspectives of events. Assumption (2) notes different perspectives of participants and hence leads into the assumptions (3) to (6), which note human cognitive limitations that affect the ability to report events. For effective outcomes, researchers need to attend to "both blades of the scissors" (Simon, 1990; Todd & Gigerenzer, 2003) where one blade is environmental issues and the other is cognitive limitations: studying "only one blade is not enough; it takes both for the scissors to cut." The first of the six assumptions follows.

(1) B2B relationships include interactions among four-plus persons. For example, a buyer in a customer firm interacts with a vendor's sales representative and each reports their discussion with one or more persons in their respective firms. The metaphor of listening-to-one-hand-clapping has some relevancy in describing research that reports on interviews or survey answers of only one person who is a participant in a B2B context. Single-respondent research may present only one perspective of events among many and is therefore not sufficiently representative of the depth of meaning of events to be temporally and spatially transferable (Nicholson et al., 2009).

(2) Because participants differ in their perspectives and prior experiences to some important extent in B2B contexts, this contributes to the "multiple perspectives" of the events to which the research relates so that important differences occur in their descriptions of B2B processes and the causes and outcomes of these processes. To clarify and deepen knowledge of what is happening and how participants interpret thinking, actions, and outcomes, case study researchers prefer to observe meetings and interview two-plus persons that interact in B2B contexts. For example, case study researchers prefer to interview a B2B buyer and a B2B vendor separately as well as to observe their face-to-face

meetings rather than rely on responses to a survey from one or the other participant.

Figure 1 illustrates these ideas as well as emphasizes the point that B2B contexts and processes involve several time periods (days, weeks, months, and years). Case study researchers have a strong preference to apply a triangulation of methods in collecting data – interviews of participants, analyses of documents, and direct observation of events such as meetings that are relevant for the same B2B process. They do this to address two issues noted below in more depth: the inability of participants to articulate the processes of intuitive decisions and actions and the varying perspectives of different observers. Triangulation is important in order to establish analytic generalizability and construct validity (Healy & Perry, 2000). Case study researchers tend to interview the same persons on more than one occasion because they recognize that B2B processes are dynamic and occur over several time periods, and hence that time issues are important to interaction in business relationships (Medlin, 2004).

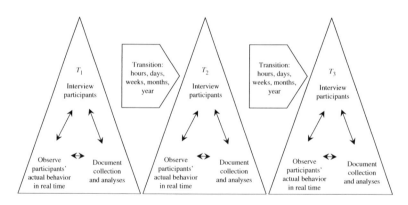

Figure 1. Triangulation in CSR. *Note*: Showing only three time periods is arbitrary; the key point: the case study researcher often prepares written narratives of his or her interviews, direct observations, and document analyses; then, these narratives are presented to selected participants in the following time period to verify that the narratives include the details reported, observed, and found in the previous time period. For examples, see Nutt (1993) and Howards and Morgenroth (1968).

(3) Most thinking occurs unconsciously; humans have limited access to their unconscious thoughts (Wegner, 2002; Wilson, 2002). Dane and Pratt (2007) discuss in-depth the importance of "nonconscious" decision-making to management and point out that in many situations intuitive decision-making is superior to, or a very useful additional tool to, rational decision-making. The naturalistic decision-making paradigm (Lipshitz, Klein, Orasanu, & Salas, 2001), which relies on the concept of intuitive decision making, has been used to explain "how proficient decision-makers are able to cope, and to perform relatively well in the face of complicated real-life challenges" (Vanharanta & Easton, 2010). Vanharanta and Easton (2010) analyze meetings to show the intuitive nature of decisions based on Klein's (1999) recognition-primed decision making (RPD) model and to show how RPD applies to managers forming business-to-business network pictures and using these network pictures to make decisions in their dealing with other network firms.

The extensive occurrence of unconscious thinking means that respondents in business-to-business research, even though they may have a genuine wish to do so, simply cannot fully verbalize situations, because they are not conscious of their own intuitive thought processes which lead to decisions. Hence the need for triangulation of data and techniques in order to uncover information that the managers cannot articulate. For example, in addition to interviews, the researcher might employ direct observation of firm processes, as was used by Vanharanta and Easton (2010) above and which is one of the CSR techniques described below.

(4) Humans edit their thoughts before responding to questions to defend their egos, to appear rational, and to hide information that they believe is best kept confidential to themselves and/or their firm — especially when talking with an interviewer for the first time or when completing a written survey. Figure 2 illustrates these third and fourth assumptions in the context of a buyer and seller in a B2B context — along with the researcher observing their interaction. Managers also attempt, as do others, to achieve consonance of information through a drive to "cognitive consistency" (Simon & Holyoak, 2002) whereby conflicts in information are resolved in the mind. This inevitably

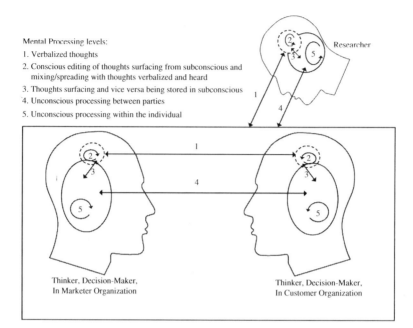

Mental Processing levels:
1. Verbalized thoughts
2. Conscious editing of thoughts surfacing from subconscious and mixing/spreading with thoughts verbalized and heard
3. Thoughts surfacing and vice versa being stored in subconscious
4. Unconscious processing between parties
5. Unconscious processing within the individual

Researcher

Thinker, Decision-Maker,
In Marketer Organization

Thinker, Decision-Maker,
In Customer Organization

Figure 2. The Multiple Mental Processes in Research on Industrial Marketing-Buying Thinking.

results in changes in perceptions of events and processes and consequent distortions, despite the best intentions of interview or survey respondents. As Simon, Snow, and Read (2004, p. 815) note, there are dynamic changes of cognitive elements, which go "from evidence to conclusions and from conclusions back to evidence" and that "consonance is restored by changing the elements that are in dissonant relations, adding consonant ones, or decreasing the importance of the dissonant elements."

Consequently, case study researchers employ methods that include but go beyond asking questions; these additional methods include document analysis (Pettigrew, 1973, 1975, 1995), direct observation (Mintzberg, 1979), and forced metaphor elicitation techniques (Von Wallpach & Woodside, 2009); the CSR techniques described below include some of these methods.

(5) Thinking and making decisions in B2B relationships include creating "satisficing" (Simon, 1956) rules — decision-makers do not attempt to identify and select optimal solutions even when they report doing so. Rather, they create and apply

simple heuristics (rules that represent paths to accepting and rejecting options) (Gigerenzer & Todd, 1999) and employ intuitive, perhaps more emotive, decision-making processes that do not attempt to use all the complex information that may be available in a rational process (Prietula & Simon, 1989).

(6) Satisficing rules involve yes/no mental paths that include two or more attributes — not a compensatory evaluation involving summing-up −3 to +3 scores on 5 or so attributes. B2B decision-makers do not use compensatory heuristics even when they report doing so (Woodside & Wilson, 2000). Consequently, research on "key success factors" (Cooper, 1998) is insufficient for forecasting B2B behavior accurately; no one key success factor is sufficient or necessary in accepting or rejecting an option in a B2B context. Identifying key success paths (KSPs) and key failure paths (KFPs) is necessary for accurately forecasting B2B outcomes. This chapter includes examples of KSPs and KFPs.

Figure 3 serves to illustrate the core assumptions that this section presents. Note in Figure 3 that time and observability represent the *X* and *Y*-axis, respectively. Unlike most respondent self-report surveys, time and observability are principal explicit dimensions in most case studies. B2B CSR recognizes that B2B relationships-enactments include specific events (milestones) that connect with each other through time and that group meetings occur before, during, and after these enactments. As Figure 3 indicates, the same persons do not participate in all group meetings that represent B2B relationship enactments: this fact has implications for observability. Sentiments and beliefs in Figure 3 include implicit and explicit attitudes (positive and negative feelings) and cognitions (perceptions of associations among two or more attributes, behaviors, and outcomes).

Groups as well as individuals form implicit and explicit sentiments and beliefs (SBs). SBs, behavior, and events relationships are dynamic; they mutually influence one another as participants struggle to make sense of what is happening, what should happen next, and what did happen just recently. Consequently, sensemaking about past, present, and future contexts and framing issues and opportunities is a core activity by participants in B2B contexts. Antecedents, processes, and outcomes of participants' sensemaking activities are frequently the major foci in B2B CSR.

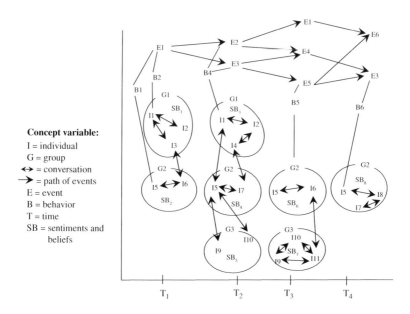

Figure 3. Concepts and Propositions in CSR. *Source*: Original figure Adapted from Calder (1977, Figure 14.2, p.198).

Most CSR requires substantial amounts of time to collect data in real-life settings – a key conclusion from studying Figure 3 and the assumptions about B2B contexts. Participants' self-reports in one-shot surveys are a poor meal and miss documenting the dynamics and nitty-gritty details of B2B processes including implicit SBs. To clarify and deepen understanding, this chapter includes example CSR summaries that display these assumptions and how they operate in specific B2B contexts. The examples come from exemplar studies that employ CSR methods.

EXEMPLAR METHODS IN CSR IN B2B CONTEXTS

This section includes brief descriptions of five CSR methods that appear in the B2B literature. These methods include "direct research" and observing B2B processes, decision systems analysis (DSA), ethnographic decision tree modeling (EDTM), content analysis, degrees-of-freedom analysis (DOFA), and fuzzy-set qualitative comparative analysis (see FS/QCA.com). The discussion includes references for readers seeking additional sources for study; the study of the original studies is necessary for honing skills in CSR in B2B contexts. The discussion is not exhaustive; Woodside (2010) provides expositions of additional methods that are applicable in B2B CSR.

Direct Research and Observing B2B Processes

Direct research includes going into B2B contexts and observing the activities and interviewing the participants in B2B processes. Direct research applies Mintzberg's (1979, p. 582) definition of a strategy, "Defining a strategy as a pattern in a stream of decisions, our central theme has been the contrast between 'deliberate' strategies, that is, patterns intended before being realized, and 'emergent' strategies, patterns realized despite or in the absence of intentions."

Direct research includes observing B2B contexts with the researcher in situ for a week, one month, several months, to a year or longer. Direct research includes a triangulation of data collected and the heart of the method is on-site interviews and face-to-face observations of B2B processes. The following description of one direct method study includes case studies of deliberate and emergent strategies "of periods of 30 or more years" (Mintzberg, 1979, p. 582).

> This is a large project, at the present time involving a number of months of on-site research in each organization. We first spend a good deal of time reading whatever historical documents we can find, in order to develop thorough chronologies of decisions in various strategy areas. Then we switch to interviews to fill in the gaps in the decision chronologies and to probe into the reasons for breaks in the patterns (i.e., for strategic changes). (Mintzberg, 1979, p. 582)

Mintzberg (1979) describes the following seven "themes" in his CSR studies that relate to B2B contexts. (1) The research is purely descriptive (not prescriptive) as much as possible. (2) The research relies on simple — in a sense, inelegant — methodologies (liking sitting in a manager's office and observing what she does).

(3) The research has been as purely inductive as possible. Inductive research includes two essential steps according to

Mintzberg (1979). The first is detective work, the tracking down of patterns, consistencies. "One searches through a phenomenon looking for order, following one lead to another. But the process itself is not neat (Mintzberg, 1979, p. 584). The "creative leap" is the second step in induction.

> The fact is that there would be no interesting hypothesis to test if no one ever generalized beyond his or her data. Every theory requires that creative leap, however small, that breaking away from the expected to describe some-thing new. There is no one-to-one correspondence between data and theory. The data do not generate the theory − only researchers do that − any more than the theory can *be proved* true in terms of the data. All theories are false, because all abstract from data and simplify the world they purport to describe. Our choice, then, is not between true and false theories so much as between more and less useful theories. (Mintzberg, 1979, p. 584)

(4) The research is, nevertheless, systematic in nature: specific kinds of data are collected systematically. See Woodside's (2010) discussion on "property space analysis" for systematic sampling to include cases of extreme behavior to achieve description and explanation of pure types − not just the most typical cases.

(5) Research measurement is in real organizational terms. The researcher does not insist on forcing the B2B relationships into abstract categories. For an example of a definition and mea-surement in natural categories, see Van Maanen's (1978) study of "The Asshole."

(6) The research, in its intensive nature, ensures that systema-tic data are supported by anecdotal data. Mintzberg offers the following insights about this sixth theme:

> For while systematic data create the foundation for our theories, it is the anecdotal data that enable us to do the building. Theory building seems to require rich descrip-tion, the richness that comes from anecdote. We uncover all kinds of relationships in our "hard" data, but it is only through the use of this "soft" data that we are able to "explain" them, and explanation is, of course, the pur-pose of research. (Mintzberg, 1979, p. 587)

Woodside (2010) presents anecdotal evidence of lying to a customer by a sales representative in a B2B context – not to suggest that lying always occur in such environments but that lying does occur sometimes in some specific circumstances (e.g., when a sales rep's product repeatedly fails to perform).

(7) The research seeks to synthesize, to integrate diverse elements into configurations of ideal or pure types. B2B relationships are sometimes constant over weeks and months and sometimes dynamic for short spurts; they include all kinds of lags and discontinuities. Because relationships in real-life are asymmetrical rather than symmetrical, configural descriptions of B2B relationships are most useful and more accurate than structural equation models of these same relationships (see the FS/QCA discussion below in this chapter and Ragin, 2008; Woodside, 2010).

Eichenwald (2000) and Woodside and Samuel (1981) are two exemplar direct research studies that include participant observation (PO) in B2B contexts. In *The Informant* (Eichenwald, 2000) an executive in an international manufacturing firm becomes an undercover researcher (with hidden cameras and listening devices) to collect data showing his colleagues planning and doing illegal price-fixing deals with executives in other firms.

In most studies PO data collection is obtrusive with the organizations' members knowing that a researcher is present for the purposes of observing, describing, and explaining what is occurring in the organization. Woodside and Samuel (1981) apply an ethnographic approach to develop flow diagrams of the information processes and decision making stages of corporate and plant executives in developing corporate purchasing agreements with suppliers.

The two-year, direct-observational case study by Cyert, Simon, and Trow (1956) is essential reading for honing skills in CSR methods in B2B contexts. Cyert et al. (1956) propose four "clements" (i.e., behavioral principles) from their study of a firm's decision process focusing on the "feasibility of using electronic data-processing equipment [a mainframe computer] in a medium size corporation that engages both in manufacturing and in selling through its own widely scattered outlets." During the study, the focal firm's executives met with representatives of different vendors, held numerous committee meetings, hired two consulting firms to help the firm make sense of the situation and their need for a mainframe computer, and finally decided to back-away from the problem – and postponed making any decision other than continue-to-wait.

The four principles represent the cornerstones of "a behavioral theory of the firm" (Cyert & March, 1963); this theory focuses on describing and explaining vaguely defined, non-programmed problems and opportunities.

We use brackets and CAPITAL LETTERS to summarize the four principles and to stress that the principles always occur – implicitly and/or explicitly – for non-programmed or semi-programmed decision-making in B2B contexts and elsewhere.

1. The alternatives are not usually "given" but must be sought, and hence it is necessary to include the search for alternatives as an important part of the process. [CREATE SEARCH ROUTINES FOR ALTERNATIVES.]
2. The information as to what consequences attach to which alternatives is seldom a "given," but, instead, the search for consequences is another important segment of the decision-making task. [CREATE SEARCH ROUTINES FOR CONSEQUENCES.]
3. The comparisons among alternatives are not usually made in terms of a simple, single criterion like profit. One reason is that there are often important consequences that are so intangible as to make an evaluation in terms of profit difficult or impossible. In place of searching for the "best" alternative, the decision-maker is usually concerned with finding a satisfactory alternative, one that will attain a specified goal and at the same time satisfy a number of auxiliary conditions. [CREATE SATISFICING HEURTISTICS.]
4. Often, in the real world, the problem itself is not a "given," but, instead, searching for significant problems to which organizational attention should be turned becomes an important organizational task. [HONE SENSEMAKING SKILLS.] (Cyert et al., 1956, p. 237)

Cyert et al. (1956) is an insider's study in the B2B CSR literature – a well-spring reference for the reports that follow its publication (Mintzberg, Raisinghani, & Theoret, 1976; Na, Marshall, & Woodside, 2009; Vyas & Woodside, 1984). Note that the fourth principle relates directly to Weick's (1995) classic, *Sensemaking in Organizations*.

Sensemaking is interpreting a context and mentally reviewing appropriate responses (e.g., search, create heuristics, decide, act now, and wait) in the context. Though still missing explicitly in many B2B case study reports, sensemaking is a critically important CSR research topic in B2B and critically important for executives to do well. Creating and testing the effectiveness of executive training courses focusing explicitly on honing sensemaking skills in B2B contexts is a worthy focus for future research.

Decision Systems Analysis (DSA)

DSA includes building ethnographic and generalized visualizations (maps) and text explanations of the sensemaking steps, interactions of people, decision processes, and outcomes in real-life B2B contexts. DSA is one operational method for Mintzberg's seventh theme: building theoretical configurations of what happens in organizations.

Hulbert, Farley, and Howard (1972) were the first to describe the theory and empirical steps of doing DSA in B2B contexts. Examples with elaborations of the method in B2B contexts include the following studies: Capon and Hulbert (1975), Howard, Hulbert, and Farley (1975), Hulbert (1981, 2003), Johnston and Bonoma (1981), Na et al. (2009), and Vyas and Woodside (1984).

Figure 4 is an example map from a DSA of the thoughts, decisions, and outcomes involving manufacturers, distributors, and customers in the United States office furniture industry. Woodside (2003) provides additional maps and explanations of the configural processes in this B2B context.

View Figure 4 as a specific example of the visual generalization of B2B processes that Figure 3 presents. Note that several individuals and firms appear in Figure 4 during what appears at first blush to be a "muddling through process" (Lindblom, 1959). DSA helps to clarify and deepen understanding of real-life B2B processes — removes the mud in the context and cataracts from the eyes of the viewer.

Ethnographic Decision Tree Modeling (EDTM)

EDTM includes the following characteristics: data on search for information, sensemaking, creating heuristics, and choice in non-

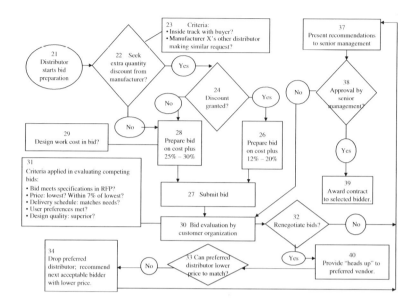

Figure 4.   Contingency Model of Large Order Marketer Bid Preparation and Buyer Award Process.

programmed or semi-programmed decisions are collected in real-life field settings. The researcher asks or observes an individual or group of decision-makers thinking aloud or role playing as they perform the process once-per-several (usually $n < 20$) individuals or groups or several-times (usually $n > 20$) for the same in individual or group. EDTM includes creating binary flow models leading to specific decision outcomes (e.g., accept versus reject a new product or increase, decrease, or keep price the same) and tests the efficacy of the models to predict outcomes in a holdout sample of cases.

Gladwin (1989) and colleagues provide several insightful ethnographic studies set in B2B contexts. Her studies include creating composite EDTM representations of real-life B2B decisions. For example, "In Eastern Zambia, this methodology was used to study the decisions of small-scale farmers [121 case studies], including female headed households (FHHs), to adopt agroforestry innovations in the form of improved fallows, researched by ICRAF, the International Centre for Research on Agroforestry, and recently promoted and extended by World Vision International, and monitored by the University of Florida Soils CRSP (collaborative research support program)" (Gladwin,

Peterson, & Mwale, 2002). Gladwin's studies focus on cognitive science reporting on the thinking and deciding processes that are representative of cases of individuals and firms engaging in sensemaking and deciding about the same issue (e.g., adopting or rejecting an agroforestry innovation).

Using data in Phillips (1968), Montgomery (1975) provides a "gatekeeper analysis" of the multiple decision processes of the same supermarket buying committee deliberating on accepting or rejecting carrying 124 manufacturers' product proposals; the 124 case studies. The resulting analysis has several characteristics of EDTM. Figure 5 is a decision tree model that the thinking and deciding process of one supermarket buying committee (supermarket executives and not consumers shopping in supermarkets) created from Montgomery's (1975) gatekeeper analysis.

Note in Figure 5 that no one simple antecedent condition is sufficient or necessary in causing accept and reject outcomes. The committee first considers whether or not the manufacturer's (M) reputation is strong; a strong reputation is not sufficient to decide to accept the manufacturer's new product. If the reputation is strong, a second issue arises: Is the product in the proposal significantly new? The configuration (causal recipe) of strong reputation and significantly new product is sufficient for the committee

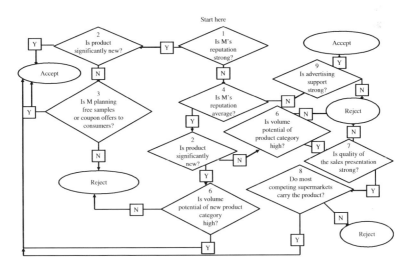

Figure 5. An Ethnographic Decision Process Model of Supermarket Committee Buying Decisions about a Manufacturer's (M's) New Product Offering. *Source*: Adapted from Montgomery (1975).

to accept the manufacturer's proposal. Note that this configuration is not necessary for gaining acceptance – other routes (paths) lead to acceptance. Note that a manufacturer with a weak reputation can propose a new product that gains acceptance (yes responses in path 1 → 4 → 9).

Several paths lead to rejection. Even a proposal from a manufacturer with a strong reputation faces rejection if such a manufacturer does not have a significantly new product and fails to provide substantial promotional support.

EDTM captures and shows an important principle in behavioral (real-life) decision making. Identifying "key success factors" can be misleading since no simple antecedent condition is sufficient or necessary to cause a given outcome. Describing and explaining "key success paths" and "key failure paths" are usually necessary to have an accurate understanding of B2B decision processes.

Howard and Morgenroth (1968) and Morgenroth (1964) provide EDTMs of decisions makers in the same petroleum company making pricing decisions. Their analysis includes the use of a holdout sample to test the predictive validity of the final version of the study's EDTM. The two papers are essential readings in CSR in B2B contexts.

Woodside and Wilson (2000) provide EDTMs of individual and group decisions of both a manufacturer and customer firms for industrial solvents. The study describes a substantial variance in price-settings for different decision paths by the manufacturer. The study confirms the view that multiple, complex, antecedent conditions (causal recipes or configurations) rather than simple antecedent conditions are sufficient (but each recipe is not necessary) for causing a high price with other causal paths leading to a low prices.

Content Analysis

Examining written communications such as minutes of meetings is one example of content analysis. Asking participants to read and help revise drafts of EDTM's and a researcher's written case report on the participants' decision processes is another example of content analysis.

Pettigrew's (1975, 1995) longitudinal analysis of written communications among senior, middle, and first-line managers is an example of content analysis of multiple communications written and read by participants (and Pettigrew as a researcher) in a B2B context. Pettigrew's findings support his conclusion that the middle-manager revised and controlled both the content and flow of communications in ways unrecognized by senior and first-line managers. Pettigrew concludes that the middle-manager's gatekeeper's actions enabled him to direct both the senior managers and first-line managers to accept his views about selecting and rejecting competing vendors. Thus, the title of Pettigrew's seminal chapter, "the industrial purchasing decision as a political process."

Morgenroth's (1964) remarkable chapter includes several revisions of EDTMs — each revision is based on content analysis by participants in the decision processes to earlier versions of Morgenroth's maps. Thus, the researcher asked the participants to further reflect and help revise the researcher's interpretations and mapping of the decision process. Morgenroth kept returning to the participants for follow-up interviews and new versions of his maps until both he and the participants were satisfied with the accuracy and completeness of the final EDTM.

Emic interpretations are the interpretative (sensemaking) views of a participant as to what has happened, what is happening now, and what will happen next. Etic interpretations are the interpretative (sensemaking) views of the researcher about what has happened, what is happening now, and what will happen. Morgenroth (1964) reports multiple-rounds through several time periods (t_i) of emic and etic interpretations of documents (maps) of how participants in a firm make pricing decision, for example: $emic_1 \rightarrow etic_2 \rightarrow emic_2 \rightarrow etic_3 \rightarrow emic_3 \rightarrow etic_3$. Such a reflective content analysis represents a hermeneutic spiral to achieve highly accurate and complete interpretations — both explicit and implicit interpretations. Hermeneutics refers to the study of interpreting texts including the study of how to improve the accuracy in interpreting.

Woodside, Pattinson, and Miller (2005) and Pattinson and Woodside (2008) propose a five-level hermeneutic analysis framework. Figure 6 summarizes the initial levels of understanding and research on B2B decision making — up to four levels of hermeneutic analysis. Level I depicts the specific interpretations of the B2B executives descriptions and explanations of what happened and why it happened for a focal decision making issue. In Figure 1 the Level I analysis shows that mental models are crafted and revised during the decision and action under study — at time t.

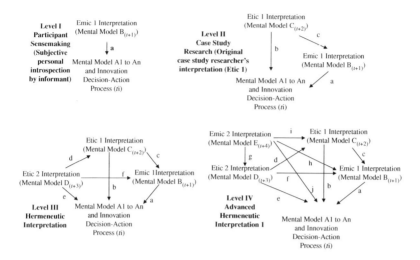

Figure 6. Hermeneutic Interpretation of Sensemaking in B2B Innovation Decisions-Action Processes. *Source*: Adapted from Woodside et al. (2005, p. 366)

The executive's later ($t + 1$) interpretation and reporting of what happened represents both a summary and an elaboration of the mental models originating during the decisions-actions. These self-reporting interpretations are subject to self-editing, memory failure, and personal prejudices and biases (Wegner, 2002).

The hermeneutic analysis framework breaks through the current (early 21st century) dominant logic in B2B research which usually stops at collecting Level I data. Arrow **a** in Figure 1 represents a summary of what the participants in the enterprise report about the decision process under study.

Level II recognizes that a participant's t + 1 interpretation of what happened at a previous time, and why it happened, is one view of specific situations, decisions, and outcomes. This participant's emic view does not reflect a complete or a completely accurate account of reality. The researcher provides further commentary and often judgments (arrow **c**) on the participant's sensemaking account. The researcher collects (arrow **b**) additional interviews with other participants and/or analyzes documents to confirm, deny, and elaborate on the participant's report. Most B2B case study research extends to Level II research (see Woodside, 2003).

Level III analysis supports Langley, Mintzberg, Pitcher, Posada, and Saint-Macary (1995, p. 277) "suggestion 5 (to), reanalyze previously analyzed decision processes not just new ones." Level III provides two etic interpretations with an additional time period and usually independent researchers. Etic 2 interpretations include commentaries of etic 1, emic 1, and mental models and decision process at the time of the original situation — relationships **d**, **f**, and **e**, respectively. Level III analysis here includes chronologically mapping events of the decision process and outcomes reported by the etic 1 researcher. In this framework, the etic 2 researcher applies decision systems analysis (DSA, see Howard et al., 1975) based on the text of the original case study done by the etic 1 researcher. Woodside et al. (2005) provide a detailed package of extended DSA using a DSA model, an events chronology map and sets of cognitive maps (for more detail see Woodside et al., 2005). Level III analysis may contain content analysis supported by software tools including TACT (TACT, 1997) and NVivo (QSR International, 2002).

Level IV analysis incorporates an additional round of interviewing of one or more of participants involved in the case study reported by the etic 1 researcher. Participants are asked questions initially related to the etic report mainly addressing accuracy, completeness, and key elements within the report. They are then asked questions that address accuracy, completeness and suggested updates to the etic 2 material presented to them, which in turn constitute updates to the etic 1 case study account.

Level V analysis includes reinterpretation of all prior emic and etic sets of interpretations. Level V analysis is classifiable as an advanced hermeneutic interpretation because the analysis includes three rounds of separate etic interpretations that help builds toward sensemaking views of the whole case study.

Degrees-of-Freedom Analysis (DFA)

DFA is the attempt to deepen understanding and accuracy in a case study by identifying how well the features in the case match competing explanations (normative theories and theories-in-use by participants) about what has happened and the explanations to the causes and outcomes relevant to what has happened.

Campbell (1975) introduces and advocates DFA in case study research. He maintained that this pattern-matching activity is analogous to having degrees-of-freedom in a statistical test:

> In a case study done by an alert social scientist who has thorough local acquaintance, the theory he uses to explain the focal difference also generates predictions or expectations on dozens of other aspects of the culture, and he does not retain the theory unless most of these are also confirmed. In some sense, he has tested the theory with *degrees of freedom* [emphasis added] coming from the multiple implications of one theory. (Campbell, 1975, pp. 181–182)

Such analysis considers case data quantitatively because the researcher notes the degree of match to the theory in terms of "hits and misses." How many hits are necessary to "confirm" the theory? Simple statistical tests are useful for noting whether or not the number of hits or misses is greater than that expected by chance. Or, the researcher may conduct DFA purely to note the absolute number of confirmed predictions for the sake of basic knowledge development (without worrying about whether results are "statistically significant"). This aspect of degrees-of-freedom analysis is consistent with Denzin and Lincoln's (1994) observation, as follows.

> Nor does qualitative research have a distinct set of methods that are entirely its own. Qualitative researchers use semiotics, narrative, content, discourse, archival, and phonemic analysis, *even statistics* [emphasis added]. (Denzin and Lincoln's, 1994)

The contribution of DOF is in demonstrating how researchers can link "traditional" (i.e., logical positivistic) hypothesis testing procedures to examine theoretical propositions in case study research. This approach is one way of achieving a "critical test" (Carlsmith, Ellsworth, & Aronson, 1976) that is, testing the relative empirical strengths and contextual relevancy of competing theories. See Woodside (2010) for details and statistical testing of DFA in B2B contexts.

Fuzzy-Set Qualitative Comparative Analysis (FS/QCA)

The FS/QCA method bridges quantitative and qualitative approaches because the methods in this tool kit are simultaneously qualitative and quantitative (Ragin, 2008, p. 82). FS/QCA focuses on analyzing alternative combinations of antecedent conditions that represent causal complexity rather than the analysis of net effects; FS/QCA identifies causal recipes (specific combinations of causally relevant ingredients relating to an outcome) and thereby unravels causal complexity.

FS/QCA builds on set theory and fuzzy sets (Zadeh, 1965) analysis using Boolean algebra rather than linear algebra. Examining all logically possible combinations of causal conditions makes it possible to construct experiment design-like contrasts (where only one causal condition at a time is allowed to vary) and thus offers a thorough analysis of the effects of relevant causal conditions. In effect, the impact of each cause is examined in all logically possible contexts (the $2k$ configurations of conditions, k = number of causal conditions) (Ragin, 2008, p. 125).

The following discussion is a brief introductory example of FS/QCA. A fuzzy set scale allows for fine gradations of the degree of membership in a causal conditional recipe. A fuzzy set is viewable as a purposively calibrated scale transformation of a continuous variable. Such calibration is possible only through the use of theoretical and substantive knowledge that is essential in the specification of the three qualitative breakpoints (full membership = 1.0; full non-membership = 0.0; and maximum ambiguity – the crossover point = 0.5) (Ragin, 2008, p. 30).

Figure 7 illustrates the creation of three fuzzy set purposively calibrated scales from case data in a business-to-business process

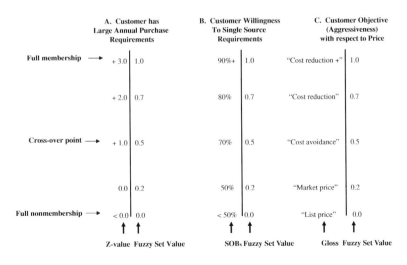

Figure 7.   Fuzzy Set Scaling Examples.

study of marketing and purchasing industrial chemicals (Woodside & Wilson, 2000). Less than 1% of all customers for the large manufacturer of industrial chemicals were fully in the membership of customers with large purchase requirements. Customers with purchase requirements for the category of chemicals in this study are classifiable more out than in the large customer requirements membership. The manufacturer classifies customers willing to single source 90% plus of their purchase requirements for the category as fully in the membership of customer willing to single source.

Customers buying 50 percent of their requirements from this manufacturer are classifiable as more out than in membership of willing to single source. Customers aggressively demanding price reductions plus additional benefits (e.g., the manufacturer building storage facilities for the category on the customers' site at no charge) are classifiable as fully in the membership of customer aggressive with respect to price setting. Customers demanding "cost avoidance" objectives (i.e., price increases less than published inflation rates for the category) are classifiable at the crossover point. Customers expressing willingness to pay "market prices" for the category are classifiable as more out than in membership for customer aggressiveness with respect to price.

Three common operations on fuzzy sets are set negation, set intersection ("logical and"), and set union ("logical or"). "Logical and" compound sets form by the combination of two or more sets, an operation commonly known as set intersection. With fuzzy sets, taking the minimal membership score of each case in the sets that are combined, accomplished a "logical and," that is, a set intersection.

Table 1 includes the fuzzy set scores and the set intersection of their three-way combination (causal recipe) for eleven customers in the study of marketing and buying of industrial chemicals. The midlevel dots are used to indicate set intersection (combination of aspects) for the three causal conditions (A B C). Note the intersection scores are equal to the lowest score from the three prior columns in Table 1. The intersection value indicates the degree each case is more in or out of the intersection membership.

Negation: a fuzzy set can be negated to indicate the degree that the case is not a member of the set. To calculate the membership of a case in the negation of fuzzy set A, simply subtract its membership in set A from 1.0 as follows: (Membership in set ~A) $= 1.0 - $ (Membership in set A) or $\sim A = 1.0 - A$, where "~"

Table 1:   Fuzzy Set Scores for Customer SOB Awarded to X.

Customer Case Number	A. Large Customer	B. Willingness Single Source	C. Price Objective	Y. Customer SOBx	A B C Annual Agreement
1	1.0	.9	.7	.9	.7
2	.9	.6	.7	.8	.6
3	.8	.9	.2	1.0	.2
4	.5	.5	.9	.3	.3
5	.9	.2	.9	.6	.2
6	.5	.2	.2	.2	.2
7	.3	.9	.2	.3	.2
8	.6	.7	.9	.1	.1
9	.4	1	.3	.9	.1
10	.3	.1	.4	.1	.1
11	.2	.6	.9	1.0	.6

indicates negation. Thus, for customer case number 1, its membership in (Not a member of the large customer group) has a negative score of 0.1. Note that negation membership, "not a large customer," is asymmetric to membership in the target concept of small customer membership, that is, a customer can be more in the out than in the large customer membership (Not a member of large customers) and still not be full member of the small customer membership. This point holds for the other two causal conditions (B and C) in Table 1. Dual coding of key causal conditions has important theoretical benefits.

Logical "or": two or more sets also can be joined through the logical or: the union of sets. The logical or directs the researcher's attention to the maximum of each case's memberships in the component sets. A case's membership in the set formed from the union of two or more fuzzy sets is the maximum value of its memberships in the component sets. The addition sign is used to indicate logical or, for example the logical or membership for case number 1 for the combination of the three causal conditions in Table 1 equals: $A + B + C = 0.9$.

With fuzzy sets, membership scores in one set (a causal condition or a combination of causal conditions) that are less than or equal to their corresponding membership scores in another set (e.g., the outcome) indicates a subset relationship. Observe in Table 1 that the causal recipe membership score for A B C are consistently less than or equal to their corresponding membership scores in customer share of business awarded to firm X (the chemical manufacturer marketing the category) in the study — with the exception of customer case number 11.

Figure 8 shows the plot of the causal recipe of the intersection representing the conjunction of the causal conditions (A B C) and the outcome membership of customer share of business awarded to firm X. The pattern of results is consistent with an argument of sufficient causation — an upper-left triangular plot, with the degree of membership in the causal combination of the horizontal axis and the degree of membership in the outcome on the vertical axis, signals the fuzzy set relation.

The plot in Figure 8 shows sufficiency but not necessity for the conjunction of A B C on the outcome membership. Other paths to high membership scores on the outcome condition exist but this observation does not take away from the finding of sufficiency in high membership scores in the causal recipe resulting in high membership scores in the outcome condition — the argument of sufficiency but not necessity permits multiple paths to high scores for the outcome condition.

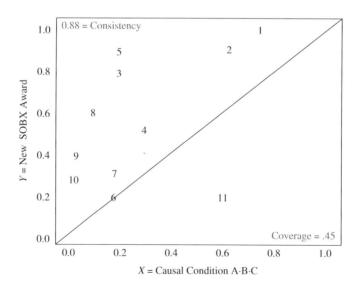

Figure 8. Plot of Y (New SOBx Award) by Causal Condition A B C (n = Customer Case Number). *Note:* Consistency ($Y_i \leq X_i$) = $\sum[\min (X_i, Y_i)]/\sum(X_i)$ = 3.3/6.4 = .88 with customer case number 11. Coverage ($X_i \leq Y$) = $\sum[\min X_i, Y)]./\sum(Y_i)$ = 2.9/6.4 = .45 including customer case number 11.

Measures of Associations

Consistency, like significance, signals whether or not an empirical connection merits the close attention of the investigator. If findings from the membership analysis are inconsistent with the hypothesized relation, then the hypothesis or conjecture is not supported (Ragin, 2008, p. 45). Coverage, like strength, indicates the empirical relevance or importance of a set-theoretic connection. Coverage estimates assess the proportion of cases following a path to high outcome scores; coverage is a straightforward indicator of the empirical importance of a causal combination (Ragin, 2008, p. 55). Equations and examples of the calculations for consistency and coverage appear in Table 2.

The formulas and specific estimates for consistency and coverage for the causal combination (conjunction A B C) appear at the bottom of Figure 4. The evaluation of the set relationships between the causal recipe and the outcome condition indicates high consistency and moderate amount of coverage.

Table 2:   Calculation of Consistency and Coverage from Calibrated Scores for X and Y.

Case	A • B • C (X_i) SOB (Y_i)	SOB (Y_i)	Minimum (X_i, Y_i)
1	0.7	1	0.7
2	0.6	0.9	0.6
3	0.2	0.8	0.2
4	0.3	0.5	0.3
5	0.2	0.9	0.2
6	0.2	0.5	0.2
7	0.2	0.3	0.2
8	0.1	0.6	0.1
9	0.1	0.4	0.1
10	0.1	0.3	0.1
11	0.6	0.2	0.2
Total	3.3	6.4	2.9

Consistency: 2.9/3.3 = 0.879

Coverage: 2/9/6.4 = 0.453

Note: Consistency ($Y_i \leq X_i$) = $\sum$ [min (X_i, Y_i)]/$\sum$(X_i) = 2.9/3.3 = .88.
Coverage ($X_i \leq Y_i$) = $\sum$[min X_i, Y,)]/$\sum$(Y_i) = 2.9/6.4 = .45.

The uniqueness of case number 11 in the findings in Table 1 and Figure 4 merits further attention and its discussion permits extending Gibbert's (2006) observations about "generalizing about uniqueness." Further discussion about customer 11 with the manufacturer marketing the category resulted in confirmation of this customer's unique relationship with this marketer. The manufacturer sales manager reported monthly complaints by this customer and continuing attempts to renegotiate prices during the annual contract. While this sales manager did not use the expression, customer 11 reflects the industrial customer equivalent to Van Maanen (1978) "The Asshole," in his study of a distinct but familiar type of person to the police. Thus, unique findings indicate a paradox worthy of further investigation. "Generalizability demands the research findings are not idiosyncratic to the firm or the sample of firms studied" (Gibbert, 2006, p. 124). Thus, the researcher should look for the presence of further assholes or other seemingly unique cases before concluding that adding condition D is relevant for model building and testing.

Creating a fourth causal condition, $\sim$D = "not an Asshole" would place all customers in Table 1 above the crossover point (0.5) except for customer 11. Customer 11's low score on this causal condition ($\sim$D = 0.00 for customer 11) would shift his A B C $\sim$D conjunction score to the left and result in high consistency for this more complex causal recipe.

Note that Table 1 and Figure 8 examine only one causal condition's relation to the outcome condition. Additional causal conditions warrant examination and these include A, B, C, A B, A C, B C, $\sim$A $\sim$B $\sim$C, as well as $\sim$A·B·C, and others. Ragin, Drass, and Davey (2007) provide a software program to ease the calculations involved in creating complex conditions and estimating their consistency and coverage (www.fsqca.com).

USEFUL STRATEGY AND THEORY IMPLICATIONS RESULTING FROM CASE REPORTS

This section offers a few insights into how CSR reports aid the effective application of a wide range of theories and hence of epistemologies and methodologies. Hence, they may influence planning, implementing, and evaluating strategies in B2B contexts, because B2B CSR often contain nitty-gritty identifiable details of processes relating to thinking, deciding, and doing among interacting participants that lead to successful versus unsuccessful outcomes. Several CSR methods inherently recognize that the B2B researcher needs to explicitly include time in collecting data and modeling B2B relationships (Woodside, 2006), that is generally more achievable with CSR than with, for example, cross-sectional surveys.

What does a manufacturer with an average reputation need to do to gain new product acceptance by executives in a super-market buying committee? Figure 5 indicates two strategy paths lead to acceptance for such a manufacturer. The point here is that creating accurate EDTMs is helpful for indentifying specific actions necessary to implement in specific contexts.

Why are price decreases more complex than price increases? Howard and Morgenroth (1968) provide the answer. CSR includes methods that provide valuable instruction to executives not only to be mindful in making decisions but how to go about becoming mindful.

CSR methods include the use of empirical positivistic (statisti-cal) tests. For example, using DOFA for testing the efficacies of competing theories compares hits and misses of theories to fea-tures present in a case. However, case study researchers have a natural bias against using seven-point scales. Mintzberg (1979) provides a telling explanation for this bias.

> "Hmmmm ... what have we here? The amount of con-trol is 4.2, the complexity of environment, 3.6." What does it mean to measure the "amount of control" in an organization, or the "complexity" of its environment? Some of these concepts may be useful in describing orga-nizations in theory, but that does not mean we can plug them into our research holus-bolus as measures. As soon as the researcher insists on forcing the organization into abstract categories – into his terms instead of its own – he is reduced to using perceptual measures, which often distort the reality. The researcher intent on generat-ing a direct measure of amount of control or of complex-ity of environment can only ask people what they believe, on seven-point scales or the like. He gets answers, all right, ready for the computer; what he does not get is any idea of what he has measured. (What does "amount of control" [or "trust"] mean anyway?) The result is sterile description, of organizations as categories of abstract variables instead of flesh-and-blood processes. And theory building becomes impossible. (Mintzberg, 1979, p. 586)

By direct research, content analysis, FS/QCA, and applying additional CSR methods, the researcher stays close to the data and can use alternative metrics to rigorously test the accuracy of complex antecedent conditions and paths leading to success and failure – and do so in terms that relate to real-life contexts. Such testing achieves the objective of generalizing the findings to multiple decisions made in a context (e.g., EDTM by Gladwin et al., 2002; Howard & Morgenroth, 1968) and across multiple cases (e.g., FS/QCA by Ragin, 2008; Woodside, 2010).

SUMMARY

CSR is an inquiry focusing on describing, understanding, predicting, and/or controlling the individual (i.e., process, animal, person, household, organization, group, industry, culture, or nationality). Any combination of the following purposes may serve as the major objective of CSR: description, understanding, prediction, or control. However, that deep understanding of the actors, interactions, sentiments, and behaviors occurring for a specific process through time is the principal objective by the case study researcher. The researcher should consider using explicit auto-driving tools to aid in bringing-up unconscious mental processes among informants (e.g., the hermeneutic spiral that Woodside et al., 2005; Pattinson & Woodside, 2008; describe) to overcome the cognitive limitations of reports noted in core assumptions (3)–(6) above.

A mental model of a process provided by a participant interviewed in a case study is an emic representation of reality. The interpretation of the same process provided by the case study researcher is an etic representation of reality. Etic representation in CSR often includes description and explanation of emic meaning as well as building composite accounts of the process based on data from triangulation. Triangulation includes (1) direct observation by the researcher within the environments of the case, (2) probing by asking case participants for explanations and interpretations of operational data, and (3) analyses of written documents and natural sites occurring in case environments.

Core criticisms made by case study researchers of large sample surveys consisting of interviews of one person, informal group, or organization include (1) the failure to confirm reported conversations, behaviors, and events, (2) the failure to collect the necessary detail for gaining deep understanding of the mechanics and reasons embedded in the processes examined, and the (3) use of response scales too far removed from reality of what they intend to measure. In contrast, when researchers use multiple data sources and techniques, they are more likely to deal effectively with both the environmental issues and the cognitive limitations noted in the six core assumptions early in this chapter than if they use single-instrument single-informant cross-sectional studies. They are also able to deal better with a variety of theories and paradigms, whether used individually or in blended form. This is important for marketing researchers as they use a wide range of theories.

Core variables in CSR include individual and group behaviors through time resulting in a sequence of paths of events (decisions, performance outcomes, and revelatory incidents). Beliefs and sentiments held by individuals and groups are additional core variables that CSR reports. No one CSR method is appropriate for all studies: a range of tools is appropriate.

Explanations with examples of additional CSR methods are available elsewhere (Woodside, 2010). The coverage here serves only to introduce some methods useful for doing CSR in B2B contexts.

Acknowledgments

The author gratefully acknowledges permission granted by the publisher, Elsevier, to reuse content in this chapter appearing originally in Woodside and Baxter (2013), Achieving accuracy, generalization-to-contexts, and complexity in theories of business-to-business decision processes, *Industrial Marketing Management*, 383-393.

References

Baxter, R., & Olesen, K. (2008). Using structuration theory to analyse relationship value creation Uppsala University. Symposium conducted at the meeting of the 24th IMP Conference, Uppsala, Sweden. Retrieved from http://www.impgroup.org/paper_view.php?viewPaper=6864http://www.impgroup.org/uploads/papers/6864.pdf

Brodie, R. J., Saren, M., & Pels, J. (2011). Theorizing about the service dominant logic: The bridging role of middle range theory. *Marketing Theory, 11*(1), 75–91. doi:10.1177/1470593110393714

Calder, B. J. (1977). Structural role analysis of organizational buying: A preliminary investigation. In A. G. Woodside, J. N. Sheth, & P. D. Bennett (Eds.), *Consumer and industrial buying behavior*. New York, NY: Elsevier.

Campbell, D. T. (1975). Degrees of freedom in the case study. *Comparative Political Studies*, 8(3), 178–193.

Capon, N., & Hulbert, J. (1975). Decision systems analysis in industrial marketing. *Industrial Marketing Management*, 4, 143–160.

Carlsmith, J., Ellsworth, M. C., & Aronson, E. (1976). *Methods of research in social psychology*. Reading, MA: Addison Wesley Publishing Company.

Cooper, R. G. (1998). Benchmarking new product performance: Results of the best practices study. *European Management Journal*, 16, 1–17.

Cyert, R. M., & March, J. G. (1963). *A behavioral theory of the firm*. Englewood Cliffs, NJ: Prentice-Hall.

Cyert, R. M., Simon, H. A., & Trow, D. B. (1956). Observation of a business decision. *Journal of Business*, 29(October), 237–238.

Dane, E., & Pratt, M. G. (2007). Exploring intuition and its role in managerial decision making. *Academy of Management Review*, 32(1), 33–54. doi:10.5465/amr.2007.23463682

Denzin, N. K., & Lincoln, Y. S. (1994). Introduction: Entering the field of qualitative research. In N. K. Denzin & Y. S. Lincoln (Eds.), *Handbook of qualitative research*. Thousand Oaks, CA: Sage.

DeSanctis, G., & Poole, M. S. (1994). Capturing the complexity in advanced technology use: Adaptive structuration theory. *Organization Science*, 5(2), 121–147.

Eichenwald, K. (2000). *The informant*. New York, NY: Broadway Books, Inc.

Gibbert, M. (2006). Generalizing about uniqueness. *Journal of Management Inquiry*, 15(2), 145–151.

Giddens, A. (1979). *Central problems in social theory: Action, structure and contradiction in social analysis*. Berkeley, CA: University of California Press.

Gigerenzer, G., & Todd, P. M. (1999). *Simple heuristics that make us smart*. New York, NY: Oxford University Press.

Gladwin, C. H. (1989). *Ethnographic decision tree modeling*. Newbury Park, CA: Sage.

Gladwin, C. H., Peterson, J. S., & Mwale, A. C. (2002). The quality of science in participatory research: A case study from Eastern Zambia. *World Development*, 30(4), 523–543.

Healy, M., & Perry, C. (2000). Comprehensive criteria to judge validity and reliability of qualitative research within the realism paradigm. *Qualitative Market Research: An International Journal*, 3(3), 118–126. doi:10.1108/13522750010333861

Howard, J. A., Hulbert, J. M., & Farley, J. U. (1975). Organizational analysis and information system design: A decision process perspective. *Journal of Business Research*, 3(April), 133–148.

Howard, J. A., & Morgenroth, W. M. (1968). Information processing model of executive decisions. *Management Science*, 14(3), 416–428.

Howard, J. A., & Morgenroth, W. M. (1968). Information processing model of executive decision. *Management Science*, 14(3), 416–428.

Hulbert, J. (2003). Organizational analysis and information system design: A road revisited. *Journal of Business and Industrial Marketing, 18*(6/7), 509–513.

Hulbert, J. M. (1981). Descriptive models of marketing decisions. In R. L. Schultz & A. A. Zoltners (Eds.), *Marketing decisions models* (pp. 19–53). New York, NY: North-Holland.

Hulbert, J. M., Farley, J. U., & Howard, J. A. (1972). Information processing and decision making in marketing organizations. *Journal of Marketing Research, 9*(February), 75–77.

Hult, G. (2011). Toward a theory of the boundary-spanning marketing organization and insights from 31 organization theories. *Journal of the Academy of Marketing Science, 39*(4), 509–536. doi:10.1007/s11747-011-0253-6

Johnston, W. J., & Bonoma, T. V. (1981). The buying center: Structure and interaction patterns. *Journal of Marketing, 45*(Summer), 143–156.

Johnston, W. J., Leach, M. P., & Liu, A. H. (1999). Theory testing using case studies in business-to-business research. *Industrial Marketing Management, 28,* 201–213.

Klein, G. (1999). *Sources of power: How people make decisions.* Cambridge, MA: MIT Press.

Langley, A., Mintzberg, H., Pitcher, P., Posada, E., & Saint-Macary, J. (1995). Opening up decision making: The view from the black stool. *Organization. Science, 6*(3), 260–279.

Lindblom, C. E. (1959). The science of muddling through. *Public Administration Review, 19*(February), 79–99.

Lipshitz, R., Klein, G., Orasanu, J., & Salas, E. (2001). Taking stock of naturalistic decision making. *Journal of Behavioral Decision Making, 14*(5), 331–352. doi:10.1002/bdm.381

Medlin, C. J. (2004). Interaction in business relationships: A time perspective. *Industrial Marketing Management, 33*(3), 185–193.

Mintzberg, H. (1979). An emerging strategy of 'Direct' research. *Administrative Science Quarterly, 24*(December), 582–589.

Mintzberg, H., Raisinghani, D., & Theoret, A. (1976). The structure of unstructured decision processes. *Administrative Science Quarterly, 21*(2), 246–275.

Montgomery, D. F. (1975). New product distribution: An analysis of supermarket buyer decisions. *Journal of Marketing Research, 12*(3), 255–264.

Morgenroth, W. M. (1964). Method for understanding price determinants. *Journal of Marketing Research, 1*(3), 17–26.

Na, W. B., Marshall, R., & Woodside, A. G. (2009). Decision system analysis of advertising agency decisions. *Qualitative Market Research: An International Journal, 12*(2), 153–170.

Nicholson, J., Lindgreen, A., & Kitchen, P. (2009). Spatial and temporal specificity and transferability: Structuration as the relationship marketing meta-theory. *Qualitative Market Research: An International Journal, 12*(2), 187–207. doi:10.1108/13522750910948789

Nutt, P. C. (1993). The formulation processes and tactics used in organizational decision making. *Organization Science, 4*(2), 226–251.

Okhuysen, G., & Bonardi, J.-P. (2011). Editors' Comments: The challenges of building theory by combining lenses. *Academy of Management Review*, *36*(1), 6–11. doi:10.5465/amr.2011.55662498

Orlikowski, W. J. (1992). The duality of technology: Rethinking the concept of technology in organizations. *Organization Science*, *3*(3), 398–427.

Pattinson, H. M., & Woodside, A. G. (2008). Capturing and (re)interpreting complexity in multi-firm disruptive product innovations. *Journal of Business & Industrial Marketing*, *24*(1), 61–76.

Penrose, E. T. (1959). *The theory of the growth of the firm*. Oxford: Basil Blackwell.

Pettigrew, A. M. (1973). *The politics of organizational decision making*. London: Tavistock.

Pettigrew, A. M. (1975). The industrial purchasing decision as a political process. *European Journal of Marketing*, *9*(March), 4–19.

Pettigrew, A. M. (1995). Longitudinal field research on change: Theory and practice. In G. P. Huber & A. H. Van De Ven (Eds.), *Longitudinal field research methods* (pp. 91–125). Thousand Oaks, CA: Sage.

Phillips, L. A. (1968). *An exploratory study of factors which determine the initial distribution of selected categories of products on supermarket shelves*. Unpublished Master's Thesis. Sloan School of Management. Massachusetts Institute of Technology, Cambridge.

Prietula, M. J., & Simon, H. A. (1989). The experts in your midst. *Harvard Business Review*, *67*(1), 120–124.

QSR International. (2002). *NVivo, V 1.3, WINDOWS XP*. Retrieved from www.qsr.com.au

Ragin, C. C. (2008). *Redesigning social inquiry: Fuzzy sets and beyond*. Chicago, IL: Chicago University Press.

Ragin, C., Drass, K., & Davey, S. (2007). *Fuzzy-set/qualitative comparative analysis 2.0*. Retrieved from http://www.u.arizona.edu/Bcragin/fsQCA/software.shtml

Sarason, Y., Dean, T., & Dillard, J. F. (2006). Entrepreneurship as the nexus of individual and opportunity: A structuration view. *Journal of Business Venturing*, *21*(3), 286–305. doi:10.1016/j.jbusvent.2005.02.007

Simon, D., & Holyoak, K. J. (2002). Structural dynamics of cognition: From consistency theories to constraint satisfaction. *Personality & Social Psychology Review (Lawrence Erlbaum Associates)*, *6*(4), 283–294.

Simon, D., Snow, C. J., & Read, S. J. (2004). The redux of cognitive consistency theories: Evidence judgments by constraint satisfaction. *Journal of Personality & Social Psychology*, *86*(6), 814–837.

Simon, H. A. (1956). Rational choice and the structure of the environment. *Psychological Review*, *63*, 129–138.

Simon, H. A. (1990). Invariants of human behavior. *Annual Review of Psychology*, *41*(1), 1.

Skinner, B. F. (1966). Operant behavior. In W. K. Honig (Ed.), *Operant behavior: Areas for research and application* (pp. 12–32). New York, NY: Appleton-Century-Crofts.

TACT. (1997). Retrieved from http://www.indiana.edu/~letrs/help-services/QuickGuides/about-tact.html

Todd, P. M., & Gigerenzer, G. (2003). Bounding rationality to the world. *Journal of Economic Psychology, 24*(2), 143–165. doi:10.1016/s0167-4870(02)00200-3

Vallaster, C., & de Chernatony, L. (2006). Internal brand building and structuration: The role of leadership. *European Journal of Marketing, 40*(7/8), 761–784.

Van Maanen, J. (1978). The asshole. In P. K. Manning & J. Van Maanen (Eds.), *Policing: A view from the street.* Santa Monica, CA: Goodyear Publishing. Retrieved from http://petermoskos.com/readings/Van_Maanen_1978.pdf

Vanharanta, M., & Easton, G. (2010). Intuitive managerial thinking; the use of mental simulations in the industrial marketing context. *Industrial Marketing Management, 39*(3), 425–436. doi:10.1016/j.indmarman.2007.08.012

Vargo, S. L., & Lusch, R. F. (2004). Evolving to a new dominant logic for marketing. *Journal of Marketing, 68*(1), 1–17.

Von Wallpach, S., & Woodside, A. (2009). Theory and practice of enacted internal branding: Theory, practice, and an experiential learning case study of an Austrian B2B company. In M. Glynn & A. G. Woodside (Eds.), *Business-to-business brand management* (Vol. 15, pp. 389–425). Advances in Business Marketing and Purchasing. Bingley, UK: Emerald Group Publishing Limited.

Vyas, N., & Woodside, A. G. (1984). An inductive model of industrial supplier choice processes. *Journal of Marketing, 47,* 30–44.

Wegner, D. M. (2002). *The illusion of conscious will.* Cambridge, MA: Bradford Books, MIT Press.

Weick, K. E. (1995). *Sensemaking in organizations.* Thousand Oaks, CA: Sage.

Wilson, T. D. (2002). *Strangers to ourselves: Discovering the adaptive unconscious.* Cambridge, MA: Belknap.

Woodside, A. G. (2003). Middle-range theory construction of the dynamics of organizational marketing-buying behavior. *Journal of Business & Industrial Marketing, 18*(4/5), 309–335.

Woodside, A. G. (2006). Advancing systems thinking and building microworlds in business and industrial marketing. *Journal of Business & Industrial Marketing, 21*(1), 24–29.

Woodside, A. G. (2010). *Case study research: Theory, methods and practice.* Bingley, UK: Emerald Group Publishing Limited.

Woodside, A. G., & Baxter, R. (2013). Achieving accuracy, generalization-to-contexts, and complexity in theories of business-to-business decision processes. *Industrial Marketing Management, 42,* 383–393.

Woodside, A. G., Pattinson, H. H., & Miller, K. E. (2005). Advancing hermeneutic research for interpreting interfirm new product development. *Journal of Business & Industrial Marketing, 20,* 364–379.

Woodside, A. G., & Samuel, D. M. (1981). Observation of centralized corporate procurement. *Industrial Marketing Management, 10,* 191–205.

Woodside, A. G., & Wilson, E. J. (2000). Constructing thick descriptions of marketers' and buyers' decision processes in business-to-business relationships. *Journal of Business & Industrial Marketing, 15*, 354–369.

Yin, R. K. (1994). *Case study research*. Thousand Oaks, CA: Sage.

Zadeh, L. (1965). Fuzzy sets. *Information and Control, 8*, 338–353.

CHAPTER

5 Performing Triple Sensemaking in Field Experiments

Arch G. Woodside, Alexandre Schpektor and Richard Xia

ABSTRACT

This chapter describes the complementary benefits of model-building and data analysis using algorithm and statistical modeling methods in the context of unobtrusive marketing field experiments and in transforming findings into isomorphic-management models. Relevant for marketing performance measurement, case-based configural analysis is a relatively new paradigm in crafting and testing theory. Statistical testing of hypotheses to learn net effects of individual terms in MRA equations is the current dominant logic. Isomorphic modeling might best communicate what executives should decide using the findings from algorithm and statistical models. Data testing these propositions here uses data from an unobtrusive field experiment in a retailing context and includes two levels of expertise, four price points, and presence versus absence of a friend ("pal" condition) during the customer-salesperson interactions ($n = 240$ store customers). The analyses support the conclusion that all three approaches to modeling provide useful complementary information substantially above the use of one or the other alone and that transforming findings from such models into isomorphic-management models is possible.

Keywords: Configural analysis; field experiment; fuzzy-set qualitative comparative analysis; multiple regression analysis; isomorphic-management model

Introduction

This chapter presents nitty-gritty details and discusses the benefits resulting from comparing case-based algorithms and variable-based dominant-logic of statistical modeling and testing of hypotheses using the same set of data. The objective here is to demonstrate Gigerenzer's (1991) conclusion, "Scientists' tools are not neutral," that is, the tools applied affect how theory is (re)constructed and the conclusions that follow from data analyzing using these tools.

The study provides an example of building isomorphic-management models by transforming findings from tests of algorithm and statistical models into cognitions-in-context modeling for management decisions. Thus, the study shows how to use tools to construct effective contingency-decisions that apply Simon's (1990) perspective — human rational behavior requires recognizing the influence of configurations of cognitions and contexts.

The study here illustrates the high value in using both multiple regression analysis (MRA) and an algorithm approach (fuzzy-set qualitative comparative analysis or fsQCA) for acquiring unique and complementary information from marketing data. This study is unique and valuable in actually showing how configural analysis complements statistical analysis of how marketing treatment variables (e.g., price and salesperson messages) and a measured consumer variable (a customer characteristic brought into the specific selling-buying context) affect purchase and profit.

The study is also unique in demonstrating how to convert algorithm and statistical modeling into isomorphic-management models. The study examines statistical and configural modeling using data from an unobtrusive field experiment. The paper presents visuals of nuances in the analyses to deepen understanding of the benefits resulting from modeling and doing data analyses using all three approaches to testing and improving theory. While Wagemann and Schneider (2007) propose that steps in applying both statistical and algorithm analytical methods are useful, the study here appears to be the first to actually show the value in doing so. The study here goes beyond doing both by suggesting "SAIM" – statistical, algorithm, isomorphic-management modeling) – as a step toward achieving use-by-executives of findings from testing statistical and algorithm models.

Case-based algorithms stress the reality of equifinality – multiple recipes that occur in their association with a high score in an outcome: the issue is never whether or not a variable has a significant net effect influence on a dependent variable. Variable-based studies focus on the finality of whether each variable is valuable or not, alone or in an interaction of variables, in predicting the value of a dependent variable: the primary issue is on reporting the "net effect," that is, the direct plus indirect influence of each independent variable on a dependent variable.

Case-based algorithms stress the reality of causal asymmetry (Fiss, 2011; Ragin, 2008) – that is, the idea that the causes leading to the presence of an outcome of interest may be quite different from those leading to the absence of the outcome. This view stands in contrast to the common correlational understanding of causality, in which causal symmetry is assumed because correlations are by their very nature symmetric; for example, if one models the inverse of high performance, then the results of a correlational analysis are unchanged except for the sign of the coefficients (Fiss, 2011).

Ragin (2008) expands on two considerations. First, the combination of three-to-six antecedent conditions presents a level of complexity not easily interpreted in statistical modeling of three-way to six-way interaction effects in MRA. Second, in real-life relationships of configurations and an outcome condition (e.g., purchase or high profit) are asymmetrical and not symmetrical – for asymmetrical relationships more than one combination occurs for a configurative score representing an algorithm and an outcome condition. Statistical modeling applies and tests for the assumption of symmetry – high scores for the outcome condition associate with high scores for each independent variable and low scores for the outcome condition associate with low scores for the independent variable. These two contrasting views appear in Figures 1a and b.

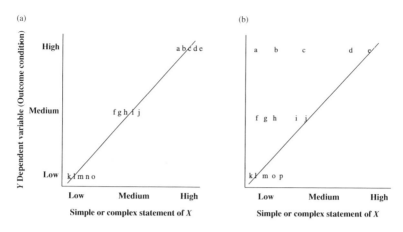

Figure 1. Symmetrical (a) and Asymmetrical (b) Relationships between *X* and *Y* for 15 Cases of Synthetic Data.

The asymmetric relationship in Figure 1b indicates that a high score in statement *X* associates with a high score in *Y* while acknowledging that *Y* can be high when *X* is low – other *X* recipes occur that result in high values for *Y*. An algorithm is judged to be useful only if the algorithm shows that high values in *X* associate with high values in *Y*.

While the use of algorithms occurs frequently in real-life decision-making (Woodside, Ko, & Huan, 2012), their use is infrequent though highly valuable in scholarly reports (e.g., McClelland, 1998). Consequently, the next section describes the use of Boolean algebra-based software (fsQCA.com, i.e., fuzzy-set qualitative comparative analysis) for testing algorithms. The objective of the study here is to encourage comparisons in thinking and data analyses using both algorithm and statistical tools.

The section "Unobtrusive Field Experimentation" summarizes an unobtrusive field experiment – where participants are not informed that they are participants in the study before, during, or after a treatment is administered. The section "Findings for Empirical Positivistic Analysis" presents traditional analysis and findings for the data from the experiment. The section "Findings from the FSQCA" presents analyses using fsQCA. The next section is a discussion that compares the benefits and limitations of the two methods. The section "Limitations, Conclusions, and Recommendations" concludes with recommendations for advancing marketing theory and practice.

Stating and Testing Algorithm Models

The proposal that Boolean algebra and set theory are useful for describing algorithms of combinations of antecedent conditions that lead to a given outcome of interest relates to proposals of asymmetric relationships. Here is an example of an algorithm: the combination of low price (~price), shopping alone (~pal), and a highly expert sales message (E) results in a sale. (The tilde symbol, "~" represents the negation of the antecedent condition.)

Equations (1a) and (1b) are alternative ways of stating this algorithm (the mid-level dot ("•") represents the logical "and" relationship). These equations indicate that this Boolean algebraic model expresses that the combination of all three conditions is sufficient for a purchase to occur (not that this expression is a necessity just that its occurrence is sufficient for a purchase outcome).

$$\sim price\_c \bullet \sim pal\_c \bullet expert\_c \rightarrow purchase\_c \qquad (1a)$$

$$\sim price\_c \bullet \sim pal\_c \bullet expert\_c \leq purchase\_c \qquad (1b)$$

Both versions (Eqs. (1a) and (1b)) indicate the same proposal that a high value in the conjunctive antecedent model, ~price_c • ~pal_c • expert_c, leads to a high value in the outcome condition, that is, purchase. A customer shopping alone AND exposed to a low price AND receiving a highly expert sales message will buy the focal product. These equations state that high values of the antecedent combinatory statement, ~price_c • ~pal_c • expert_c, are less than the high values the outcome condition, purchase_c. (The postscript, "_c" indicates a calibrated score rather than an original value for a given condition. For the purchase condition, codes for the original data usually include 0.00 for non-purchase and 1.00 for purchase; the recommended (Fiss, 2009) calibrated codes for such dummy codes for purchase_c = 0.01 and 0.99 – the fsQCA.com software performs better with this slight modification to the two scores rather than using the original dummy-coded scores. However, dummy codes of 0.00 and 1.00 often work well when using fsQCA.com and are used in the following examples in this chapter.)

Computationally, all conditions in these equations (price, pal, expert, and purchase) are scores calibrated from original values – analogous to z transformations of original data using matrix algebra. "Condition" in algorithm analysis is analogous to "variable" in statistical analysis.

CALIBRATION

Calibrated scores for use in Boolean algebra range from 0.00 to 1.00 (or 0.01 to 0.99 for older versions of the fsQCA.com software). If a specific price point is the highest for a range of prices, the price-point code would equal 0.99. Alternatively, the lowest price-point code would equal 0.01.

If "pal" represents a customer shopping with a friend, the calibrated score of this level of the condition, pal, equals 1.00. If high and low expert levels are used in a field experiment, the score for low expert would be 0.00 and the score for high expertise would be 1.00. Using Boolean algebra, the specific score for the combination of $\sim$price_c $\bullet$ $\sim$pal_c $\bullet$ expert_c equals the lowest score appearing in this combination. Thus, for $\sim$price_c = 0.00, $\sim$pal_cl = 0.00, expert_c = 1.00 the combination score equals 0.00.

In many studies calibration of scores in fsQCA reflect the perspective that variation in data for a given condition varies in its information usefulness. For example, assume that you have 10 countries with single letter names: A, B, C, D, E, F, G, H, I, and J. The median household incomes (USD) respectively for these 10 countries are follows: 500; 700; 800, 1,500; 3,000; 5,000; 7,000; 9,000; 14,000; 22,000. The fsQCA calibration procedure asks the researcher to identify three membership points from theory and prior evidence that are necessary for the calibration: the threshold point indicating full non-membership in the condition (equal to 0.05); the crossover point between non-membership and membership that indicates maximum ambiguity; and the threshold point indicating full membership in the condition.

If the condition is "high income countries" (hi_income_c) and the three points are defined by theory and prior evidence to equal 1,000, 4,000, and 10,000, then the calibrated scores for the 10 countries are follows: A = .03; B = .04; C = .04; D = .08; E = .27; F = .62; G = .82; H = .92; I = .99; J = 1.00. This calibration indicates the two countries (I and J) have full membership scores in the condition, high income, and three countries have full non-membership scores of not being high income countries (A, B, and C). Calibration results in scores comparable across conditions as well as corrects for data values that distort information relevant for testing theory – discarding data that seem to represent "statistical outliers" does not occur in calibration and fsQCA.

The calibrated values for "not high income countries" (~hi_income_c_) is the negation of these values, for example, for country A, ~hi_income_c = .97. Note that "low income" does not have the same meaning as "not high income" and the calibration for low income would not be equal to "not high income." Calibration for low income is not done here; Ragin (2008) and Woodside and Zhang (2013) provide additional details and examples on how to perform calibrations.

Assume a researcher has data for six cases of consumers shopping for a product that is being market tested at three price points: $1.98, $2.98; and $3.98. Table 1 shows hypothetical data for the six cases in a "thought experiment" (a "gedanken" in German, see Cohen, 2005).

Notice the details in Table 1. The first case (customer 1) is exposed to price-point $1.98 (i.e., price_c = 0.01 and ~price_c = 0.99) and she/he is shopping alone − thus, pal_c = 0.00 and ~pal_c = 1.00. The first customer is exposed to an expert sales message: expert_c = 1.00.

Table 1 includes data for just one combinatory model: ~price_c • ~pal_c • expert_c. The value for this model for case 1 equals 0.99 • 1.00 • 100; this value is equal to 0.99 remembering that the lowest value in this combination represents its Boolean conjunction. The data for case 1 indicates that the customer purchased the focal product (i.e., purchase_c = 1.00).

Index calculations for "consistency" and "coverage" appear in Table 1. According to Ragin (2008), set-theoretic "consistency" gauges the degree to which the cases sharing a given combination of conditions agree in displaying the outcome in question. That is, consistency indicates how closely a perfect subset relation of whales is approximated by a causal recipe of a configuration of antecedent conditions. Consistency is analogous to significance metrics (e.g., r, a correlation) in statistical hypothesis testing. Ragin suggests that a configural model should achieve a consistency ≥ 0.80 to be useful and the fsQCA.com permits testing for consistency of models beginning at 0.70.

The consistency computation in Table 1 indicates that the model works well! Even though only case 1 has a high membership score in this model, among the six cases when a case has a high model score, the outcome condition (purchase) indicates full membership (1.00). The numbers in Table 1 indicate membership scores and not original scaled values.

Table 1:   Computation to Estimate Consistency for Six Cases.

A case	B Price	C pal	D expertise	E purchase	F price_c	G ~price_c	H ~pal_c	I expertice_c	J ~price_c • ~pal • expert_c	K purchase_c	L min(Ji, Ki)
1	$1.98	No	Yes	Yes	0.01	0.99	1.00	1.00	0.99	1.00	0.99
2	$1.98	No	No	No	0.01	0.99	0.00	0.00	0.00	0.00	0.00
3	$2.98	No	Yes	Yes	0.50	0.50	1.00	1.00	0.50	1.00	0.50
4	$2.98	Yes	Yes	Yes	0.50	0.50	0.00	1.00	0.00	1.00	0.00
5	$3.98	No	No	No	0.99	0.01	1.00	0.00	0.00	0.00	0.00
6	$3.98	Yes	No	Yes	0.99	0.01	0.00	1.00	0.00	1.00	0.00
7	Total								1.49	4.00	1.49

Consistency = $\Sigma \min(Ji, Ki)/\Sigma J = 1.49/1.49 = 1.00$.
Coverage = $\Sigma \min(Ji, Ki)/\Sigma K = 1.49/4.00 = 0.37$.

Table 1 includes purchases by four customers and non-purchases by two customers. The findings for the conjunctive model tested in Table 1 (~price_c •; ~pal_c • expert_c) indicates that this model is irrelevant in explaining the purchases by customers 3, 4, and 6. Additional conjunctive models of the same three simple antecedent conditions (i.e., price, pal, expert) may be useful for explaining purchase. In real-life, no one Boolean or matrix based model is both sufficient and necessary usually for explaining an outcome condition. Two-to-ten models are likely to be informative explaining an outcome condition when five-to-ten antecedent conditions are under examination for combinatory influences on an outcome.

CONSISTENCY AND COVERAGE

Consistency is an index that indicates the extent that scores for the simple or complex antecedent condition is lower than their corresponding outcome condition scores. Consistency is first in importance in interpretations in QCA; without relatively high consistency (≥0.75 or 0.80) the discussion of coverage is moot.

Set-theoretic "coverage" assesses the degree to which a cause or causal combination accounts for instances of an outcome. That is, analogous to effects size (e.g., r^2) in statistical hypothesis testing, coverage gauges empirical relevance or importance. The coverage in Table 1 for the model, ~price_c • ~pal_c • expert_c, indicates coverage equal to 0.37. In particular, coverage results from 0.00 to 0.60 are intriguing. Theoretically, a model with high consistency and near zero coverage indicates a case that rarely occurs now but might be designed to occur because such a case associates with an outcome of particular interest (e.g., purchase in the context of marketing and positive-to-negative presence of a disease in the context of a medical treatment).

VISUALIZING FINDINGS FOR TESTS OF ALGORITHMS

Figure 2 is an X-Y plot of the findings for the consistency of the complex antecedent-condition model, ~price_c • ~pal_c • expert_c. Figure 2 shows that the model is consistent: high scores in the model associate with high scores in the outcome condition. Algorithm analysis makes no prediction about the relationship between Y and X for low scores for the complex antecedent-condition model. We conclude only that the model is useful for explaining high scores in Y and know that high scores in X are necessary for high scores in Y.

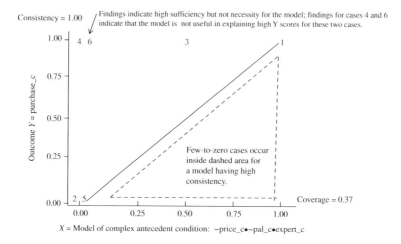

Figure 2. Visualizing the Findings for the Model ~price_c • ~pal_c • expert_c for the Synthetic Data. *Note*: *X*-axis is a conjunctive statement (i.e., a recipe) representing a complex condition that predicts high values of *Y* occur for high values of *X*; no prediction is made for low values of *X*. The findings for consistency (1.00) indicate that the model is useful, the findings for coverage (0.37) indicates that the model is representative of some.

Unobtrusive Field Experimentation

Context matters. Simon (1990, p. 7) famously proposed, "Human rational behavior is shaped by a scissors whose two blades are the structure of the task environment and the computational capabilities of the actor." This view applies to a context in which an experiment takes place – in a real-life field setting. Levitt and List (2007) provides relevant empirical evidence that human behavior varies substantially in field versus laboratory studies – humans are more cooperative and ethical in their behavior in laboratory contexts. While laboratory studies often provide useful information, their relevancy may be restricted to laboratory contexts while field experiments are likely to have greater relevancy to real-life context (cf. List, 2006).

A continuum is a useful way of viewing the obtrusiveness of a field experiment. Obtrusiveness can be very high if the procedure is a unique occurrence for the participants in the study. Here is an example of a highly obtrusive field experiment: Ehrenberg (1988) and assistants going to homes of participants for many weeks to ask household members to select one brand each from a tray containing three brands for each of four product categories — over the course of many weeks price levels and other conditions would be changed and the influences on these changes on purchases would be estimated by Ehrenberg.

The data for the present paper comes from Woodside and Davenport (1974, 1976). The study procedure by Woodside and Davenport (1972, 1976) is very low in obtrusiveness; customers participating in the study were not informed before, during, or after of their participation. The context was as close to a natural occurrence as possible.

THEORY

Theory Building from a Net Effects Perspective

From a net effects (empirical positivism statistical testing) perspective, the relevant theory that the field experiment examines includes the following hypotheses and rationales. The discussion here presents only hypotheses for demand; the hypotheses for profit are similar to the hypotheses for demand.

H1. Price increases cause decreases in demand. Price increases serve to reduce the inherent value/price relationship in the product-service perceived by the customer.

H2. A face-to-face expert versus non-expert communication by a salesperson causes demand to increase. Increases in expertise serve to increase the inherent value/price relationship in the product-service perceived by the customer.

H3. The decreases in demand due to price increases are less for high versus low expertise in the salesperson communication. The high expertise message serves to justify paying a high price for the product-service in the customer's mind.

H4. The presence of a friend, "shopping pal," versus no friend present causes a decrease in demand. The presence of a pal causes the focal shopper to think more rationally than the absence of a pal. The pal may remind the focal shopper that the original purpose of the shopping did not include buying the product-service or responding favorably to the salesperson's suggestion to buy the product-service. A quick note: the findings are opposite of H4's prediction.

H5. The presence of a friend (pal) versus no friend (no pal) increases the negative impact of price increases on demand decreases. The presence of a pal prompts the focal shopper to recognize the low value/price ratio when price is high — the shopper is more vigilant about price in the pal present versus absent condition. The findings do not support H5; a hypothesis quite different from H5 receives support.

H6. The increase in demand due to the expert versus non-expert message is greater for the no-pal versus pal condition. The focal shopper relies on the likely negative view of the pal to counteract the impact on demand of the expert versus non-expert message. The findings do not support H6.

H7. A three-way interaction effect occurs: the decrease in the impact of price on demand for the expert versus no-expert condition is greatest when no pal is present versus pal absent. Figure 3 is a visual of this three-way interaction. The findings do not support H7; findings opposite to H7 occurred in the field experiment about to be reported.

Theory Building from a Causal Recipe Perspective

No similar to many studies that apply statistical modeling with hypotheses of optimal pricing and related management decisions (Shah, Gor, & Jhaveri, 2012), the following propositions apply a causal recipe perspective of how antecedent conditions influence the score (low versus high) for an outcome condition (e.g., demand). No one simple condition such as price, expertise, or pal is sufficient

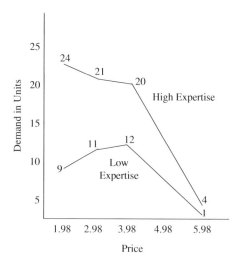

Figure 3.   Effects of Price and Salesman Expertise.

for influencing demand. A combination of conditions is sufficient but not necessary for a high score in an outcome condition. Because causal recipes consider the impact of alternative ingredients in different recipes, proposals for optimality of anyone condition (e.g., price) based on the net effect of the condition are non-applicable – decisions differ depending on context and algorithms always include findings for multiple relevant contexts.

The following causal recipes are sufficient in that a high score in the recipe associates with a high score in the outcome condition:

$$\text{Expert} \bullet \text{Pal} \leq \text{Demand} \tag{2}$$

$$\text{Expert} \bullet \sim \text{Price} \leq \text{Demand} \tag{3}$$

$$\text{Expert} \bullet \sim \text{Pal} \bullet \sim \text{Price} \leq \text{Demand} \tag{4}$$

$$\sim \text{Expert} \bullet \text{Pal} \bullet \text{Price} \leq \sim \text{Demand} \tag{5}$$

Figure 2 shows an X-Y plot for sufficiency but not necessity recipes that would support Eq. (4). Eq. (5) refers to the negation of demand, that is, an equation proposed that results in low scores for demand (close to no customer buys for high scores for Eq. (5)). While not appearing in Eq. (5) versus 4, causal asymmetry is often central to crafting theory using configural thinking, that is, the cause of not buying or failure include conditions in their recipes that differ from the conditions associating with buying or success.

THE UNOBTRUSIVE FIELD EXPERIMENT

The study uses the data of an unobtrusive field experiment (Woodside & Davenport, 1972, 1976). The experiment was set in a retail store, and the product was the "HC-2001 Head and Capstan Cleaner kit," which was a novel product with somewhat complex technology at the time of the study and was considered to be important since tape players were popular music players during the age of the experiment. The kit includes two felts pads, head cleaning solutions, and cartridge to be used to clean 8-track players. The product was only introduced to the market during the month of the experiment and none of the firm's six major competitors has the same kind of product to offer in time because of the relatively quick launch of the product by the firm.

The salesperson tried to induce the customers who just bought some tapes to consider buying the tape cleaner kit; customers were assigned randomly to different treatment conditions. Each salesperson-customer exchange includes two treatment conditions: a salesperson expertise level and a price-point. Two salesperson expertise message (expert vs. non-expert) and four price points ($1.98, $2.98, $3.98, $5.98) make the total of eight different treatment combinations. Thirty customers were assigned randomly to each of the eight combinations; thus, the total sample size of the study is 240 customers.

Data were also collected on whether or not the customers were shopping with or without someone else (a "measured" or "chronic" variable, the "pal" condition) when they were making the purchase decision. Since this antecedent is not manipulated in the experiment in each condition, the number of customers with pal (or without pal) can range between 0 and 30.

The unobtrusive nature of the experiment is signified by the fact that the subjects were not informed as to the condition they were assigned, the salesperson did not know beforehand what price-message combination was to be applied next (a random set of instructions as to the message and price to apply next appeared on separate pages placed beneath the cash register), and the customers could not see any other possible prices or other expertise level except the only price on the 6″ by 6″ card in front of them when the salesperson introducing the product to them. The procedure occurred in a natural shopping setting. Further details of the unobtrusive field experiment procedures and experiment context appear in Woodside and Pitts (1974, 1976).

In this study, the antecedents include four prices, expertise and non-expert sales messages, and customer with/without pal. To further the exploration of the initial study, the present study includes "profit" to the outcome in addition to "purchase" because profit is an important criterion to marketing response.

For the antecedents for expertise and pal, the calibration includes 0.00 and 1.00 because there are two scores available for each condition. For the antecedent price, the calibrated membership scores for each price in the study, price points of $1.98, $2.98, $3.98, and $5.98 include 0.05, 0.27, 0.74, and 0.96, respectively. For the outcome condition of the study, purchase is either 0 or 1; but for the high profit outcome set, the highest to the lowest profits possible include 4.98, 2.98, 1.98, 0.98, and 0.00; the calibrations for these profits include 0.99, 0.75, 0.50, 0.25 and 0.01.

Table 2 is a summary showing the calibrations (i.e., the scores for the specific points or levels of each condition). Two different calibration scales for profit appear in Table 2: an "exuberant profit" scoring scale and a "normal profit" scoring scale. The exuberant scale expresses the view numerically that profits are exceptionally high when the sale returns a profit twice the cost of

Table 2: Calibrations for Price, Salesman Expertise, Purchase Pal, and Profit Conditions.

Conditions		Calibration	
Price	$1.98	0.05	
	$2.98	0.27	
	$3.98	0.74	
	$5.98	0.96	

Profit		Calibration (Exuberant)	Calibration (Normal)
	$0	0.01	0.01
	$0.98	0.33	0.25
	$1.98	0.78	0.50
	$2.98	0.95	0.75
	$3.98	0.99	0.99
Expertise Calibration	Expertise	0.99	
	Non-Expertise	0.01	
Purchase Pal Calibration	Pal	0.99	
	No Pal	0.01	
Purchase Calibration	Purchase	0.99	
	Not Purchase	0.01	

Notes: (1) In calibration for price, the calibrations of price of $1.98, $3.47, and $4.95 are for full non-membership threshold, crossover point, and full membership threshold of 0.05, 0.50, and 0.95 in fsQCA, respectively. (2) In calibration for exuberant profit, the profit of $0.05, $1.26, $2.98 are for full non-membership threshold, crossover point, and full membership threshold of 0.05, 0.50, and 0.95 in fsQCA, respectively. (3) In calibration for normal profit, a five-value fuzzy-set calibration was used. (4) Calibrations for expertise, purchase pal an purchase are crisp set values.

the item that the retailer pays. Thus, a profit of $1.98 for an item with a retail price of $2.98, the calibrated profit score is 0.78 for the exuberant scale but 0.50 for the normal scale. A gross profit is classifiable as exuberant when the profit to the retailer is $1.98 on an item costing a retailer $1.00 and the retailer's price is $2.98, versus when a retailer's markup is typically 50% of the selling price or 100% of the retailer's cost.

PREDICTIVE VALIDITY OF THE DATA IN THE EXPERIMENT

This research tests for predictive validity of the models for both statistical analysis and QCA findings. The study includes holding out half of the sample to test for predictive validity of the model from the first holdout sample on the data of the second sample, and vice versa. The study randomly selects half of the data from each of the eight groups covering in the 4 (prices) by 2 (expert levels) experiment. (Note the difference from randomly selecting half from the whole sample data.) This study examines the predictive validity to show the generalization of the MRA and fsQCA conclusion, and also to call for predictive validity testing to be a routine in future research using MRA or fsQCA.

Findings for Empirical Positivistic Analysis

The data in Table 3 include all the data points necessary to convert the information into a data file for statistical analysis (using SPSS or SAS for example) and qualitative comparative analysis (using fsQCA). Data for the control group that appear in Table 3 were not used in the analysis in this paper.

FINDINGS FROM THE STATISTICAL ANALYSIS

Figures 7 and 8 are visualizations of key findings. No statistical analyses are necessary for concluding that the findings do not support H1 for a wide range of prices. Price does not influence demand over the first three price points in the experiment. Demand does decline dramatically for the $5.98 versus the $3.98 price. A price-demand tipping point occurs for a price at some point greater than the suggested retail price of $1.98.

Looking at Figure 3, no statistical analysis is necessary for concluding that the findings support H2: 65 units were sold for

Table 3: Customer Purchase Behavior for Four Price, Two Salesman Expertise, and Two Purchase Pal Conditions.

Price	Salesman Expertise	Purchase Pal	Purchase	No Purchase	n
$1.98	Expert	Yes	13	2	15
		No	11	4	15
	Non-Expert	Yes	5	7	12
		No	4	14	18
$2.98	Expert	Yes	9	0	9
		No	12	9	21
	Non-Expert	Yes	6	6	12
		No	5	13	18
$3.98	Expert	Yes	12	1	13
		No	8	9	17
	Non-Expert	Yes	3	3	6
		No	9	15	24
$5.98	Expert	Yes	2	4	6
		No	2	22	24
	Non-Expert	Yes	1	9	10
		No	0	20	20
$1.98	Control		4	26	30

the 90 high-expertise executions versus 32 units sold for the 90 low-expertise executions across the first three price levels. Sales doubled for the high versus low expertise conditions. Unit sales were very low for both message conditions at the $5.98 price even though sales were four times greater (4 units) for the high expertise versus low expertise levels at this extreme price.

The findings in Figure 3 do not support H3. A small sales decline occurs as price increased from $1.98 to $3.98 for the expert message condition but sales increased versus declined for the low expert condition − but the increase was only from 9 to 12 units. Clearly, the pattern of these findings does not support H3.

Figure 4 illustrates findings relevant for testing H4. The findings do not support H4: sales did not decline with the presence of a purchase pal; sales increased with the presence of a purchase pal. Typically, sales occurred 75% of the times when a pal was present versus 43%percent of the times when a pal

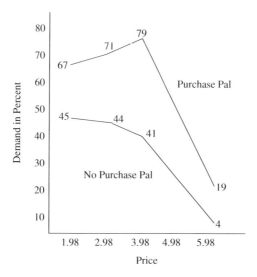

Figure 4.   Effects of Price and Purchase Pal.

was absent – a finding supporting a hypothesis opposite that of H4.

The three interaction hypothesis (H5–H7) do not receive support since the pal condition resulted in higher sales than the no pal condition – findings opposite of expectations. Possibly the focal customer was exhibiting conspicuous purchasing behavior in the pal condition and did not need to explain the decision not to buy in the no pal condition. The explanation to the counter-intuitive findings for pal awaits additional research.

Statistical Analysis

Figure 5 includes MRA findings for unit demand and profit using a quadratic function for price and expertise and pal conditions. The findings are similar for both unit demand and profits; all terms in the two equations are significant. Price has a positive and then a negative impact on unit sales and profit. Expertise has a positive impact on unit sales and profit. Pal has a positive (not a negative) impact on unit sales and profit.

Predictive Validity

The footnotes to Figures 6 and 7 provide estimates of fit and predictive validities for the MRA models for unit demand and profit

Profit

Model Summary

Model	R	R^2	Adjusted R^2	Std. Error of the Estimate
1	.497ᵃ	.247	.234	1.08684

a. Predictors: (Constant), pal, experise, price2, price

ANOVAᵃ

Model		Sum of Squares	df	Mean Square	F	Sig.
1	Regression	90.930	4	22.733	19.245	.000ᵇ
	Residual	277.585	235	1.181		
	Total	363.515	239			

a. Dependent Variable: profit
b. Predictors: (Constant), pal, experise, price2, price

Coefficientsᵃ

Model		Unstandardized Coefficients		Standardized Coefficients	t	Sig.
		B	Std. Error	Beta		
1	(Constant)	-3.205	.603		-5.313	.000
	price	2.082	.325	2.484	6.408	.000
	price2	-.259	.040	-2.534	-6.544	.000
	experise	.604	.143	.239	4.220	.000
	pal	.625	.152	.235	4.112	.000

a. Dependent Variable: profit

Purchase

Model Summary

Model	R	R^2	Adjusted R^2	Std. Error of the Estimate
1	.551ᵃ	.304	.292	.40843

a. Predictors: (Constant), pal, experise, price2, price

ANOVAᵃ

Model		Sum of Squares	df	Mean Square	F	Sig.
1	Regression	17.125	4	4.281	25.665	.000ᵇ
	Residual	39.202	235	.167		
	Total	56.327	239			

a. Dependent Variable: purchase
b. Predictors: (Constant), pal, experise, price2, price

Coefficientsᵃ

Model		Unstandardized Coefficients		Standardized Coefficients	t	Sig.
		B	Std. Error	Beta		
1	(Constant)	-.123	.227		-.542	.589
	price	.303	.122	.925	2.482	.014
	price2	-.051	.015	-1.264	-3.394	.001
	experise	.294	.054	.297	5.460	.000
	pal	.246	.057	.237	4.304	.000

a. Dependent Variable: purchase

Figure 5. Multiple Regression Models Predicting Purchase and Profit Using All Data ($n = 240$).

Sub-Sample B

Coefficients[a]

Model		Unstandardized Coefficients B	Std. Error	Standardized Coefficients Beta	t	Sig.
1	(Constant)	-.513	.428		-1.199	.233
	price	.583	.262	1.359	2.230	.028
	price2	-.102	.037	-1.663	-2.732	.007
	expertise	.333	.076	.340	4.387	.000
	pal	.232	.081	.223	2.854	.005

a. Dependent Variable: purchase

ANOVA[a]

Model		Sum of Squares	df	Mean Square	F	Sig.
1	Regression	8.532	4	2.133	12.824	.000[b]
	Residual	19.127	115	.166		
	Total	27.660	119			

a. Dependent Variable: purchase
b. Predictors: (Constant), pal, expertise, price2, price

Model Summary

Model	R	R^2	Adjusted R^2	Std. Error of the Estimate
1	.555[a]	.308	.284	.40783

a. Predictors: (Constant), pal, expertise, price2, price

Sub-Sample A

Coefficients[a]

Model		Unstandardized Coefficients B	Std. Error	Standardized Coefficients Beta	t	Sig.
1	(Constant)	-.614	.440		-1.395	.166
	price	.690	.269	1.582	2.560	.012
	price2	-.116	.038	-1.874	-3.035	.003
	expertise	.254	.078	.255	3.234	.002
	pal	.262	.083	.252	3.163	.002

a. Dependent Variable: purchase

ANOVA[a]

Model		Sum of Squares	df	Mean Square	F	Sig.
1	Regression	8.208	4	2.052	11.616	.000[b]
	Residual	20.315	115	.177		
	Total	28.524	119			

a. Dependent Variable: purchase
b. Predictors: (Constant), pal, expertise, price2, price

Model Summary

Model	R	R^2	Adjusted R^2	Std. Error of the Estimate
1	.536[a]	.288	.263	.42030

a. Predictors: (Constant), pal, expertise, price2, price

Figure 6. Findings for *Purchase* Models for Two Sub-Samples ($n = 120$ for each sub-sample) Showing the Fit Validities and Cross-Validation (Predictive Validity). *Notes:* Purchase_A = -.614 + (.690*price)-(.116*Price2) + (.254*expertise) + (.262*pal);purchase_B = -.513 + (.583*price)-(.102*price2) + (.333*expertise) + (.232*pal). Fit validity for purchase A using model A: $r = .536$; fit validity for purchase B using model B: $r = .555$. Predictive validity of the model B to estimate purchase_A: $r = .530$; predictive validity for model A to estimate purchase_B: $r = .548$.

Sub-Sample A

Coefficients[a]

Model		Unstandardized Coefficients		Standardized Coefficients	t	Sig.
		B	Std. Error	Beta		
1	(Constant)	-4.779	1.116		-4.283	.000
	price	3.310	.683	3.073	4.846	.000
	price2	-.468	.097	-3.052	-4.814	.000
	expertise	.470	.199	.191	2.366	.020
	pal	.634	.210	.247	3.025	.003

a. Dependent Variable: profit

ANOVA[a]

Model		Sum of Squares	df	Mean Square	F	Sig.
1	Regression	43.411	4	10.853	9.560	.000[b]
	Residual	130.554	115	1.135		
	Total	173.965	119			

a. Dependent Variable: profit
b. Predictors: (Constant), pal, expertise, price2, price

Model Summary

Model	R	R^2	Adjusted R^2	Std. Error of the Estimate
1	.500[a]	.250	.223	1.06548

a. Predictors: (Constant), pal, expertise, price2, price

Sub-Sample B

Coefficients[a]

Model		Unstandardized Coefficients		Standardized Coefficients	t	Sig.
		B	Std. Error	Beta		
1	(Constant)	-4.405	1.048		-4.204	.000
	price	3.005	.641	2.929	4.689	.000
	price2	-.431	.091	-2.950	-4.725	.000
	expertise	.687	.186	.294	3.692	.000
	pal	.562	.199	.226	2.821	.006

a. Dependent Variable: profit

ANOVA[a]

Model		Sum of Squares	df	Mean Square	F	Sig.
1	Regression	43.014	4	10.754	10.775	.000[b]
	Residual	114.773	115	.998		
	Total	157.787	119			

a. Dependent Variable: profit
b. Predictors: (Constant), pal, expertise, price2, price

Model Summary

Model	R	R^2	Adjusted R^2	Std. Error of the Estimate
1	.522[a]	.273	.247	.99901

a. Predictors: (Constant), pal, expertise, price2, price

Figure 7. Findings for *Profit* Models for Two Sub-Samples (n = 120 for each sub-sample) Showing the Fit Validities and Cross-Validation (Predictive Validity). *Notes:* Profit model A = -4.779 + (3.310*price) - (.468*price2) + (.470*expertise) + (.634*pal); profit model B = -4.405 + (3.005*price) - (.431*price2) + (.687*expertise) + (.562*pal). Fit validity of model A to estimate sample A profit: r = .500; fit validity of model B to estimate sample B profit: r = .522. Predictive validity of model A to estimate sample B profit: r = .510; predictive validity of model B to estimate sample A profit: r = .489

respectively. Both fit and predictive validities are "large" (Cohen, 1977) for both unit demand and profit models ($r \geq .50$).

Table 4 presents cross-tabulations for examining tests of main effects for expertise, price, and pal on unit sales. The findings support the conclusions that pal and expertise have large effects on sales and price does not for a wide range of prices.

Findings from the fsQCA

The study includes creating fuzzy truth table algorithms in order to calculate configural findings. This algorithm calculates all alternative sufficient and necessary conditions that lead to the outcome. Once conditions are put in and the outcome is specified, the algorithms will both consider and examine the relevant condition combinations, including negation, for one or more of the simple conditions that to lead to high consistency for the outcome condition. We have coded the algorithm to show recipes with a minimum consistency requirement of 0.7. Algorithms were run to show recipes for several outcomes in the following discussion.

Purchase is the first outcome run. The algorithm calculated that the recipe of expertise • pal • leads to purchase; this recipe is the only sufficient condition that leads to high consistency for the purchase outcome. Regardless of the price level, having an expert AND a pal is sufficient to achieve the outcome of a purchase. The consistency for this recipe is 0.845 and the unique coverage is 0.368.

Not purchase (~purchase) was the next outcome that was run. The algorithm calculated that three recipes are sufficient to lead to the outcome of not purchase: ~expertise • ~pal + ~pal • price + ~expertise • price with plus sign ("+") indicating the logical "or" condition. Since QCA is an asymmetric rather than symmetric tool, we do not deduce that the opposite of these recipes will lead to a purchase. Rather, causal asymmetry holds and any of these recipes lead to a non-purchase. See Figure 9 for an example of a not purchase model that includes price and not expertise. Figure 9 is another non-purchase model – not pal coupled with not expertise.

The next outcome is "exuberant" profit. The algorithm calculated that only the recipe of experitise • pal • price is sufficient to lead to the outcome of high consistency for exuberant profit.

Table 4:   Calibration Membership Scores for Antecedent and
                Outcome Conditions.

(A) Purchase by Price and Expertise

price * purchase * expertise crosstabulation

Expertise				Purchase		Total
				.01	.99	
.01	price	.05	Count	21	9	30
Low Expertise			% within price	70.0	30.0	100.0
		.27	Count	19	11	30
			% within price	63.3	36.7	100.0
		.74	Count	18	12	30
			% within price	60.0	40.0	100.0
		.96	Count	29	1	30
			% within price	96.7	3.3	100.0
	Total		Count	87	33	120
			% within price	72.5	27.5	100.0
.99	price	.05	Count	6	24	30
High Expertise			% within price	20.0	80.0	100.0
		.27	Count	9	21	30
			% within price	30.0	70.0	100.0
		.74	Count	10	20	30
			% within price	33.3	66.7	100.0
		.96	Count	26	4	30
			% within price	86.7	13.3	100.0
	Total		Count	51	69	120
			% within price	42.5	57.5	100.0
Total	price	.05	Count	27	33	60
			% within price	45.0	55.0	100.0
		.27	Count	28	32	60
			% within price	46.7	53.3	100.0
		.74	Count	28	32	60
			% within price	46.7	53.3	100.0
		.96	Count	55	5	60
			% within price	91.7	8.3	100.0
	Total		Count	138	102	240
			% within price	57.5	42.5	100.0

$phi = 0.323, p < 0.006$

Table 4:   (*Continued*)

(B) Purchase by Price and Pal

price * purchase * pal crosstabulation

Pal				Purchase		Total
				.01	.99	
.01	Price	.05	Count	18	15	33
No Pal			% within price	54.5	45.5	100.0
		.27	Count	22	17	39
			% within price	56.4	43.6	100.0
		.74	Count	24	17	41
			% within price	58.5	41.5	100.0
		.96	Count	42	2	44
			% within price	95.5	4.5	100.0
	Total		Count	106	51	157
			% within price	67.5	32.5	100.0
.99	price	.05	Count	9	18	27
Pal			% within price	33.3	66.7	100.0
		.27	Count	6	15	21
			% within price	28.6	71.4	100.0
		.74	Count	4	15	19
			% within price	21.1	78.9	100.0
		.96	Count	13	3	16
			% within price	81.2	18.8	100.0
	Total		Count	13	3	16
			% within price	81.2	18.8	100.0
Total	price	.05	Count	27	33	60
			% within price	45.0	55.0	100.0
		.27	Count	28	32	60
			% within price	46.7	53.3	100.0
		.74	Count	28	32	60
			% within price	46.7	53.3	100.0
		.96	Count	55	5	60
			% within price	91.7	8.3	100.0
	Total		Count	138	102	240
			% within price	57.5	42.5	100.0

$$\text{phi} = 0.373, \ p < .000$$

Notes: Light gray shaded entries indicate highest and dark gray shaded entries indicate lowest share purchases. Purchase share is highest for high versus low expertise and pal versus no pal for each of the four prices.

The consistency for this recipe is 0.775 and the coverage is 0.292.

The next outcome is ~exuberant profit. The algorithm calculated that two recipes are sufficient to lead to the outcome of not exuberant profit: ~expertise + ~pal. This finding shows that it does not matter what the price level is, not having an expert or not having a pal is sufficient to lead to not making exuberant profit. The solution consistency is 0.745 and the solution coverage is 0.892.

PREDICTIVE VALIDITY OF THE FSQCA MODELS

Figure 8 includes findings for testing the model pal • expertise → purchase for two subsamples of the data (n = 120 for each sample with 15 cases from each of the 8 cells in each subsample). The models perform with high consistency (>0.83) and substantial coverage (>0.36) for each model. These findings support the conclusion that the model has acceptable predictive validity.

Figure 9 is a composite model of happenings (purchase versus non-purchase for the majority of outcomes for given combinations of price, expertise, and pal conditions. Figure 9 serves as a helpful visualization of the most profitable key success path (KSP) for the retailer to apply (when possible). For highest profit, if the customer enters the context (i.e., comes to the cash register and salesperson) with a pal, the salesperson should executive the expert sales message and price the tape cleaner at $3.98. For highest profit, if the customer does bring a pal to the context, the salesperson should execute the expert sales message and price the tape cleaner at $2.98.

Figure 9 is representative of how managers might actually think – an isomorphic (i.e., in this instance, high correspondence with actual thinking processes) model that uses beliefs, evidence, and emotions that lead to a decision (Woodside et al., 2012; Woodside, Pattinson, & Montgomery, 2012). A price point that a manager selects should depend on a specific set of contextual conditions. "Depend" implies "what if" analysis and modeling processes that isomorphic models capture.

Note in Figure 9 that no one factor (i.e., antecedent condition) is sufficient of for highest profit. Key success factors (KSFs) do not exist; in isolation, there are no KSFs. In real-life only KSPs occur. Crafting and presenting findings in an isomorphic model such as Figure 9 completes the SAIM process configural research that includes statistical, algorithm, and isomorphic-management modeling.

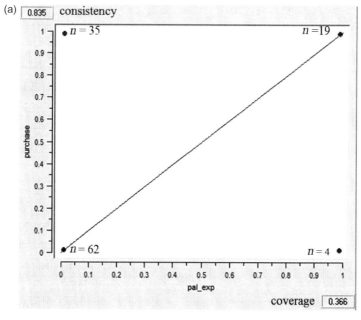

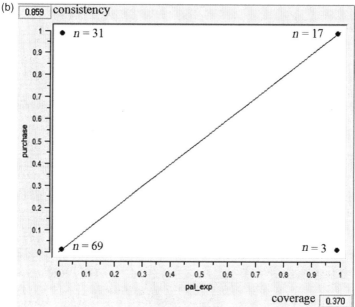

Figure 8. Testing Two Configural Models. (a) Sample 1, *n* = 120: pal•expert < Purchase; (*b*) Sample 2, *n* = 120, pal•expert < Purchase. *Notes*: This figure includes test results for predictive validity of the pal•expert → purchase. The findings support high predictive validation that the model has high consistency and similar coverage for each set of data.

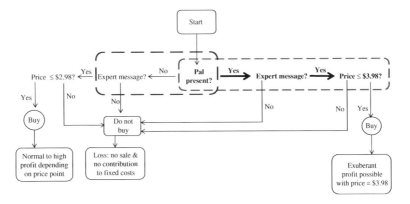

Figure 9. Isomorphic-Management Model of Outcomes for Purchase and Non-Purchase above 50% for 16 Configurations of Four Prices by Two Expertise and Two Pal Conditions. *Notes*: Most profitable process for firm appears in bold black dashed area; least profitable process for firm appears inside bold dashed area. Product will just sit there for the following model: ~pal • ~expert.

Comparing the Benefits and Limitations of the Two Methods

Being able to predict point estimates for the dependent variable is one benefit from applying MRA to data from field experiments. Given that a model has high fit validity, the second step should be taken to see if such predictions are accurate — by testing for predictive validity via a second sample of data. A model may provide acceptable fit validity and do poorly at providing acceptable predictive validity as Gigerenzer and Brighton (2009) and Woodside (2013) demonstrate.

MRA provides useful information on whether or not the net effects of dependent variables and their interactions are significant statistically. However, sometimes the focus on significance of main and interactive effects and the relative sizes of these effects — by comparing the sizes of standardized partial regression coefficients (ßs) — takes eyes away from the central issue: is the model accurate in predicting sought-after values in the dependent variable (purchase and profit). Prediction here refers to a high coefficient of determination (adjusted R^2) for the model for a holdout sample.

The predictive validities ("effect sizes") for purchase and profit are "large" (Cohen, 1977) as the findings in Figures 6 and 7 indicate. Effect sizes almost never (never) go above $r = 0.60$ and $r^2 = 0.36$ for predicting the dependent variable in field experiments because MRA provides symmetrical estimates, that is, the tool predicts low and high values for the dependent variable. QCA and fsQCA does not.

Qualitative comparative analyses provide algorithms that predict high scores for an outcome condition (e.g., purchase or profit) without making any predictions about low scores for this outcome condition. For most relationships of theoretical interest that go beyond testing the obvious, correlations between two variables top-out at about 0.60 because relationships are asymmetrical rather than symmetrical. Writing questions to test the same construct that achieve coefficient alpha (r values) above 0.80 are an exception to this fact.

Reality most often (always) includes several configurations of complex antecedent conditions whereby high scores in these conditions result in high scores in the outcome condition. Researchers should not think or craft theory in terms of "key success factors" because cases that do not fit the significant main effect between two variables always exist if the data sample is reasonable large (e.g., $n > 300$). The real issue needs to be and can be how to provide generalizations that account for nearly all the cases in a data set that have high scores for the outcome condition. Such generalization is achievable by crafting and testing alternative theories of complex configurations of antecedent conditions – "key success paths" and not key success factors.

No one factor is necessary or sufficient for a high score in an outcome condition. Even a supplier's fine reputation is insufficient for a supermarket buying committee to adopt a new product manufactured by this supplier (see Montgomery, 1975 for details). This statement does not apply to low scores in an outcome condition.

A low score on some specific simple (often unexpected) antecedent conditions can prevent a high score on an outcome condition from occurring. To illustrate, Woodside and Baxter (2013) apply Van Maanen (1978) findings for the "Asshole" in police work – the asshole is a certain type of street criminal – to industrial marketing-buying behavior. Woodside and Baxter (2013) report that being an asshole can prevent a buyer from becoming preferred customer no matter how favorable other ingredients appear in a complex antecedent condition. The key point here: causality is asymmetrical. The negation of what accounts for a key success path is not the negative scores for each of antecedents in the original key success path.

A researcher needs to treat negative outcomes (e.g., not buying and not profit) as outcomes distinct from positive outcomes. The study of failure is a field for theory and research unto itself and not the negation of the study of success. Thus, for example Weick and Sutcliffe (2001) direct attention to the study of failures and propose tenets for the highly reliable organization. The tenets include five advocacies: preoccupation with failure; reluctance to simplify interpretations; sensitivity to operations; commitment to resilience; and deference to expertise.

Similarly, for the study at hand, attention to failure indicates that coupling not expertise when a customer shops alone (~pal • ~expertise) associates with a high score on failure. However, other paths lead to high failure such as coupling high price with low expertise (price • ~expertise) – thus, telling us not to simplify interpretations. To address sensitivity to operations, coupling a moderately high price with high expertise is likely to avoid failure. For commitment to resilience: Has the retailer tried every combination of expertise with the two pal conditions and four price points? Representing deference to expertise, the field experiment provides useful knowledge about the paths to desirable outcomes as well as the paths to undesirable outcomes.

Limitations, Conclusions, and Recommendations

Though others call for comparison of theory, findings, and interpretations in the same study via MRA and QCA, the study here as well as Woodside and Zhang's (2013) comparisons of QCA with MRA theory-method reports in Henrich et al. (2010) may be the only two studies to do so. The number of available comparisons is a limitation for drawing firm conclusions.

However, the evidence and interpretations here do support extending Wagemann and Schneider's (n.d., p. 17) observation, "QCA should not be applied as the only data analysis technique in a research project." Thus, MRA should not be applied as the only data analysis technique in a research project. Researchers should take-to-heart Ragin's (1997, 2010) insights in crafting theory and in analyzing data at the case-based level: his main insight is that QCA permits generalizing beyond the individual case while at the same time observing the relevancy of each conjunctive statement (recipe) for each individual case while discussions of findings and theory at the individual case level are set aside and ignored in most studies using MRA only.

QCA is more than just a tool; the same applies in studies using MRA. Gigerenzer's (1991, p. 19) claim is worth repeating, "Scientists' tools are not neutral." The work here in revisiting and extending the analyses of the data appearing in Woodside and Pitts (1976) provides credence to Gigerenzer's claim.

Both MRA and QCA include benefits and limitations. Fortunately, the benefits and limitations of ways of thinking and analyzing data are distinct for each so that using both approaches extends the benefits of each and overcomes several limitations. The hope is that this paper confirms this observation. The benefits of modeling and generalizing beyond the individual case when maintaining a study's focus on the individual case is do-able — an exceptional benefit for acquiring skills for crafting theory and analyzing data via configural comparative methods such as fsQCA.

Acknowledgment

The authors gratefully acknowledges permission granted by the Editor-in-Chief, K.H Kuarng, International Journal of Business and Economics, to reuse content in this chapter originally appearing in Woodside, Schpektor, and Xia (2013).

References

Cohen, J. (1977). *Statistical power analysis for the behavioral sciences*. New York, NY: Academic Press.

Cohen, M. (2005). *Wittgenstein's beetle and other classic thought experiments*. Oxford: Blackwell.

Ehrenberg, A. (1988). *Repeat-buying: Facts, theory and applications* (2nd ed.). London: Edward Arnold.

Fiss, P. C. (2009). *Practical issues in QCA*. Presentation at Academy of Management 2009. Retrieved from http://www-rcf.usc.edu/*fiss/QCA_PDW_2009_Fiss_Practical_Issues.pdf

Fiss, P. (2011). Building better causal theories: A fuzzy set approach to typologies in organization research. *Academy of Management Journal, 54*, 393–420.

Gigerenzer, G. (1991). From tools to theories: A heuristic of discovery in cognitive psychology. *Psychology Review, 98*, 254–267.

Gigerenzer, G., & Brighton, H. (2009). Homo heuristicus: Why biased minds make better inferences. *Topics in Cognitive Science, 1*, 107–143.

Henrich, J., Ensminger, J., McElreath, R., Barr, A., Breet, C., Bolyanatz, A., et al. (2010). Markets, religion, community size, and the evolution of fairness and punishment. *Science, 327*, 1480–1484.

Levitt, S. D., & List., J. A. (2007). What do laboratory experiments measuring social preferences reveal about the real world? *Journal of Economic Perspectives, 21*, 153–174.

List, J. A. (2006). The behavioralist meets the market: Measuring social preferences and reputation effects in actual transactions. *Journal of Political Economy, 114*, 1–37.

McClelland, D. C. (1998). Identifying competencies with behavioral-event interviews. *Psychological Science, 9*, 331–339.

Montgomery, D. B. (1975). New product distribution: An analysis of supermarket buyer decisions. *Journal of Marketing Research, 12*, 255–264.

Ragin, C. C. (1997). Turning the tables: How case-oriented methods challenge variable oriented methods. *Comparative Social Research, 16*(1), 27–42.

Ragin, C. C. (2008). *Redesigning social inquiry. Fuzzy sets and beyond.* Chicago, IL: Chicago University Press.

Shah, N. H., Gor, A. S., & Jhaveri, C. A. (2012). Optimal pricing and ordering policy for an integrated inventory model with quadratic demand when trade credit linked to order quantity. *Journal of Modeling in Management, 7*, 148–165.

Simon, H. A. (1990). Invariants of human behavior. *Annual Review of Psychology, 41*, 1–19.

Van Maanen, J. (1978). The asshole. In P. K. Manning & J. Van Maanen (Eds.), *Policing: A view from the street.* Santa Monica, CA: Goodyear Publishing. Retrieved from http://petermoskos.com/readings/Van_Maanen_1978.pdf

Wagemann, C., & Schneider, C. Q. (2007). *Standards of good practice in Qualitative Comparative Analysis (QCA) and fuzzy sets.* Working Paper. Istituto Italiano di Scienze Umane, Palazzo Strozzi, Piazza dei Strozzi, Florence, Italy. Retrieved from http://www.compasss.org/wpseries/Wagemann%20Schneider2007.pdf

Wagemann, C., & Schneider, C. Q. (n.d.). *Standards of good practice in Qualitative Comparative Analysis (QCA) and fuzzy sets.* Working paper. Florence, Italy: Istituto Italiano di Scienze Umane. Palazzo Strozzi, Piazza dei Strozzi. Retrieved from http://www.compasss.org/wpseries/Wagemann Schneider2007.pdf

Weick, K. E., & Sutcliffe, K. M. (2001). *Managing the unexpected – Assuring high performance in an age of complexity.* San Francisco, CA: Jossey-Bass.

Woodside, A. G. (2013). Moving beyond multiple regression analysis to algorithms: Calling for a paradigm shift from symmetric to asymmetric thinking in data analysis, and crafting theory. *Journal of Business Research, 66*, 463–472.

Woodside, A. G., & Baxter, R. (2013). Achieving accuracy, generalization-to-contexts, and complexity in theories of business-to-business decision processes. *Industrial Marketing Management, 42*(3), 382–393.

Woodside, A. G., & Davenport, J. W., Jr. (1974). Effects of salesman similarity and expertise on consumer purchasing behavior. *Journal of Marketing Research, 11*, 198–202.

Woodside, A. G., & Davenport, J. W., Jr. (1976). The effects of price and sales-man expertise on customer purchasing behavior. *Journal of Business, 49,* 51–59.

Woodside, A. G., Ko, E., & Huan, T. C. (2012). The new logic in building iso-morphic theory of management decision realities. *Management Decision, 50,* 765–777.

Woodside, A. G., Pattinson, H., & Montgomery, D. B. (2012). Implemented strategies in business-to-business contexts. In M. S. Glynn & A. G. Woodside (Eds.), *Business-to-business marketing management: Strategies, cases and solutions* (pp. 323–355). Advances in Business Marketing and Purchasing. Bingley, UK: Emerald Group Publishing Limited.

Woodside, A. G., & Pitts, R. E. (1976). Consumer response to alternative selling strategies: A field experiment. In B. B. Anderson (Ed.), *Advances in consumer research* (Vol. 3, pp. 398–404). Cincinnati, OH: Association for Consumer Research.

Woodside, A. G., Schpektor, A., & Xia, X. (2013). Triple sense-making of find-ings from marketing experiments using the dominant variable based-logic, case-based logic, and isomorphic modeling. *International Journal of Business and Economics, 12*(2), 131–153.

Woodside, A. G., & Zhang, M. (2013). Cultural diversity and marketing trans-actions: Are market integration, large community size, and world religions neces-sary for fairness in ephemeral exchanges? *Psychology & Marketing, 30,* 263–276.

6

Complexity Theory, Configural Analysis, and Deepening the Service Dominant Logic

Pei-Ling Wu, Shih-Shuo Yeh, Tzung-Cheng (T.C.) Huan and Arch G. Woodside

ABSTRACT

Recognizing Gigerenzer's (1991) dictum that scientists' tools are not neutral (tools-in-use influence theory formulation as well as data interpretation), this chapter reports theory and examines data in ways that transcend the dominant logics for variable-based and case-based analyses. The theory and data analysis tests key propositions in complexity theory: (1) no single antecedent condition is a sufficient or necessary indicator of a high score in an outcome condition; (2) a few of many available complex configurations of antecedent conditions are sufficient indicators of high scores in an outcome condition; (3) contrarian cases occur, that is, low scores in a single antecedent condition associates with both high and low scores for an outcome condition for different cases; (4) causal asymmetry occurs, that is, accurate causal models for high scores for an outcome condition are not the mirror opposites of causal models for low scores for the same outcome condition. The study tests and supports these propositions in the context of customer assessments ($n = 436$) of service facets and service-outcome evaluations for assisted temporary-transformations of self via beauty salon and spa treatments. The findings contribute to advancing a nuanced theory of how customers' service evaluations relate to their assessments of overall service quality and intentions to use the service. The findings support the need for service managers to be vigilant in fine-tuning service facets and service enactment to achieve the objective of high customer retention.

Keywords: Beauty salon; complexity; configuration; contrarian; transformation

Introduction: Complexity and Customer Evaluations of Service Enactments and Outcomes

Mann Zhang reports being very happy with his new metro-look outcome following his visit, haircut, and styling at Miao's Beauty Salon & Spa; Mann also reports that he intends **not** to return to Miao's shop in the future. A second customer, Lin Chu, reports that Miao's is dark and generally unattractive inside but she gives very positive ratings to Miao for overall service quality. The first of these two anecdotal stories is an example of a "negative contrarian case" — a specific case of a positive indicator and negative outcome relationship while most other cases support a positive main effect between an indicator and an outcome. The second anecdote is an example of a "positive contrarian case" — a specific case of a negative indicator and positive outcome while most cases support a negative main effect between the indicator (e.g., poor ambience) and the outcome (e.g., overall service quality).

The next chapter contributes a radically new perspective in the service dominant logic literature (SDL, e.g., Lusch & Vargo, 2006a, 2006b; Vargo & Lusch, 2004a, 2004b; Vargo & Lusch, 2006; Vargo & Morgan, 2005) in three principal ways. The study here explains how complexity theory provides a solid foundation for advancing a radically new SDL theory; describes how the use of Boolean algebra and asymmetric analytics rather than matrix algebra and symmetric analytics provides a means for testing major tenets of complexity theory in SDL contexts;

presents an empirical study of complexity theory tenets that includes comparing findings from symmetric testing with the alternative logic of asymmetric testing. The study's four foundational footings include (1) prior work that emphasizes how method selection affects theory perspective (Gigerenzer, 1991); (2) the contention that the low R^2's obtained in regression analysis lead to false conclusions about the ability of socioeconomic variables as well as attitudinal measures to substantially explain variance in dependent variables since R^2 is a measure of a model's ability to predict individual rather than group behavior (Bass, Tigert, & Lonsdale, 1968); (3) how models applying Boolean-based asymmetric analytics (Ragin, 2008) solves the symmetric analytic problems observed by Bass et al. (1968) by transcending variable and case level data analysis; and (4) advances in applying McClelland's (1998) algorithm solutions for overcoming the limitations of symmetric-based (e.g., ANOVA and regression) analytics. The findings support the perspective that such thinking and testing of complexity theory tenets via asymmetric methods provides a radically new and useful advance to the SDL literature.

Examining data on customer evaluations of their service experiences (Chang, Tseng, & Woodside, 2013) supports the following observation. A few-to-substantial numbers of cases occur in studies that have independent (X) and dependent (Y) contrarian relationships to the hypotheses tested and supported by the main findings. For example, some customers dissatisfied with their service experiences and outcomes also respond that they intend to return to this same service provider while other customers highly satisfied with their service experiences and outcomes respond that they intend-not-to-return. Such cases are identifiable in data sets even when MRA indicates highly statistical significance in support of the main effects that positive evaluations of service facets and enactments associate with positive intentions-to-return. The study here proposes and demonstrates the use of configural analysis and modeling of indicator combinations of contrarian cases to deepen understanding of such relationships.

Second, and beyond the discussion of contrarian case analysis, focusing analytics on net effects restricts insight because no single independent variable (X) explains substantial amounts of variation in customers' positive and negative evaluations (Y's) — most observed relationships are asymmetrical but the tools used predominately in service research test for symmetrical relationships (Ragin, 2008). For this reason, analysis of variance

(ANOVA), correlation, and multiple regression models (MRAs) offer low-to-moderate explanatory effect sizes of variations in evaluation outcomes under investigation (e.g., customer assessments of overall service quality and intention-to-use the service in the future). MRA findings in the customer service evaluation and satisfaction literature mostly report adjusted (for sample size) coefficients for determination (adj. R^2's) less than 0.50 and usually less than 0.25. In contrast to such MRA findings, useful asymmetric configural models provide algorithms indicating that all or nearly all cases with relatively high values in the configural antecedent statements have relatively high values in the outcome condition – the "outcome condition" is analogous to the dependent variable in MRA.

The present study demonstrates the use of asymmetric tools for predicting high scores for an outcome condition using complex configurations that typically include combinations of three-to-seven simple antecedent conditions. To do so, the study includes testing for the associations of high scores for the complex antecedent conditions and high scores for the outcome conditions using appropriate computer software for performing such tests (e.g., fsQCA.com). Asymmetric testing makes no predictive claims for how an outcome (Y) relates to low configural indicator (X) scores – that is, Y scores are both low and high when X scores are low. The idea of creating and confirming the accuracy of configural statements associating with high scores for an outcome has great appeal for service executives because such configural statements indicate that if the service provider enacts combinatory service condition C•T•H•Z or G•H•W•S, an attractive outcome will occur (e.g., customers experiencing each of these two complex antecedent combinations report high likelihood of using the service provider again) – the capital letters. The consonants (C, T, H, S, W, and Z) in the two configural statements represent specific service facets and the mid-level dot, "•", indicates the logical "and" procedure. For a beauty salon and spa, the consonants might include C = credentials of stylists and trainers; T = appealing aroma, temperature, lighting; H = attractive product displays; S = skill of personal service provider; W = pleasing word-of-mouth communications; Z = attractive architecture, decorations, and wallpaper.

The second configural statement (i.e., G•H•W•S) indicates that a different configural statement from the first one associates with high scores in the outcome condition. Frequently, a few complex statements associate with high scores for an outcome condition. Different complex configural statements accurate in predicting high scores for the outcome condition usually include some of the same as well as unique individual cases. A logical "and" is a procedure in Boolean algebra whereby the total expression is equal to the lowest score occurring among the simple antecedents within the complex statement. Thus, for a specific case (customer) might respond with scores calibrated to include $C = .95$; $T = 1.00$; $H = .80$; $Z = .87$, then $C \bullet T \bullet H \bullet Z = .80$.

The numerical scores are calibrated scores — a calibrated score is the result of a procedure of transforming original scores into membership scores for each specific antecedent or outcome condition — similar in purpose to transforming raw scores to z-scores in statistical hypothesis testing in regression analysis. Calibrated scores range from 0.00 to 1.00 for measures of all conditions — both antecedent and outcome conditions. A score of 0.80 for a complex antecedent condition would be quite high in most studies using fsQCA. If the configural model, $C \bullet T \bullet H \bullet Z$, was accurate/useful, then high scores (say for nine cases for this statement) among the cases in the study (e.g., $n = 20$ to 3,000), would associate with the occurrence of high scores in an outcome condition (e.g., eight of the nine cases have high scores in the outcome condition). Thus, if the analysis supports high accuracy for identifying high scores in the outcome condition, the expression in model 1 receives support as a useful model in predicting such occurrences:

$$C \bullet T \bullet H \bullet Z \leq U \tag{1}$$

where U equals scores for an outcome condition such as the customer's overall satisfaction with the service experienced. In research using Boolean algebra and testing for alternative configurations associating with high scores for an outcome condition, a "+" indicates "or" in a statement expressing different complex conditions:

$$(C \bullet T \bullet H \bullet Z) + (G \bullet H \bullet W \bullet S) \leq U \tag{2}$$

Eq. 2 indicates that high scores for two complex antecedent configurations lead to the same outcome — high scores in U. Note that H appears in both complex models but each statement has combinations of simple antecedent conditions unique unto itself.

Following this introduction, the next section presents core tenets of complexity theory. The section that follows describes the business context of the empirical study. The section on complexity theory proposes complexity theory tenets for the specific industry business context. The next section covers the method of the study. Findings are described next. After this, the contributions of the study for theory and service management practice are discussed. The last section concludes and includes limitations and recommendations for additional research.

Complexity Theory in Service Research

Most cases in a data set will have low scores for any given complex antecedent condition that predicts high scores in an outcome accurately for asymmetric models. Low scores on the complex antecedent condition associate with both low and high scores on the outcome condition. Figure 1c illustrates such an asymmetric sufficient-but- not-necessary relationship for 26 hypothetical cases. For clarity purposes, Figure 1 includes displays of rectangular, symmetric, and asymmetric necessary-but-not-sufficient relationships. Unlike a symmetric Pearson r index (a symmetric

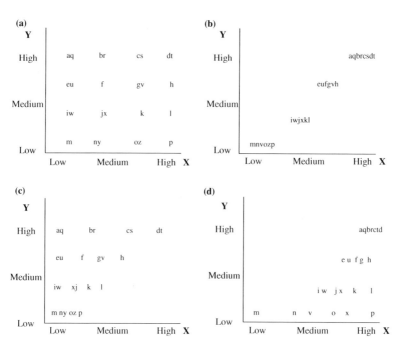

Figure 1. Hypothetical Relationships where X is a Complex Configural Condition (e.g., C•T•H•Z) and Y is a Service Outcome Condition (e.g., Customer Intention-to-Return). (a) Rectangular. (b) Symmetrical. (c) Asymmetric — Sufficient but Not Necessary. (d) Asymmetric — Insufficient but Necessary.

relationship appears visually in Figure 1b), Boolean-related indexes for measuring the consistency of a given complex antecedent statement are unaffected by low and high scores for the outcome scores. Given the occurrence of contrarian cases in nearly all data sets, r's and adjusted R^2 values almost never exceed 0.50 except for measuring reliability for multiple items in a scale for one construct; such symmetric-focused studies rarely consider modeling the indicators for the contrarian cases.

The major tenets of complexity theory and qualitative comparative analysis (QCA) are relevant for attempting to deepen accurate explanation of how customers evaluate facets of services, enactments, and outcomes. These tenets include the proposition that a few (not one) of many possible paths lead to the same outcome, that is, "equifinality" occurs – alternative asymmetric combinations of indicators (i.e., algorithms) are sufficient but no one combination is necessary for accurately predicting customers' highly positive evaluations of service performance and high intentions to return to the same service provider.

A second complexity theory proposition is that, "Relationships between variables can be non-linear with abrupt switches occurring, so the same "cause" can, in specific circumstances, produce different effects" (Urry, 2005, p. 4). Thus, high customers' intentions to return may associate with an outcome of high overall service-quality assessments "in specific circumstances [contexts]" and an increase in demand may be an outcome of low overall service-quality assessments in other specific contexts. The same point is relevant for service antecedent and outcome conditions.

The complexity turn to service research and theory includes the tipping-point tenet as Urry (2005) and Gladwell (2002) describe. Gladwell (2002) describes that if a system passes particular thresholds with minor changes in the controlling variables, switches occur such that a liquid turns into a gas, a large number of apathetic people suddenly tip into a forceful movement for change. "Such tipping points give rise to unexpected structures and events whose properties can be different form the underlying elementary laws" (Urry, 2005, p. 5). In asymmetric service research models such tipping points frequently involve replacing a negative with a positive response to one issue in a string (path) of questions-answers within a given complex configuration of antecedent conditions. Examples of such "causal complexity" (Ragin, 2000) appear in the empirical findings of the present study.

Service Provider and Customer Contexts in the Beauty and Spa Industry

A planned objective of the study was to test tenets of complexity theory in a highly-intense personal service industry. The study focuses on a service high in physical and social contacts between customers and service providers – the beauty salon/spa industry. Several ethnographic studies of customers and stylists, physical-wellness trainers, and beauty salon/spa managers support the consistent finding that service enactments in this industry usually include 15 to 180 minutes of physical touching related to holding, shampooing/washing, massaging, hair-cutting, hair plucking, nail-filing, applying polish, waxing, hair-washing and dyeing, applications of lubricants/cosmetics, wrapping, drying, pedicures, and selling of cosmetics often with discussions, recommendations, and purchases of cosmetic products (Grimlin,1996; Otnes, Ilhan, & Kulkarni, 2012; Sharma Black, 2001; Toerien & Kitzinger, 2007; Üstüner & Thompson, 2012).

In this high-touch•high-talk industry, the customer (and frequently the service provider) often engage in personal communications – storytelling – about issues in life including relationships with significant others during service enactments. Both high-touch and high-talk together is a configurative statement that is integral within beauty and spa industry. Sharma and Black (2001, p. 926) report beauty therapists taking on a counsellor-like role when, for example, "clients confide about their family or marital problems in the course of a treatment." Toerien and Kitzinger (2007, p. 654) emphasize, "… the relational side of salon work is far more pervasive than such instances imply. Emotional labor includes, crucially, the successful personalizing of an encounter that is utterly routine for the therapist." As Sharma and Black (2001, p. 928) express, "At all costs the client must not feel that she is on a 'production line' served by a robot." Such lengthy and deep personal/physical touching and verbal communications offer rich, multi-step contexts representing multiple combinations of potentially positive and negative facets of service enactments – much more so than typical service enactments in most retail settings (e.g., department stores, banks, clothing stores, supermarkets, pharmacies, and gas stations).

The global personal care industry is valued at $300 billion by Kline & Company and growing by 4.5% annually (Matthews, 2013). The U.S. hair care services industry alone includes about 86,000 establishments (82,000 beauty salons; 4,000 barber shops) with combined annual revenue of about $20 billion (Beauty Salon Business Overview & Trends, 2012). The spa industry includes $14 billion sales in the United States in 2012 (Big Five Statistics, 2013). In China, "beauty is big business" – the country's cosmetics market is worth $26 billion a year, making it the third-largest globally. Euromonitor, a research firm, believes the cosmetics industry in China will grow 8% annually now through 2017. "Wages for the legions of 'beauty assistants'" are rising at double-digit rates annually in China (*The Economist*, 2014, p. 57).

Applying Complexity Theory Tenets in the Beauty and Spa Industry

Figure 2 summarizes a general complexity theory (GCT) relevant for the beauty and spa industry – and to the entire discipline of service research following a few minor modifications. Rather than using primarily a boxes-and-arrow approach (cf. Sirgy, Grewal, & Mangleburg, 2000), the GCT visual employs Venn diagrams to indicate the primary configural nature of complex antecedent conditions that indicate high scores in outcome conditions. This section describes major tenets of the GCT for the beauty salon and spa industry that are relevant for the retailing service sector more generally. The three bold-lines with upper case arrows (A, B, C) in Figure 2 represent the major flows of configural relationships that the theory predicts; the three dotted-lines with lower case arrows (d, e, f) indicate peripheral routes that are likely to have lower consistencies in predicting high scores for outcome conditions.

The first Venn diagram (left side of Figure 2) expresses the tenet that specific demographic configurations of customers affect their perceptions/evaluations of service facets and their overall assessment of service enactments. For clarity, only four simple demographic antecedents appear in Figure 2; of course, additional demographics are possible to include and are worthy of examination. With four demographics, 16 combinations occur: four simple antecedent conditions, six two-way, four three-way,

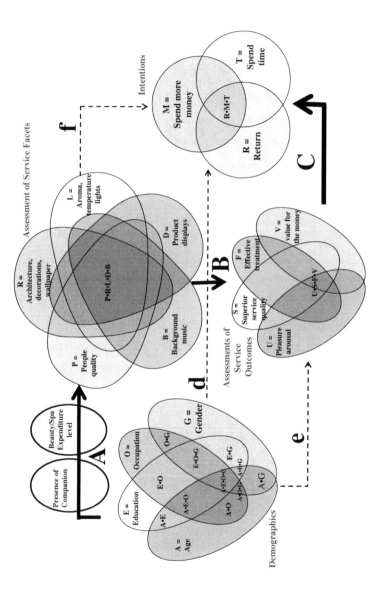

Figure 2. Foundational Complex Configural Model. *Notes:* Thick arrows indicate propositions regarding effective algorithms; thin and dotted arrows indicate predictions of low accuracy.

and one four-way complex configurations. In comparison to the use of Boolean-based algorithm analysis and as Ragin (2008) emphasizes, considering these combinations as two-way, three-way, and four-way interaction effects in symmetrical statistical tests is difficult to interpret and to explain and presents multicollinearity problems.

Because the literature in the behavioral sciences associates "hypothesis" with "statistical hypothesis testing" and because testing for the adequacy of complex configurations in predicting outcome scores usually includes consistency metrics and does not include statistical hypothesis testing, "tenet" is the term in-use here to express testable precepts of complexity theory in service research contexts. Testing for the statistical influence of configurations (i.e., algorithms) for accuracy in predicting high scores for an outcome condition is possible and does appear in the literature (e.g., McClelland, 1998).

T1: COMPLEX DEMOGRAPHIC CONFIGURATIONS AFFECT CUSTOMER EVALUATIONS OF SERVICE FACETS

The first core tenant (T1) in the GCT is that a few of the complex demographic configurations are indicators of high evaluation scores in the (a) simple and (b) collective customer evaluations of service facets. Arrow A in Figure 2 is a visual of these evaluations. The four demographics simple antecedents combine in a "truth table" (Ragin, 2008) in more than 16-ways because one or more of the simple antecedent may be negative in a given antecedent and one or two of the simple antecedents may be irrelevant for a given configuration's influence on an outcome condition. For example, $\sim$A$\bullet$E$\bullet$O$\bullet\sim$G is a complex configuration representing a young adult ($\sim$A), high education completion (E), high occupational status (O) and a male ($\sim$G where G represents female gender), where sideways tilde ("$\sim$") represents negation (e.g., 1-A = $\sim$A). If the impact is a high score on outcome U is about the same for $\sim$A$\bullet$E$\bullet$O$\bullet\sim$G and A$\bullet\sim$E$\bullet$O$\bullet\sim$G, then simplifying the two models to $\sim$A$\bullet$O$\bullet\sim$G — this model indicates high scores for this model associates with high U scores no matter the E score.

A truth table or "property space" (Lazarsfeld, 1937) analysis expresses all the combinations possible among the simple antecedent conditions. For four simple antecedents at three levels each (negation, absent, and positive), a total of 81 combinations are possible (3^4 = 81). For six simple antecedent conditions having

3 levels for each, 729 combinations occur theoretically. In configural analysis of data, not all theoretically possible combinations appear among the data, especially in small sample ($n \leq 30$) studies – empty cell combinations are identified as "remainders" in configural asymmetric research.

T2: CAUSAL ASYMMETRY: DEMOGRAPHIC CONFIGURATIONS LEADING TO NEGATIVE OUTCOMES ARE NOT THE MIRROR OPPOSITES OF DEMOGRAPHIC CONFIGURATIONS LEADING TO POSITIVE OUTCOMES

The second core tenet (T2) in the GCT is that (a) a few of the complex demographic configurations are indicators of low evaluation scores in the (a) simple and (b) collective customer evaluations of service facets and (b) this second group of complex antecedent configurations indicating a negative outcome (~U) are not mirror opposites of the first set of indicators. Thus, "causal asymmetry" (Fiss, 2011; Fiss, Marx, & Cambré, 2013) occurs in explaining and predicting U versus ~U. For example, occupational status (O) may often appear in configurations accurate in explaining high scores for an outcome (U) but O may be irrelevant in explaining low scores for the same outcome (~).

T3: UNIQUE COMPLEX ANTECEDENT CONFIGURATIONS ARE SUFFICIENT BUT NOT NECESSARY FOR HIGH SCORES IN AN OUTCOME CONDITION

The third core tenet (T3) for demographics configurations: no simple antecedent condition (A, E, O, or G) is sufficient or necessary for explaining high scores in a given service facet or overall evaluations of the service facets (an outcome U for service facets). GCT recognizes that alternative combinations of antecedents will indicate a high score in an outcome – more than one path exists for high scores to occur in an outcome condition. Thus, one complex configuration can be sufficient but it is not necessary for the occurrence of a high score in the outcome condition.

T4: SIMPLE ANTECEDENT CONDITIONS CAN BE NECESSARY BUT THEY ARE INSUFFICIENT FOR INDICATING HIGH SCORES IN AN OUTCOME CONDITION

Simple antecedent statements may be necessary but are insufficient for a high score in an outcome because several ingredients constitute a service enactment (Figure 1d) — just as several ingredients are necessary in baking a delicious cake. GCT does not focus on comparing the relative size of the net effect of each simple condition in a given configural model; GCT focuses are describing, explaining, and predicting high outcome scores by complex (2+) antecedent conditions.

Note that none of the tenets in the GCT refer to symmetric predictions — they do not include any predictions about low scores or high scores for an outcome when low scores occur in the complex antecedent conditions — in this aspect the GCT tenets are less restrictive than symmetric testing of hypotheses. At the same time, the GCT is more restrictive in its prediction requirement of consistently high scores in U by a few complex antecedent conditions — the consistency rule usually applied in configural research is that all or nearly all scores of U should be equal to or above the main diagonal of scores in an XY plot (Figure 1c) where X is the complex configural antecedent condition and Y is the outcome condition (U or ~U).

T5: WITHIN DIFFERENT COMPLEX ANTECEDENT COMBINATIONS, SIMPLE ANTECEDENT CONDITIONS MAY APPEAR AS A POSITIVE AND NEGATIVE INFLUENCE ON AN OUTCOME

T5: A simple antecedent conditions is a positive indicator in some configurations and a negative indictor in other configurations on high scores in an outcome condition — whereby the outcome condition is U or ~U. For example, older customers (A) may contribute positively to high score evaluations of service facets of a beauty salon/spa; younger customers (~A) may contribute positively to high score evaluations of service facets of a beauty salon/spa. Both A and ~A may contribute negatively to high-to-low evaluation scores of service facets of a beauty salon/spa. The valence (sign) of influence of a simple antecedent depends upon what additional simple conditions constitute a given complex configuration.

This tenet (T5) in complexity theory advances beyond rational economic theory of rational consumer behavior to explain seeming anomalies. Consider the question, "Can an increase in price associate with increasing demand?" Rational economic theory predicts only a decreasing price and increasing demand relationship. Yet, empirical studies support the perspective that price increases associate with demand increases in certain contexts (Leibenstein, 1950; Milgrom & Roberts, 1986).

T5 expresses the perspective that both a positive and negative influence occurs for most simple antecedent conditions — each simple condition has a positive and negative influence on an outcome depending upon the specific complex configurations in which the simple antecedents appear.

T6: THE PRESENCE OF A COMPANION WITH THE CUSTOMER MODIFIES HOW A CUSTOMER EVALUATES SERVICE FACETS

A "purchase pal" is a family member, friend, colleague from work, or an acquaintance that the customer knows beforehand or develops a friendship at the shopping site that may influence the customer's assessment and purchases while experiencing the service enactment (Chebat, Haj-Salem, & Oliveira, 2012; Woodside & Sims, 1976). Purchase pals may increase the customer's confidence to commit to service enactments (e.g., hair coloring) that s/he might otherwise postpone. Purchase pals may provide the "voice of reason" to block the customer's action to embrace a "daring do" (Hielscher, Fisher, & Cooper, 2009). T6 expresses the perspective that the mere presence of purchase pals affects how customers assess service facets. Such a modifying influence may be a positive or negative influence depending on what other ingredients appear in specific configurations (e.g., the presence of purchase pals may occur more frequently with young customers ($\sim$A) versus older customers (A) assuming that more youthful customers are less able to rely on their own assessments of outcomes of prior service enactments than older customers).

T7: BEAUTY/SPA EXPENDITURE LEVELS MODIFY THE INFLUENCE OF DEMOGRAPHIC CONFIGURAL INFLUENCES ON SERVICE FACETS

Customers spending relatively high levels of money for service enactments may be more vigilant in judging service facets than other customers — big spenders occupy different "money worlds" versus small spenders (cf. Tatzel, 2002). Big spenders may expect to receive hands-on service from senior versus junior staff members, the use of the best cosmetics, special pampering and seating, and speedy compliance to requests. Consequently large expenditures (L) may have a positive as well as a negative modifying influence in different demographic configuration influences on service facet evaluations.

The same may occur for the negation of large expenditures ($\sim$L). The negation of big spending does not necessarily associate with the high or low scores in an outcome condition – much depends on the demographics of the big versus smaller spender: ~L may associate with one or other depending on the presence/ absence of additional ingredients in the demographic configurations that do associate with low (high) scores in the outcome condition. Configuratively, L may combine with ~O (negation of occupational status) and ~E (negation of education) to produce a particularly high vigilant affect; L•~O~E are customers with low occupational status, low education, with high expenditures for the service – possibly for a very special occasion since such a configuration would not be expected to occur frequently.

CONFIGURATIONS OF CUSTOMER SERVICE-FACET EVALUATIONS AFFECT OVERALL SERVICE OUTCOMES AND INTENTIONS TOWARD THE SERVICE PROVIDER

T8 to T12 in the GCT application to beauty salon/spa indicate relationships among service facets and outcomes – the two center Venn diagrams in Figure 2 and arrow B. The five service facets appearing in Figure 2 include people (e.g., stylist) quality; architectural features; ambience – aroma, temperature, lighting; product displays; and background music. Sufficient number of personnel is a sixth service facet in the study but does not appear to reduce the level of complexity in Figure 2.

The selections of service facets, service outcomes, and intentions for the study are based on a literature review of both empirical positivistic studies (Babin & Darden, 1995; Baker, Parasuraman, Grewal, & Voss, 2002; Bitner, 1995; Bloemer & De Ruyter, 1998; Donovan & Rossiter, 1982; Donovan, Rossiter, Marcoolyn, & Nesdale, 1994; Hudson & Gilbert, 2000; Mathwick, Malhotra, & Rigdon, 2001; Mitchell, 2001; Sharma & Stafford, 2000) and ethnographic studies (Barber, 2008; Grimlin,1996; Otnes et al., 2012; Sharma & Black, 2001; Toerien & Kitzinger, 2007; Üstüner & Thompson, 2012) relating to service industry studies in general and the beauty salon/spa industry in particular.

The general theoretical perspective regarding service facets is that they serve as both outcomes and antecedent conditions. Service facets are ingredients in service enactments. Different configurations of service facets affect high scores in service outcomes. Four service outcomes appear in Figure 2: pleasure arousal; superior service quality; effective treatment; value for the money. The empirical study here also includes analyzing complex antecedent configurations indicating high scores for positive and the negation scores for each of these four outcomes.

The study includes the examination of three customer intentions toward the beauty salon/spa: intentions to return; booking additional time per session to cover additional services; and spending more money during future sessions. The study includes analyzing complex antecedent configurations indicating high scores for positive and the negation scores for each of these three intentions. Because the reasoning supporting the specific tenets regarding service facets' influence on service outcomes and due to space limitations, the remaining tenets are stated without elaboration. Using a net effects approach, prior empirical findings using symmetrical testing (i.e., multiple regression analysis) support the general perspective that specific service facets influence patient/client/customer assessments of service outcomes (e.g., Woodside, Frey, & Daily, 1989).

T8: Complex service-facet configurations affect high scores for customer evaluations of service outcomes. T9: Causal asymmetry occurs, that is, service facet configurations leading to negative outcomes are not the mirror opposites of demographic configurations leading to positive outcomes. T10: Unique configurations of service facets are sufficient but each is not necessary for high scores for service outcomes to occur. T11: Simple service-facet antecedent conditions can be necessary but are insufficient for high scores for an outcome condition. T12: Simple antecedent service facets can have a positive and negative influence on an outcome – the valence depends upon the presence of specific additional service facets in complex antecedent configurations.

Similarly, following the general framework by Woodside et al. (1989) of how customer evaluations of service enactments influence satisfaction and intention outcomes, configurations of service outcomes are principal indicators of customers' service intentions. Arrow C in Figure 2 is a visual of this perspective and the five final tenets in the complexity theory of beauty salon/spa services. T13: Complex service-outcome configurations affect high scores for customer intentions relating to the service provider. T14: Causal asymmetry occurs, that is, service outcome configurations leading to low intention scores are not the mirror opposites of outcome configurations leading to high intention scores. T15: Unique configurations of service outcomes are sufficient but each is not necessary for high scores for service intentions to occur. T16: Simple service-outcome antecedent conditions can be necessary but are insufficient for high scores for an intention condition. T17: Simple service-outcome antecedents can have both a positive and negative influence on intentions – which depends upon what other simple conditions make-up the complex configurations indicating high scores in the outcome condition.

Method

The present study includes an empirical examination of the 17 complexity tenets in the context of evaluations by customers of a large beauty salon/spa located in Changhua City. (Changhua City is located in Changhua County, west-central Taiwan. The county has a population of 1.3 million inhabits – the second largest county by population in Taiwan.) The specific beauty salon/spa has 28 full-time employees including 11 front-line professionals, 6 junior staff personnel and trainees; 5 immediate supervisors, 3 senior supervisors, and 2 owner-executives. The owners requested anonymity of the name of the salon/spa in this research.

A quota convenience sample of customers was asked to complete a survey on-site after receiving and paying for a service experience. The quota was based on coverage of age and gender segments of the salon/spa so that the sampled respondents matched the salon/spa's population share of young (<30), middle-aged (30–50), and older (>50) customers and its ratio of female to male customers. The survey was completed by samples representative of five age groups by both genders. The survey was completed anonymously by each respondent. Each respondent was urged to be open and forthcoming in answering. A small gift was given to each respondent for participating in the study.

SURVEY INSTRUMENT

Along with the demographic questions, customers were asked a total of 31 assessment questions and 4 buying intention questions. Most respondents completed the survey in less than five minutes. The intention for the study was that the constructs would include multiple-item five-point scales (very poor to very good and very much disagree to very much agree; this goal was achieved with high Cronbach alpha's and clear rotated factor structures for nearly all constructs).

The survey comprises five parts including store environment, experiential value, store image, buying intention, and socio-demographic items. Prior studies informed the development these items. The store environment part of the questions comprised 15 questions that can be allocated in three sub-categories namely social, ambience, and design (Baker et al., 2002). Experiential value aspects of questions were designed based on the work of Mathwick et al. (2001), which further divide into four dimensions, namely customer return on investment (ROI), esthetics, playfulness, and service excellence.

The store image items were designed based on prior research (Mitchell, 2001). The study incorporated items from prior studies in four sub-categories of store image – namely product, facility, service, and price images – to include twelve questions. The buying intention measure comprised four questions based on works regarding customer loyalty (Hudson & Gilbert, 2000). The above questions are in 5-point Likert scales where 1 denotes strongly disagree and 5, strongly agree. The final part of the questionnaire includes respondents' socio-demographic information, such as age, gender, marital status, education level, occupation, and yearly salary.

The assessment survey items in the survey appear in Appendix A. Summaries of the quartimax-rotated factor structures for most of the individual items in the survey appear in Tables B1 and B2. The factor structures for the items for constructs in the scale support the conclusion that constructs are distinct and usefully describe specific service facets, outcomes, and intentions. Cronbach alpha is above 0.70 for each of the multi-item constructs for service facets and outcomes.

RESPONDENTS

A total of 436 customers responded to the survey; the response rate was 75% of customers asked to participant. "No time, sorry," was the principal reason offered for not agreeing to participate. The majority of the respondents were female ($n = 383$, 88%). In terms of age groups, only 16 respondents were less than 21 years old, which is reasonable since young respondents may not be able to afford the service; 32% of the respondents were between 21 and 30 years old, 29% between 31 and 40 years old, 22% between 41 and 50 years old, and 13% were 51 or older. A total of 147 respondents reported having a university degree (34%), followed by high school equivalent education

(n = 138, 32%), and technical college (n = 94, 22%). Very few respondents reported having secondary school, primary school, or post-graduate degrees. In terms of occupation, 139 respondents (32%) worked in service industries, 64 worked as business managers (15%), 56 were full-time housekeepers (13%), and 44 were freelancers (10%). Very few respondents were retired, industrial workers, or farmers.

The beauty salon/spa is a relative luxury service in Taiwan, which means only adult respondents with sufficiently high incomes may afford the service. Indeed, only 232 respondents (53%) reporting spending more than NT$1,500 per visit (1.00 NT$ = 0.033 USD in 2014). Only 118 respondents (27%) report spending more than NT$1,000. Since spa is an intimate experience, more than half (n = 239, 55%) of the respondents visited by themselves. Others visit with friends (n = 77, 18%) or family members (n = 72, 16%). Only 37 respondents went with colleagues (9%).

Findings

To learn what variable associations indicate by a conventional data analysis perspective, some preliminary symmetrical testing was done. Correlations and cross-tabulations were run to examine the associations among the four principal sets of constructs: demographics, customer assessments of service facets, service outcome assessments, and customers' intentions toward the service provider. Following this preliminary analysis, asymmetrical fsQCA data analyses were performed to examine major tenets of complexity theory. This section first reports on the findings for the symmetrical tests followed by the findings for the configural asymmetric tests.

CORRELATION AND CROSS-TABULATION FINDINGS

Tables 1 and 3 and Figure 3 provide collections for socioeconomic variables, customer service-facet assessments, service outcome assessments, and intentions. From Table 1, a meta-analysis for the thirty correlations for the socioeconomic and service-facet assessments results in an average r = .032 with an estimated range of 0.016–0.049 – thus indicating a statistically significant small effect size. These findings support Bass et al. (1968) observations that symmetric tests indicate minor relationships among

Table 1: Correlations of Demographics with Service Facet Evaluations.

		Demographics					Service Facets					
		Age	Female_v_male	Education	House Keeper	Service Worker	Arch_dec_wall	People_quality	Aroma_temp_lights	Music	Displays	Sufficient Number of Personnel
Age	Pearson correlation	1	.007	−.201**	.219**	−.296**	.090	.016	.012	−.001	.070	.017
	Sig. (two-tailed)		.892	.000	.000	.000	.062	.733	.806	.985	.144	.730
	N	436	436	436	436	436	436	436	436	436	436	436
female_v_male	Pearson correlation	.007	1	.054	.059	.104*	.081	.091	.074	.096*	.116*	.011
	Sig. (two-tailed)	.892		.256	.220	.030	.090	.058	.123	.046	.015	.820
	N	436	436	436	436	436	436	436	436	436	436	436
Education	Pearson correlation	−.201**	.054	1	−.227**	.039	.022	.137**	.025	−.016	.033	.015
	Sig. (two-tailed)	.000	.256		.000	.411	.654	.004	.602	.737	.485	.739
	N	436	436	436	436	436	436	436	436	436	436	436
Housekeeper	Pearson correlation	.219**	.059	−.227**	1	−.263**	.042	.024	−.019	.030	.040	.028
	Sig. (two-tailed)	.000	.220	.000		.000	.381	.617	.700	.534	.410	.560
	N	436	436	436	436	436	436	436	436	436	436	436
Serviceworker	Pearson correlation	−.296**	.104*	.039	−.263**	1	−.057	.038	.019	.024	−.069	−.020
	Sig. (two-tailed)	.000	.030	.411	.000		.239	.426	.698	.616	.151	.677
	N	436	436	436	436	436	436	436	436	436	436	436

arch_dec_wall	Pearson correlation	.090	.081	.022	.042	−.057	1	.524**	.478**	.402**	.651**	.481**
	Sig. (two-tailed)	.062	.090	.654	.381	.239		.000	.000	.000	.000	.000
	N	436	436	436	436	436	436	436	436	436	436	436
people_quality	Pearson correlation	.016	.091	.137**	.024	.038	.524**	1	.478**	.402**	.651**	.481**
	Sig. (two-tailed)	.733	.058	.004	.617	.426	.000		.000	.000	.000	.000
	N	436	436	436	436	436	436	436	436	436	436	436
aroma_temp_lights	Pearson correlation	.012	.074	.025	−.019	.019	.478**	.524**	1	.598**	.467**	.375**
	Sig. (two-tailed)	.806	.123	.602	.700	.698	.000	.000		.000	.000	.000
	N	436	436	436	436	436	436	436	436	436	436	436
Music	Pearson correlation	−.001	.096*	−.016	.030	.024	.402**	.454**	.598**	1	.385**	.413**
	Sig. (two-tailed)	.985	.046	.737	.534	.616	.000	.000	.000		.000	.000
	N	436	436	436	436	436	436	436	436	436	436	436
Displays	Pearson correlation	.070	.116*	.033	.040	−.069	.651**	.520**	.467**	.385**	1	.443**
	Sig. (two-tailed)	.144	.015	.485	.410	.151	.000	.000	.000	.000		.000
	N	436	436	436	436	436	436	436	436	436	436	436
Sufficient number of personnel	Pearson correlation	.017	.011	.016	.028	−.020	.481**	.556**	.375**	.413**	.443**	1
	Sig. (two-tailed)	.730	.820	.739	.560	.677	.000	.000	.000	.000	.000	
	N	436	436	436	436	436	436	436	436	436	436	436

Note: Correlations indicate few significant symmetric relationships among demographics and service facet evaluations. Correlations among service facet evaluations are significant and medium in effect size.

		Demographics					Experience Assessments and Intentions				
		Age	female_v_male	Education	housekeeper	serviceworker	arousal_pleasure	effective_treatment	return	spendmore_time_money	superior_service_quality
Age	Pearson correlation	1	.007	-.201**	.219**	-.296**	-.041	.038	-.071	-.139**	.000
	Sig. (two-tailed)		.892	.000	.000	.000	.398	.426	.138	.004	.999
	N		436	436	436	436	436	436	436	436	436
female_v_male	Pearson Correlation	.007	1	.054	.059	.104*	.088	.057	.037	-.031	.073
	Sig. (two-tailed)	.892		.256	.220	.030	.066	.238	.442	.519	.126
	N	436		436	436	436	436	436	436	436	436
Education	Pearson correlation	-.201**	.054	1	-.227**	.039	.101*	.026	.062	.011	.091
	Sig. (two-tailed)	.000	.256		.000	.411	.035	.594	.197	.812	.056
	N	436	436		436	436	436	436	436	436	436
housekeeper	Pearson correlation	.219**	.059	-.227**	1	-.263**	.039	.077	.045	.037	.016
	Sig. (two-tailed)	.000	.220	.000		.000	.416	.110	.352	.439	.731
	N	436	436	436		436	436	436	436	436	436
serviceworker	Pearson correlation	-.296**	.104*	.039	-.263**	1	.102*	.044	.084	.024	.016
	Sig. (two-tailed)	.000	.030	.411	.000		.033	.360	.079	.621	.732
	N	436	436	436	436		436	436	436	436	436
arousal_pleasure	Pearson correlation	-.041	.088	.101*	.039	.102*	1	.483**	.480**	.407**	.609**
	Sig. (two-tailed)	.398	.066	.035	.416	.033		.000	.000	.000	.000
	N	436	436	436	436	436		436	436	436	436
effective_treatment	Pearson correlation	.038	.057	.026	.077	.044	.483**	1	.390**	.319**	.527**
	Sig. (two-tailed)	.426	.238	.594	.110	.360	.000		.000	.000	.000
	N	436	436	436	436	436	436		436	436	436
return	Pearson correlation	-.071	.037	.062	.045	.084	.480**	.390**	1	.647**	.520**
	Sig. (two-tailed)	.138	.442	.197	.352	.079	.000	.000		.000	.000
	N	436	436	436	436	436	436	436		436	436
spendmore_time_money	Pearson correlation	-.139**	-.031	.011	.037	.024	.407**	.319**	.647**	1	.439**
	Sig. (two-tailed)	.004	.519	.812	.439	.621	.000	.000	.000		.000
	N	436	436	436	436	436	436	436	436		436
superior_service_quality	Pearson correlation	.000	.073	.091	.016	.016	.609**	.527**	.520**	.439**	1
	Sig. (two-tailed)	.999	.126	.056	.731	.732	.000	.000	.000	.000	
	N	436	436	436	436	436	436	436	436	436	436

Highest r

Figure 3. Correlations of Demographics with Experience Assessments and Intentions. *Notes*: Correlations includes few significant symmetric relationships among demographics and experience assessments and Intentions. Correlations among outcomes, experience assessments, and intentions are positive and highly significant.

socioeconomic and dependent customer-related variables – while other data analysis methods indicate major relationships among these same variables.

Table 1 includes the highly significant correlations among the service facets which would result in multi-collinearity problems in regression analyses. However, these correlations are all below 0.70 and sufficiently low to conclude that each construct is measure a unique service facet.

The 25 correlations for the socioeconomic variables and customer evaluations of service outcome and intentions in Figure 3 include 23 non-significant findings with the correlations ranging from $-.139$ to $+.102$ – again supporting the conclusion that symmetric test findings have zero to small effects on customer assessments. Figure 3 correlations among service facet constructs and with service intentions are significant statistically and medium in effect sizes.

Table 2 includes correlations among service facets and intentions. As expected, the correlation among the two intention constructions – spend more money on next visit and intention to return, is the highest correlation within Figure 3 and Table 2 ($r = .647$). The findings in Table 2 indicate medium effect sizes among service facets and intentions – about at the same levels as the correlations among service outcomes and intentions. Such findings support the conclusion that dotted arrow f should be replaced by a solid arrow having the same emphasis as arrow B in Figure 2.

Table 3 provides correlations for service facet evaluations, service outcomes, and intentions. The "quick clustering" (Kamen, 1970) at the bottom of Table 3 shows the largest correlations; these appear on double-headed arrows – the purpose of quick clustering is to visualize the findings to ease interpretation. The main conclusion is that the three categories of customer judgments associate significantly. Customer outcome evaluations of service quality delivered appears to be a central linkage between service facet evaluations, other service outcomes, and intention measures.

Figure 4 and Table 4 present examples of the presence of contrarian cases. Figure 4 is a cross of two service outcome evaluations: effective treatment and service quality delivered. On a variable by variable basis, the phi^2 measure indicates a positive large effect size (Cohen, 1977). A substantial majority of cases with positive evaluations about receiving effective treatment give positive evaluations about the delivered overall service quality;

Table 2:   Correlations of Beauty Salon/Spa Facets and Intentions.

		Ambience						Intentions	
		Arch_dec_wall	People_qual	Aroma_temp_see	Music	Display	Sufficient Number of Personnel	Return	Spendmore_time_money
arch_dec_wall	Pearson correlation	1	.524**	.478**	.402**	.651**	.481**	.455**	.357**
	Sig. (two-tailed)		.000	.000	.000	.000	.000	.000	.000
	N	436	436	436	436	436	436	436	436
people_qual	Pearson correlation	.524**	1	.544**	.454**	.520**	.556**	.420**	.386**
	Sig. (two-tailed)	.000		.000	.000	.000	.000	.000	.000
	N	436	436	436	436	436	436	436	436
aroma_temp_see	Pearson correlation	.478**	.544**	1	.598**	.467**	.375**	.339**	.316**
	Sig. (two-tailed)	.000	.000		.000	.000	.000	.000	.000
	N	436	436	436	436	436	436	436	436
Music	Pearson correlation	.402**	.454**	.598**	1	.385**	.413**	.320**	.253**
	Sig. (two-tailed)	.000	.000	.000		.000	.000	.000	.000
	N	436	436	436	436	436	436	436	436

display	Pearson correlation	.651**	.520**	.467**	.385**	1	.443**	.381**	.333**
	Sig. (two-tailed)	.000	.000	.000	.000		.000	.000	.000
	N	436	436	436	436	436	436	436	436
Sufficient number of personnel	Pearson correlation	.481**	.556**	.375**	.413**	.443**	1	.368**	.325**
	Sig. (two-tailed)	.000	.000	.000	.000	.000		.000	.000
	N	436	436	436	436	436	436	436	436
return	Pearson correlation	.455**	.420**	.339**	.320**	.381**	.368**	1	.647**
	Sig. (two-tailed)	.000	.000	.000	.000	.000	.000		.000
	N	436	436	436	436	436	436	436	436
Spendmore_time_money	Pearson correlation	.357**	.386**	.316**	.253**	.333**	.325**	.647**	1
	Sig. (two-tailed)	.000	.000	.000	.000	.000	.000	.000	
	N	436	436	436	436	436	436	436	436

Table 3:   Correlations of All Dimensions of Customers' Evaluations and Intentions.

	Touch	People_quality	Aroma_temp_lights	Music	Displays	Sufficient Number of Personnel	Value for money	Superior_service_quality	Arousal_pleasure	Effective_treatment	Return	Spendmore_time_moeny
Touch	1.000	.524	.478	.402	.651	.481	.458	.486	.447	.374	.455	.357
people_quality	.524	1.000	.544	.454	.520	.556	.402	.458	.459	.425	.420	.386
aroma_temp_lights	.478	.544	1.000	.598	.467	.375	.347	.391	.454	.333	.339	.316
Music	.402	.454	.598	1.000	.385	.413	.299	.374	.341	.279	.320	.253
Displays	.651	.520	.467	.385	1.000	.443	.398	.458	.452	.409	.381	.333
Sufficient number of Personnel	.481	.556	.375	.413	.443	1.000	.405	.406	.355	.329	.368	.325
value for money	.458	.402	.347	.299	.398	.405	1.000	.523	.460	.453	.548	.562
superior_service_quality	.486	.458	.391	.374	.458	.406	.523	1.000	.609	.527	.520	.439
arousal_pleasure	.447	.459	.454	.341	.452	.355	.460	.609	1.000	.483	.480	.407
effective_treatment	.374	.425	.333	.279	.409	.329	.453	.527	.483	1.000	.390	.319

Return	.455	.420	.339	.320	.381	.368	.548	.520	.480	.390	1.000	.647
spendmore_time_moeny	.357	.386	.316	.253	.333	.325	.562	.439	.407	.319	.647	1.000

Quick Cluster Summary

touch $\xleftrightarrow{.65}$ displays

people_quality $\xleftrightarrow{.52}$

$\xleftrightarrow{.52}$

$\xleftrightarrow{.54}$ aroma_temp_lights

$\xleftrightarrow{.56}$ sufficient_number_people

aroma_temp_lights $\xleftrightarrow{.60}$ music

arousal_pleasure $\xleftrightarrow{.61}$ superior_service_quality $\xleftrightarrow{.53}$ effective_treatment

$\xleftrightarrow{.49}$

superior_service_quality $\xleftrightarrow{.55}$ return

valueformoney $\xleftrightarrow{.56}$ spendmore_time/money $\xleftrightarrow{.65}$ return

208   PEI-LING WU ET AL.

			Very low (1–15)	Low (16)	Medium (20)	High (20)	Very high (25)	Total
effective treatment groups	Lowest (1–48)	Count	20	19	21	10	2	72
		% within effective treatment groups	27.8	26.4	29.2	13.9	2.8	100.0
	Low (60–64)	Count	10	14	69	16	13	122
		% within effective treatment groups	8.2	11.5	56.6	13.1	10.7	100.0
	Middle (75–80)	Count	1	2	30	28	10	71
		% within effective treatment groups	1.4	2.8	42.3	39.4	14.1	100.0
	High (100)	Count	2	4	16	32	26	80
		% within effective treatment groups	2.5	5.0	20.0	40.0	32.5	100.0
	Highest (125)	Count	1	5	28	16	41	91
		% within effective treatment groups	1.1	5.5	30.8	17.6	45.1	100.0
Total		Count	34	44	164	102	92	436
		% within effective treatment groups	7.8	10.1	37.6	23.4	21.1	100.0

Cases supporting the large main effect: A→O. Negative contrarian cases indicating ~A→O. service quality groups. Positive contrarian cases indicating A→~O. phi = .629, p < .000

Figure 4. Two Outcomes: Effective Treatment and Service Quality Segments. *Notes*: A = antecedent condition (e.g., effective treatment); O = outcome condition (e.g., service quality). The significant main effect relationship indicates a large effect size (Cohen, 1977), phi^2 = .40. However, negative and positive contrarian cases still occur; the positivistic model does not account for such contrarian cases.

similarly, a substantial majority of cases with negative evaluations about effective treatment have negative evaluations about delivered service quality. However, both negative and positive contrarian cases do occur. A total of 41 negative and 12 positive contrarian cases occur. The findings include two cases with highly negative effective treatment evaluations and highly positive service quality evaluations. The findings include one case with highly positive effective treatment evaluation and a highly negative evaluation for delivered service quality. Rather than ignore such cases in reports only on a positive main effect, fuzzy-set qualitative comparative analysis (fsQCA) models both positive and negative routes to high scores in an outcome condition.

Table 4 demonstrates the occurrence of both negative and positive contrarian cases for a service outcome (customer evaluations of delivered service quality) and intention to return to the service provider. The numbers of negative and positive contrarian cases are nearly identical. Note in Table 4 that the phi^2 indicates a large effect size; yet, contrarian cases occur. What combination of antecedent conditions includes negative contrarian cases that indicate highly positive outcome scores? What combination of antecedent conditions includes positive contrarian cases that indicate high scores in the negation of the outcome condition?

Table 4: Service Quality and Return Intention Segments.

| | | | Return_5groups | | | | | |
			4–9	12–15	16	20	25	Total
service quality groups	Very low (1–15)	Count	17	4	9	3	1	34
		% within service quality groups	50.0	11.8	26.5	8.8	2.9	100.0
	Low (16)	Count	10	18	10	4	2	44
		% within service quality groups	22.7	40.9	22.7	9.1	4.5	100.0
	Medium (20)	Count	5	14	101	24	20	164
		% within service quality groups	3.0	8.5	61.6	14.6	12.2	100.0
	High (20)	Count	2	5	43	31	21	102
		% within service quality groups	2.0	4.9	42.2	30.4	20.6	100.0
	Very high (25)	Count	2	2	26	18	44	92
		% within service quality groups	2.2	2.2	28.3	19.6	47.8	100.0
Total		Count	36	43	189	80	88	436
		% within service quality groups	8.3	9.9	43.3	18.3	20.2	100.0

Notes: Positive contrarian cases (light gray shaded) indicating A–~O.
Negative contrarian cases (dark gray shaded) Indicating ~A→O.
phi = .736, p <.000.
~A→O = low score for the antecedent condition leads to high score for the outcome condition.
A→~O = high score for the antecedent condition leads to low score in the outcome condition.
The two sets of contrarian cases are counter to the main large effect size (phi^2 = .54) positive relationship, A → O.

(A negation outcome condition is equal to one minus the calibrated outcome score; the next section describes calibrating scores in fuzzy-set QCA.)

CALIBRATION

The use Boolean algebra in the study of the influence of complex configurations of antecedent conditions requires transforming original scaled values to fuzzy-set values for both antecedent and outcome conditions. All fuzzy-set values for all simple conditions range from 0.00 to 1.00 and these values indicate the degree of membership of the case in each condition. The set membership scores that result from calibrating original scores into fuzzy-set scores are not probabilities, but instead are transformations of ordinal or interval scales into degree of membership in the target set. "In essence, a fuzzy membership score attaches a truth value, not a probability, to a statement (e.g., the statement that a country is in the set of development countries") (Ragin, 2008, p. 183).

Ragin (2008) emphasizes that fuzzy sets, unlike conventional variables, must be calibrated. "Because they must be calibrated, they are superior in many respects to conventional measures, as they are used in both quantitative and qualitative social science. In essence, I argue that fuzzy sets offer a middle path between quantitative and qualitative measurement. However, this middle path is not a compromise between the two; rather, it transcends many of the limitations of both" (Ragin, 2008, p. 174).

Much of variation captured by ratio-scale indicators such as age and income is simply irrelevant to the distinction by low and high values. The original values must be adjusted on the basis of accumulated substantive knowledge in order to be able to interpret low versus high scores in a way that resonates appropriately with existing theory (cf. Ragin, 2008, p. 18). Ragin points out that there is a world of difference between living in a country with a gross national product (GNP) per capita of \$2,000 and living in one with a GNP per capita of \$1,000; however, there is virtually no difference between living in one with a GNP per capita of \$22,000 and living in one with a GNP per capita of \$21,000. Calibration of fuzzy-set measures addresses such issues directly.

Fuzzy-set calibration makes use of external information on the degree to which cases satisfy membership criteria and not inductively derived determination (e.g., using sample means). Criteria need to be set for three breakpoints in fuzzy-set calibration with endpoints of 0.00 for full non-membership to 1.00 for full membership. The breakpoints include 0.05 for threshold for full non-membership, 0.50 for the crossover point of maximum membership ambiguity; and 0.95 for the threshold of full membership. Determination of the three breakpoints permits calibration of all original values into membership values using a direct method and an indirect method (see Ragin, 2008). Similar to the mathematics involved in calculating partial standardized regression coefficients for variables in MRA using the Statistical Packages for the Social Sciences (SPSS), performance of the mathematical calculations to calibrate all membership scores for a simple condition can be done by using a software routine in the program, www.fs/QCA. See Ragin (2008, pp. 104–105) for an example of using this procedure.

The original values in 5-point Likert scale can be calibrated so that 1 = 0.05; 2 = 0.25; 3 = 0.50; 4 = 0.75; 5 = 0.95. This procedure was done in the study here. However, if respondents scores ignore an extreme score such as 1 or 5 on a Likert scale, the calibration scores would have been adjusted accordingly; for example, if one or two respondents among 100 + respondents provided a strongly disagree response (score of "1") among several Likert items, then the calibration would have been 1 = 0.00; 2 = 0.05; 3 = 0.33; 4 = 0.67; 5 = 0.95.

INDEX METRICS FOR MEASURING CONSISTENCY AND COVERAGE OF A COMPLEX CONFIGURATION

The consistency index gauges the degree to which the cases share a simple or complex condition in displaying the outcome in question – consistency is analogous to a correlation in statistical analysis. The coverage index in fsQCA assesses the degree to which a simple and complex causal condition (recipe) "accounts for" instances of an outcome condition – coverage is analogous to a r^2 in statistical analysis. In QCA a consistency index above 0.80 with a coverage index of 0.45 indicates high membership scores in the outcome condition for nearly all high scores in the antecedent statement and a substantial share of the cases fitting an asymmetric sufficiency distribution. Consistency $(Xi \leq Yi) = \sum \{min (Xi, Yi)\}/\sum(Xi)$ where Xi is case i's membership score in set X; Yi is case i's membership score in the outcome condition, Y; $(Xi \leq Yi)$ is the subset relation in question; and "min" dictates selecting the lower of the two scores. Coverage $(Xi \leq Yi) = \sum \{min(Xi, Yi)\}/\sum(Yi)$. The formula for coverage of Y by X

substitutes $\sum(Yi)$ for $\sum(Xi)$ in the denominator of the formula for consistency. See Ragin (2008) and Woodside (2013a) for elaborations and numerical examples.

Due to substantial space requirements necessary to fully describe the method, this section only provides an introduction to the theory and use of QCA. Ragin (2008) provides an extensive description of theory and method of QCA; a user's manual and software for QCA is available at www.fsQCA.com. QCA studies cases as configurations of causes and conditions rather treating each independent variable in a given analysis as analytically distinct and separate as done in conventional quantitative methods. "The key difference between the two is captured in the idea of a causal 'recipe' — a specific combination of causally relevant ingredients linked to an outcome. In set-theoretic work, the idea of a causal recipe is straightforward, for the notion of combined causes is directly captured by the principle of set intersection" (Ragin, 2008, p. 9).

T1: RECEIVES SUPPORT — COMPLEX DEMOGRAPHIC CONFIGURATIONS DO INDICATE CUSTOMER EVALUATIONS OF SERVICE FACETS

The findings in Table 5 support T1. Four models with complex antecedent conditions that include various demographic characteristics along with companionship and expenditure levels indicate high scores in the outcome condition for customer evaluations of people quality. Note in Table 5 that the first model has a consistency index equal to 0.941 and a unique coverage index equal to 0.026. The model includes six ingredients — customers visiting without a companion who are housekeepers, not service workers, who are females with low education, and they are young.

$\sim$ companion• $\sim$ servicew•housekeeper•female• $\sim$ edu• $\sim$ age

£people quality   (3)

The XY plot of model 3 appears at the bottom of Table 5. Each dot in the XY plot represents one or more cases (i.e., customers) in the study — some customers have the same scores in the plot. Note that the low scores for model 3 associate with low and high scores for the outcome, people quality evaluations. Model 3 predicts only that high scores in the complex statement indicate high scores in the outcome condition.

Table 5: Demographic, Companion, Beauty Saloon/Spa Expenditure Algorithm Models Predicting High People Q (Service Professional Evaluations).

Model[a]	Raw Coverage	Unique Coverage	Consistency
1 ~compan*~servicew*housek*female*~educ_c*~age_c	0.025859	0.025859	0.941345[b]
2 ~spa_expend_c*~compan*~servicew*~housek*~female*educ_c*~age_c	0.005423	0.005423	0.938776
3 spa_expend_c*compan*servicew*~housek*~female*~educ_c*~age_c	0.004401	0.004401	0.957265
4 Spa_expend_c*compan*servicew*~housek*female*educ_c*age_c	0.033443	0.033443	0.928026

solution coverage: 0.069127

solution consistency: 0.935638

Notes: The presence of companion contributes positively and negatively to the outcome (high score in people_q) depending on the additional antecedents in each of these four complex antecedent conditions – it is not so much a question of whether or not companion influences the outcome but under what circumstances (contingencies) companion does so.

[a]For example, model 1 states a case (customer) with a high score for no companion, not a service worker, a housekeeper, female, with low education and young will give a high score in service professional evaluations.

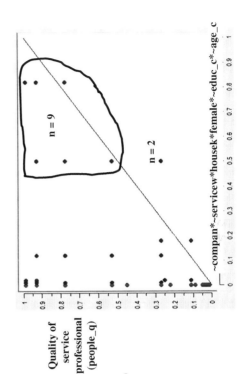

Quality of service professional (people_q)

~compan*~servicew*housek*female*~educ_c*~age_c

b

Note in Table 5 that the negation of companion (i.e., no companion appears in three of the four models). Model 4 in Table 5 represents older female service workers with high education, high expenditure, with a companion in tow. The models in Table 5 indicate that the impacts of the simple antecedent conditions are not always positive or negative or even always present. Life — including evaluations of service experiences and outcomes — is too complex to be captured by reports of main effects and net effects.

Spa expenditures need not be high for high people quality evaluations by customers. High spa expenditures appear in two of the four models in Table 5 and the negation of spa expenditures appears in one of the models. Spa expenditures are excluded from model 1 in Table 5. Such findings support basic tenets of complexity theory — both a simple antecedent condition can have a positive, negative, and no relationship with an outcome conditions depending on the conditional statement (i.e., recipe) of complex antecedent conditions associating with high scores in a particular outcome condition. Due to space limitations, findings for the associations of other demographic•companion•expenditure models for service facet evaluations other than people quality do not appear here but these additional findings support T1 as well.

Additional findings also support T1 for a complex demographic, companion, and expenditure condition indicating high overall scores for all service facets (i.e., P•R•L•D•B for service facets in Figure 1). The top portion of Table 6 reports the specific complex model for this compound outcome condition. This model indicates that a young female with low education who is a housekeeper spending few funds and visiting alone to have high scores for overall service facets. Note that the Y in a model can be a compound statement or two or more conditions rather than a statement of a simple outcome condition.

T2: RECEIVES SUPPORT — CAUSAL ASYMMETRY OCCURS — DEMOGRAPHIC ANTECEDENT CONFIGURATIONS LEADING TO NEGATIVE OUTCOMES ARE NOT THE MIRROR OPPOSITES OF DEMOGRAPHIC CONFIGURATIONS LEADING TO POSITIVE OUTCOMES

The findings in Tables 7a and 7b support T2. The outcomes for these models are return intentions. Table 7a predicts high scores in return intentions using demographics and service outcome

Table 6: Models Predicting High Global Outcomes.

(A) Model (Only One) for High Score for Overall Service Facets

	Raw Coverage	Unique Coverage	Consistency
~spa_expend_c*~compan*~servicew*housek*female*~educ_c*~age_c	0.021547	0.021547	0.908832

solution coverage: 0.021547

solution consistency: 0.908832

Note: Customers with high scores in the configuration of low expenditure per spa visit, visiting without a companion, a housekeeper, not a service worker, and is a female, with low education and are young give high evaluations overall to service facets.

Models for High Scores for not Overall Service Facets	Raw Coverage	Unique Coverage	Consistency
compan*~housek*~female*~educ_c*~age_c	0.023858	0.015350	0.977240
compan*spa_expend_c*~servicew*~housek*~female*~educ_c	0.019135	0.010696	0.941880
~compan*spa_expend_c*servicew*~housek*~educ_c*~age_c	0.051537	0.051537	0.938053
compan*~spa_expend_c*~servicew*housek*female*educ_c	0.051537	0.051537	0.981859
~compan*~spa_expend_c*~servicew~ housek*~female*educ_c*age_c	0.005105	0.004862	1.000000
compan*~spa_expend_c*~servicew~housek*~female*educ_c*age_c	0.012745	0.009932	0.978667

solution coverage: 0.116201

solution consistency: 0.957642

Table 6:   (Continued)

(B) Service Facet Models for High Scores for Overall Service Outcomes

	Raw Coverage	Unique Coverage	Consistency
~p_disp_c*~music_c*arom_temp_li*peop_s_c*peopq_c	0.162999	0.013673	0.803952
music_c*~arom_temp_li*~peop_s_c*peopq_c*arch_c	0.132606	0.033770	0.812556
p_disp_c*~music_c*arom_temp_li*peop_s_c*arch_c	0.289748	0.117718	0.823423
solution coverage: 0.337700			
solution consistency: 0.777224			

Note: Positive people evaluations (for quality or sufficient number of people) appear in all three models for high evaluations for overall service outcomes (i.e., the configuration pleasure arousal, effective spa treatment, overall service quality, and value for the money.

(C) Models of Service Outcomes Predicting Overall Intentions

	Raw Coverage	Unique Coverage	Consistency
p_arousal_c*value_m_c	0.696970	0.113648	0.821986
value_m_c*eff_treat_c	0.645502	0.62181	0.846482
solution coverage: 0.759150			
solution consistency: 0.811979			

Table 7a: Outcome Models with Demographics and Service Outcome Evaluations Predicting High Return Intentions.

	Raw Coverage	Unique Coverage	Consistency
~servicew*~housek*educ_c*~age_c*eff_treat_c*serqual_c	0.174005	0.067611	0.967676
~servicew*~housek*female*educ_c*spa_expend_c*eff_treat_c*~p_arousal_c	0.094602	0.005378	0.949062
servicew*~housek*female*educ_c*~age_c*~spa_expend_c*serqual_c	0.082276	0.005211	0.970832
~servicew*housek*female*spa_expend_c*~eff_treat_c*serqual_c*~p_arousal_c	0.024853	0.002405	0.982827
~servicew*housek*female*~educ_c*age_c*spa_expend_c*serqual_c	0.057322	0.005211	0.972238
servicew*~housek*female*educ_c*~age_c*serqual_c*p_arousal_c	0.139197	0.035376	0.945112
~housek*female*educ_c*spa_expend_c~eff_treat_c*serqual_c*p_arousal_c	0.204771	0.026757	0.954829
~servicew*housek*female*~educ_c*eff_treat_c*serqual_c*p_arousal_c	0.058258	0.012861	0.961942
servicew*~housek*female~age_c*spa_expend_c*~eff_treat_c*serqual_c*~p_arousal_c	0.032469	0.005746	0.987805
~servicew*female*~educ_c*~age_c*spa_expend_c*~eff_treat_c*serqual_c*~p_arousal_c	0.042457	0.002572	0.973946
~servicew*housek*female*~educ_c*~spa_expend_c*~age_c*~eff_treat_c*~serqual_c*~p_arousal_c	0.009587	0.003975	0.993079
~servicew*housek*female*~educ_c*~age_c*spa_expend_c*~eff_treat_c*p_arousal_c	0.095137	0.003775	0.974008
~servicew*~housek*female*~educ_c*~age_c*spa_expend_c*~eff_treat_c*p_arousal_c	0.052412	0.012026	0.981238
servicew*~housek*female*~educ_c*age_c*spa_expend_c*serqual_c*~p_arousal_c	0.026757	0.004576	0.968561
servicew*~housek* female*~educ_c*age_c*eff_treat_c*serqual_c*~p_ arousal_c	0.027759	0.003407	0.965157
~servicew*female*educ_c*age_c*spa_expend_c*eff_treat_c*serqual_c*p_arousal_c	0.160877	0.030131	0.961469
~servicew*~housek*~female*~educ_c*~age_c*~spa_expend_c*~eff_treat_c*serqual_c*~p_arousal_c	0.006681	0.002439	1.000000

Table 7a: (Continued)

	Raw Coverage	Unique Coverage	Consistency
servicew*~housek*~female*~educ_c*~age_c*spa_expend_c*eff_treat_c*~serqual_c*p_arousal_c	0.004075	0.004075	1.000000
~housek*female*~educ_c*age_c*spa_expend_c*eff_treat_c*serqual_c*~p_arousal_c	0.065874	−0.000000	0.986987
~ servicew*female*~educ_c*age_c*spa_expend_c*eff_treat_c*serqual_c*~p_arousal_c	0.068413	−0.000000	0.993692
~ servicew*~housek*female*age_c*spa_expend_c*eff_treat_c*serqual_c*~p_arousal_c	0.092832	−0.000000	0.961925

solution coverage: 0.588023

solution consistency: 0.951616

Table 7b: Outcome Models with Demographics and Service Outcome Evaluations Predicting the Negation of Return Intentions.

	Raw Coverage	Unique Coverage	Consistency
~servicew*~housek*educ_c*~age_c*~serqual_c*~value_m_c*~p_arousal_c	0.186842	0.060085	0.874315
~servicew*~housek*female*~educ_c*~age_c*~eff_treat_c*~serqual_c*~value_m_c	0.083577	0.024810	0.873089
~servicew*~housek*~female*~educ_c*~age_c*~eff_treat_c*~serqual_c*~p_arousal_c	0.036593	0.002342	0.874126
~servicew*~housek*~female*~educ_c*age_c*~eff_treat_c*~serqual_c*~p_arousal_c	0.036958	0.027957	0.876736
~servicew*female*~educ_c*age_c*~eff_treat_c*~serqual_c*~value_m_c*~p_arousal_c	0.117096	0.019760	0.883490
servicew*~housek*female*educ_c*~eff_treat_c*~serqual_c*~value_m_c*~p_arousal_c	0.100410	0.007684	0.893229
servicew*~housek*female*educ_c*~age_c*~eff_treat_c*~serqual_c*~p_arousal_c	0.097629	0.004757	0.877054
~servicew*female*educ_c*age_c*eff_treat_c*~serqual_c*~value_m_c*~p_arousal_c	**0.131733**	**0.019906**	**0.871249**
servicew*~housek*female*educ_c*~eff_treat_c*serqual_c*~value_m_c*~p_arousal_c	0.051449	0.004391	0.863636
~servicew*housek*female*age_c*~eff_treat_c*~serqual_c*~value_m_c*~p_arousal_c	0.048302	0.000439	0.887097
~servicew*female*housek*educ_c*age_c*serqual_c*~value_m_c*~p_arousal_c	0.033738	0.000000	0.874763

solution coverage: 0.459748
solution consistency: 0.857727

Table 7c: Service Outcomes and Overall Intentions.

	Raw Coverage	Unique Coverage	Consistency
value_m_c*~serqual_c	0.332971	0.010501	0.779580
~value_m_c*serqual_c	0.493947	0.055815	0.745373
~serqal_c*~p_arousal_c	0.427943	0.001552	0.852887
~eff_treat_c*~serqual_c	0.486188	0.001914	0.835466
~value_m_c*~p_arousal_c	0.463427	0.002793	0.819220
~value_m_c*~eff_treat_c	0.558244	0.008121	0.789928
solution coverage: 0.764277			
solution consistency: 0.731872			

evaluations as indicators. Table 7b predicts high scores in the negation of return intentions; Table 7b answers the question what service outcomes drives which customers away. Both Tables 7a and 7b include unique complex antecedent conditions which include demographic, companion, expenditure level, and service outcome conditions. Notice that in both intentions to return and the negation of returning include age and ~age, as well as female and ~female, as well as education and ~education. Consequently, the focus on main effects of age, gender, and education is misplaced if the objective is to identify which customers are likely to return and which are likely not to return. At first blush while the findings in Tables 7a and 7b appear to be overly complex, such customer recipes are easy to process by service workers and managers. (The findings of Table 7c are described later.)

Note that the negation of service-quality evaluation appears in two of the models, positive service-quality evaluations appear in 16 models in Table 7a, and service-quality evaluation does not appear in three of the models. None of the models in Tables 7a include both the negation of service quality and the negative of effective treatment evaluations. All the models in Tables 7b — the negation of return intentions — includes either the negation of service quality or the negation of effective treatment or both evaluations.

T3: RECEIVES SUPPORT — UNIQUE COMPLEX ANTECEDENT CONFIGURATIONS ARE SUFFICIENT BUT NOT NECESSARY FOR HIGH SCORES IN AN OUTCOME CONDITION

With the exception of finding only one model is consistent in predicting high scores for overall service facet evaluations (top of

Table 6), T3 receives support. Several complex antecedent conditions are sufficient for predicting high scores for each of the unique service facets, the service outcomes, and the intention conditions. Note the Panel B in Table 6 includes three complex service-facet models predicting high scores for overall service outcomes. Panel C in Table 6 includes two service outcome models predicting high scores for overall intentions toward the service provider.

T4: RECEIVES SUPPORT — SIMPLE ANTECEDENT CONDITIONS CAN BE NECESSARY BUT THEY ARE INSUFFICIENT FOR INDICATING HIGH SCORES IN AN OUTCOME CONDITION

Figure 5 is an example of a service facet support T4. Having a sufficient number of professional service providers is a necessary condition that is insufficient for high overall outcome scores. Notice in Figure 5 that all scores for overall outcome scores are relatively low when scores are low for this antecedent condition. When scores are high for the number of people sufficient scores,

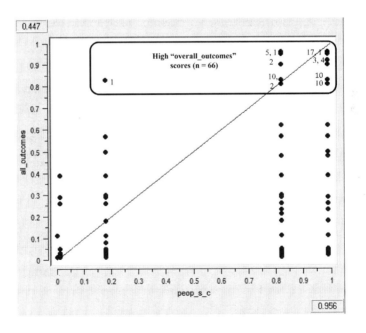

Figure 5. Sufficient Number of Professional Service Providers: Indicates a Necessary but Insufficient Condition (Numbers indicate number of cases (customers). *Note:* 65 of 66 cases high "all_outcome" scores have high scores in evaluating the beauty salon/spa but The majority of cases with high scores in beauty/salon/spa have low "all_outcome" scores.

the overall outcome scores are high and low — Figure 5 is most similar to Figure 1d. Failing to provide sufficient numbers of professional service providers can hurt but doing so is not sufficient for high scores in the overall outcome following the service enactment/experience.

T5: RECEIVES SUPPORT — WITHIN DIFFERENT COMPLEX ANTECEDENT COMBINATIONS, SIMPLE ANTECEDENT CONDITIONS MAY APPEAR AS A POSITIVE AND NEGATIVE INFLUENCE ON AN OUTCOME

Nearly all the models in all the tables support T5. Thus, contrarian cases occur in data — such cases show that high X indicates high Y, low Y, and not anything about Y. The negation of X indicates high Y, low Y, and not anything about Y. Which of these three relationships occur for the outcome and the negation of the outcome depends upon what other simple antecedent condition co-join with X. The bottom-line is that the focus on the net effect of X on Y typically offers a meager explanation versus the sophisticated and useful explanations that complex antecedent conditions provide.

T6: RECEIVES SUPPORT — THE PRESENCE OF A COMPANION WITH THE CUSTOMER MODIFIES HOW A CUSTOMER EVALUATES SERVICE FACETS

The findings in Tables 5 and 6 support T6. The presence and absence of a companion within complex antecedent conditions contributes to high scores for people quality assessments and overall service facet quality — and this contribution appears consistently in the configural models. These findings fit well inside Shakespeare's *As You Like It* monologue by the melancholy Jaques in Act II Scene VII, "All the world is a stage" as well as Goffman's (1959) *Presentation of Self in Everyday Life*.

What may be surprising is that for the majority of models the absence rather than the presence of a companion contributes to increases in specific and general service facet evaluations. Note that next to the top of Table 6 that four of the six **negation** models for overall service facet evaluation includes the presence of a companion. Possibly customers may transform into critiques as well as actors in the presence of companions but identify more often with the service provider when companions are absent.

Whatever the process, the absence/presence of companions influences customer assessments of service facets consistently.

T7 RECEIVES SUPPORT — BEAUTY/SPA EXPENDITURE LEVELS MODIFY THE INFLUENCE OF DEMOGRAPHIC CONFIGURAL INFLUENCES ON SERVICE FACETS

Both high and low customers' beauty/spa expenditure levels contribute positively to customers' service facet evaluations — which depends upon what additional ingredients are included in the alternative complex antecedent configurations. Spending more versus less money does not equate consistently to higher or lower customer service-facet evaluations. What appears to receive support is that service providers need to insure that appropriate care in crafting service facets is presented that complement the expenditures customers make.

CONFIGURATIONS OF CUSTOMER SERVICE-FACET EVALUATIONS DO INFLUENCE OVERALL SERVICE OUTCOMES AND INTENTIONS TOWARD THE SERVICE PROVIDER

T8 receives support: complex service-facet configurations affect high scores for customer evaluations of service outcomes. Panel B in Table 6 includes three models of complex service-facet antecedents and service outcomes. T9 receives support: unique configurations of service facets are sufficient but each is not necessary for high scores for service outcomes to occur. Panel B in Table 6 includes three models that are very high in consistency in predicting high scores for service outcomes. T10 receives support: simple service-facet antecedent conditions can be necessary but are insufficient for high scores for an outcome condition. Tables 8a and 8b provide details. T11: Simple antecedent service facets can have a positive and negative influence on an outcome — the valence depends upon the presence of specific additional service facets in complex antecedent configurations. Tables 8a—8d include antecedent service-facet evaluations affecting the four service outcomes. Note that the valences of specific service facets vary within the different complex antecedent conditions.

T12 receives support: complex service-outcome configurations affect high scores for customer intentions relating to the service provider. Panel B in Table 6 includes two specific models with high consistency for the relationship for service-outcome configurations and customer intentions. The bottom of Figure 6

Table 8a: Algorithm Models where High Service Facet Scores Predict High Pleasure Arousal.

	Raw Coverage	Unique Coverage	Consistency
1. ~p_disp_c*arom_temp_li*peopq_c*~arch_c[a]	0.171143	0.029206	0.914117
2. p_dosp_c*arom_temp_li*peop_s_c*~peopq_c	0.226139	0.065384	0.899023
3. p_disp_c*~music_c*~arom_temp_li*peop_s_c*peopq_c	0.130198	0.017502	0.906614
4. music_c*~arom_temp_li*~peop_s_c*peopq_c*arch_c	0.079542	0.005727	0.935565
5. p_disp_c*music_c*peop_s_c*peopq_c*~arch_c	0.235637	0.040766	0.937447
6. ~music_c*arom_temp_li*peop_s_c*~arch_c	0.175519	0.034008	0.955461

solution coverage: 0.430365

solution consistency: 0877238

[a]For example, model 1 includes negation of product display quality, aroma/temperature/lighting, people (service professional) quality, and not architecture/décor. Note that high scores in people quality appears in five of the six models and one model includes low scores in people quality (contrarian cases).

Table 8b: Algorithm Models Where High Service Facet Scores Predict High Service Quality.

	Raw Coverage	Unique Coverage	Consistency
p_disp_c*peop_s_c*arch_c	0.644455	0.087184	0.907581
p_disp_c*arom_temp_li*peop_s_c*~peopq_c	0.226182	0.009770	0.949511
p_disp_c*music_c*peop_s_c*peopq_c	0.568186	0.016373	0.922092
~p_disp_c*~music_c*arom_temp_li*~peop_s_c*~arch_c	0.086040	0.015631	0.923689
p_disp_c*~music_c*~arom_temp_li~peopq_c*arch_c	0.104737	0.002931	0.933914
~p_disp_c*~music_c*arom_temp_li*peop_s_c*peopq_c	0.099347	0.000034	0.947013
music_c*~arom_temp_li*~peop_s_c*peopq_c*arch_c	0.078763	0.006030	0.978243
music_c*arom_temp_li*peop_s_c*~peopq_c*arch_c	0.209406	0.007917	0.965367
p_disp_c*music_c*~arom_temp_li*~peop_s_c*~peopq_c*~arch_c	0.080346	0.010039	0.921917
~p_disp_c*arom_temp_li*peop_s_c*peopq_c*~arch_c	0.143108	0.000000	0.936301
music_c*arom_temp_li*peo_s_c*peopq_c*~arch_c	0.222073	0.005592	0.938898

solution coverage: 0.774323

Solution consistency: 0.881495

Table 8c: Algorithm Models Where High Facet Scores Predict High Value-for-the-Money Outcome.

	Raw Coverage	Unique Coverage	Consistency
~p_disp_c*~music_c*arom_temp_li*peop_s_c*peopq_c	0.114723	0.015957	0.904329
music_c*~arom_temp_li*~peop_s_c*peopq_c*arch_c	0.094154	0.023359	0.922061
p_disp_c*~music_c*arom_temp_li*peop_s_c*arch_c	0.203382	0.013172	0.923730
p_disp_c*~music_c*peop_s_c*peopq_c*arch_c	0.222125	0.027139	0.908085

solution coverage: 0.275049

solution consistency: 0.896265

Table 8d: Algorithm Models Where High Facet Scores Predict High Effective Spa Treatment Outcome.

	Raw Coverage	Unique Coverage	Consistency
p_disp_c*~arom_temp_li*peo_s_c*peopq_c	0.247795	0.077464	0.871345
p_disp_c*~music_c*~arom_temp_li*peopq_c*~arch_c	0.136703	0.002316	0.898763
~p_disp_c*arom_temp_li*~peop_s_c*peopq_c*~arch_c	0.116840	0.021489	0.884990
~p_disp_c*~music_c*arom_temp_li*peop_s_c*peopq_c	0.123831	0.003045	0.905583
music_c*~arom_temp_li*~peop_s_c*peopq_c*arch_c	0.101660	0.006391	0.923619
p_disp_c*music_c*arom_temp_li*peop_s_c*arch_c	0.217380	0.066827	0.915959
~p_disp_c*music_c*arom_temp_li*peop_s_c*~peopq_c*arch_c	0.147851	0.028781	0.900941

solution coverage: 0.429913

solution consistency: 0.844611

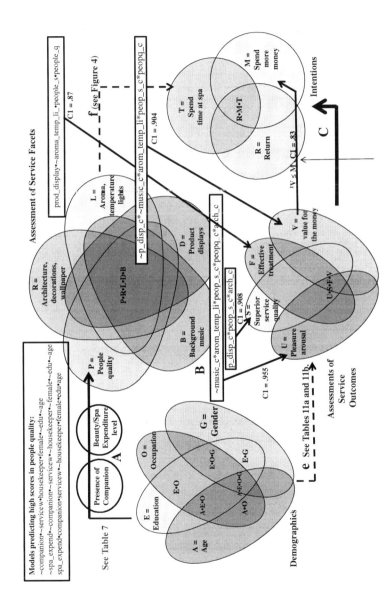

Figure 6. Specific Findings for Key Configural Models. *Note:* 1 For example, high scores for value-for-the-money predict high scores for spend more money with consistency (C1) equal to .83.

shows that value for the money alone is sufficient (but not necessary) for high intentions to return. Figure 6 is a summary visual of key findings in the study.

T13: Causal asymmetry occurs, that is, service outcome configurations leading to low intention scores are not the mirror opposites of outcome configurations leading to high intention scores. Two models indicate consistent high scores in outcome conditions and the negation of returning to the service provider:

~service_quality•~pleasure_arousal•~not_value_money ≤ not_return (4, C1 = .83, C2 = .50)

effective_treatment•~service_quality•~pleasure   arousal ≤ not_return (5, C1 = .79, C2 = .32)

where C1 = consistency and C2 = raw coverage. Note that the failure to provide pleasure arousal enters both models 4 and 5 – failure to provide pleasure arousal is necessary but not sufficient in these models to indicate the negative of returning. Table 7c provides unique service outcome models predicting the negation of overall intentions that are not the mirror opposites of the models for overall intentions that appear in Panel C of Table 6.

T14 receives support: Unique configurations of service outcomes are sufficient but each is not necessary for high scores for service intentions to occur. T15: Simple service-outcome antecedents can have both a positive and negative influence on intentions – which depends upon what other simple conditions make-up the complex configurations indicating high scores in the outcome condition. See Table 7c for specific findings.

XY PLOT FOR HIGH CONSISTENCY FOR SERVICE FACETS AND INTENTIONS TO RETURN

Figure 7 is an XY plot showing high consistency for a service facet model and intentions to return. The model show that high scores on the complex antecedent condition that includes architecture, sufficient service personnel, and product displays indicate high scores on intentions to return. While informative, this model is only one of several service facet models that support the presence of consistent models for dotted arrow f in Figure 2.

The findings in Figure 7 are amenable to statistical testing as well. The finding that 125 of 130 cases with high scores for the complex antecedent condition is statistically significant ($p < .001$).

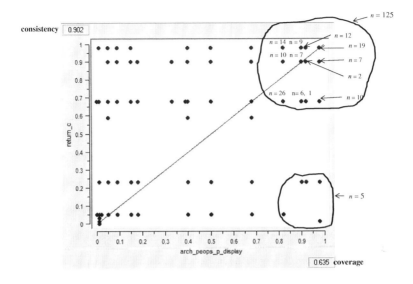

Figure 7. Algorithm for décor, sufficient people, product display predicting return intention (Décor•Sufficient_People•Product_Displays ≤ Return). *Note*: 125 customers with high score for this algorithm have high return intention membership scores above 0.65 and only 5 customers with high scores for this algorithm have member ship scores below 0.65; thus, five times more customers with high scores on the algorithm have high versus low return intentions.

SUPPORT FOR DEMOGRAPHIC ALGORITHMS INDICATING HIGH OUTCOME SCORES

Complex antecedent demographic models alone do indicate high scores for outcome conditions as well as the negation of outcome conditions. Details appear in Tables 9a and 9b. Professional working males with high education offer high scores for service outcomes and do across a range of service outcomes; see Table 9a. Older males with low education offer high scores for not pleasure arousal and not effective treatment; see Table 9b.

Contributions to Theory and Service Management Practice

Complexity theory includes the recognition that no simple condition is the cause of an outcome of interest. Several indicators act

Table 9a: Demographics Indicating High Scores in Service Outcomes.

(A) Models for Arouse Pleasure

	Raw Coverage	Unique Coverage	Consistency
educ_c*servicew*~housek*~female	0.016186	0.008217	0.968085
educ_c*age_c*servicew*~housek	0.106008	0.098040	0.904675
~educ_c*~age_c*~servicew*~housek*~female	0.021131	0.021131	0.894578
~educ_c*~age_c*~servicew*~housek*female	0.032941	0.032941	0.897287

solution coverage: 0.168297

solution consistency: 0.903552

(B) Models for Delivered Service Quality

	Raw Coverage	Unique Coverage	Consistency
educ_c*servicew*~house*~female	0.015396	0.007849	0.972341
educ_c*age_c*servicew*~housek	0.101705	0.094159	0.916515
~educ_c*~age_c*~servicew*housek*female	0.031936	0.031936	0.918605

solution coverage: 0.141491

solution consistency: 0.918635

(C) Models for Effective Treatment

	Raw Coverage	Unique Coverage	Consistency
educ_c*servicew*~housek*~female	0.019602	0.019602	0.972340
educ_c*~age_c*~servicew*housek*female	0.036459	0.036459	0.865580

solution coverage: 0.056061

solution consistency: 0.900138

(D) Models for High Value for the Money

	Raw Coverage	Unique Coverage	Consistency
educ_c*servicew*~housek*~female	0.017191	0.017191	0.919149
~age_c*~servicew*housek*female	0.052805	0.052805	0.862809
~educ_c*~age_c*servicew*~housek*~female	0.025388	0.025388	0.960844

solution coverage: 0.095384

solution consistency: 0.897081

Table 9b: Demographics Indicating High Scores for the Negation of Service Outcomes.

Model for Not Arouse Pleasure

	Raw Coverage	Unique Coverage	Consistency
~educ_c*age_c*~servicew*~housek*~female	0.055459	0.055459	0.832364

solution coverage: 0.055459

solution consistency: 0.832364

Model for Not Effective Treatment

	Raw Coverage	Unique Coverage	Consistency
~educ_c*age_c*~servicew*~housek*~female	0.042147	0.042147	0.828488

solution coverage: 0.042147

solution consistency: 0.828488

Model for the Negation of All Outcomes

	Raw Coverage	Unique Coverage	Consistency
~educ_c*age_c*~servicew*~housek	0.172276	0.091144	0.848083
~educ_c*~age_c*servicew*~housek	0.104062	0.072772	0.852941
~educ_c*~age_c*~servicew*female	0.121394	0.062760	0.813222
educ_c*age_c*~housek*female	0.322628	0.231986	0.842563
educ_c*~age_c*~servicew*~housek*~female	0.041302	0.034448	0.873956

solution coverage: 0.605354

solution consistency: 0.821484

Note: Demographic complex antecedent conditions do indicate consistent negation specific and overall outcome evaluations. Low education occurs in most of these models. High education occurs in the final two models in this table.

in combination to cause an outcome of interest. Algorithm building and testing procedures such as fsQCA focus on testing combinatory theories as indicators of an outcome of interest. Both complexity theory and fsQCA do not build and test models for both positive and negative outcome of interest – both theory and method are asymmetric in focus. Unlike attempting to build useful models in predicting both high and low scores, complexity theory and fsQCA are "positive" only in focus. "You tested positive for cancer (C)", and "The tests indicate that you do not have cancer", are both asymmetric statements; both statements test using complex antecedent conditions which examine for C and ~C outcomes.

Symmetric tests and symmetric-based theories attempt to do too much and too little. Too much: they attempt to build models to accurately predict both low and high scores. Given that positive behavior is not the mirror opposite of negative behavior, such attempts are doomed except for analysis of the reliability of items in a multi-item scale. Too little: symmetric theories and testing usually ignore contrarian cases; both negative and positive contrarian cases occur in medium to large data sets. Negative contrarian cases are cases with a negative antecedent condition for most cases having a positive outcome condition for a simple antecedent condition; the particular antecedent condition alone usually is neither sufficient nor necessary of the occurrence of the positive outcome. Both the negative contrarian case and the positive cases for the simple antecedent condition are ingredients in different complex antecedent conditions which are indicators for the positive outcome. A positive contrarian case is a case having a negative antecedent score associated with the given antecedent condition that has a positive outcome, yet this positive contrarian case does not have a negative outcome. Both the positive contrarian case and the cases with values supportive of the observed main effect are relevant to different complex models.

Simon (2009) informs in his chapter in *Simplicity, Inference and Modelling* to the beauty in "finding pattern, especially simple pattern, in the midst of apparent complexity and disorder." Simon construes parsimony itself as "pattern in the phenomena" and places it "at the root of what we mean by a scientific law." Distinguishing between simplicity and parsimony, Simon does not think we should seek "the absolutely simplest law", but "the law that is simplest in relation to the range of phenomena it explains, that is most parsimonious." Simon (2009, p. 32) refers to the following statement as one of Popper's (1961) dictums, "Science seeks parsimony, not simplicity searching for pattern in phenomena".

While at first blush the empirical complex antecedent configurations appearing in the present study may not appear to be parsimonious, they are parsimonious patterns of indicators leading to outcomes of interest. Theory and research focusing on "parsimonious patterns of asymmetric outcomes of interest" is a statement taking us far beyond the dominant logic in service research and services marketing appearing in the servicescape and "servqual" literature (e.g., Harris & Ezeh, 2008; Wakefield & Blodgett, 1996; Zeithaml, Berry, & Parasuraman, 1996). The asymmetric focus on building parsimonious patterns which accurately predict high scores in an outcome of interest (including negation outcomes) should complement ("replace" may apply here) the focus on net effects, that is, the dominating present focus on whether or not simple antecedent conditions and dependent variables relate to each other statistically significantly.

The issue of whether or not net effects relate significantly or not does not relate sufficiently to the principal aims of science or service management practice. Service delivery includes the alternative performance confluences of several service facets. A service facet performance is a pattern of behavior in a given context that involves one or more service providers and a customer alone one or more attending companions. Both the parsimonious customer patterns (e.g., demographic profiles) and enactments of service-facet patterns join together to influence service outcomes and all three may join together to influence customer service intentions. The Venn diagrams in Figure 2 better represent reality than the boxes and arrows diagrams in the servicescape and servqual literature because the Venn diagrams visualize several tenets in complexity theory. Multiple patterns occur (equifinality occurs); while one pattern may be sufficient it is not necessary for an outcome of interest to occur; contrarian cases occur and result in alternative patterns leading the same outcome as non-contrarian cases; negation models are not the mirror opposites of positive outcome models (causal asymmetry occurs).

Limitations, Suggestions for Future Research, and General Conclusion

LIMITATIONS AND SUGGESTIONS FOR FUTURE RESEARCH

This study may be the first to formally examine tenets of complexity theory in service research contexts. However, additional studies (Chang et al., 2013; Woodside, 2013b; Woodside & Zhang, 2012) are available in the service research literature that examine complex antecedent conditions as indicators of positive service outcomes. Yet, the number of studies is scant. Additional

Table 10: Complex Configurations of Service Facet Models Indicating High Scores for Arouse Pleasure for Subsamples 1 and 2.

Models from Subsample 1

	Raw Coverage	Unique Coverage	Consistency
1. p_disp_c*music_c*peop_s_c*peopq_c	0.547956	0.284139	0.836815
2. ~p_disp_c*music_c*arom_temp_li*peopq_c*~arch_c	0.184476	0.032283	0.922235
3. p_disp_c*~music_c*~arom_temp_c*peop_s_c*arch_c	0.142195	0.029235	0.855604
4. music_c*arom_temp_li*peop_s_c*~peopq_c*arch_c	0.210349	0.030016	0.872851
5. p_disp_ * music_c*~arom_temp_li*peopq_c*arch_c	0.165802	0.001094	0.852156
6. ~p_disp_c*~music_c*arom_temp_li*peop_s_c*peopq_c*~arch_c	0.104979	0.010553	0.884134

solution coverage: 0.669819

solution consistency: 0.815707

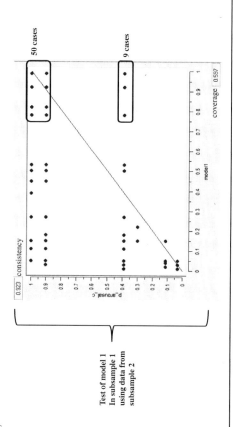

Test of model 1
In subsample 1
using data from
subsample 2

studies in additional contexts are necessary to support the useful-ness of the complexity theory and complex configural analysis.

McClelland (1998) and Gigerenzer and Brighton (2009) emphasize that a critical validation question is whether or not a model (MRA and/or an fsQCA model) predicts a dependent vari-able (outcome condition) in additional samples — holdout sam-ples that are separate data sets from the data set used to test the fit of data to theory. "Achieving a good fit to observations does not necessarily mean we have found a good model, and choosing the model with the best fit is likely to result in poor predictions", Gigerenzer and Brighton (2009, p. 114) observe. Unfortunately, only a handful of studies report on predictive validity, nearly all studies report only on fit validity (cf. Roberts & Pashler, 2000). Up until this section, the study here suffers from this unnecessary limitation.

To test for predictive validity, the sample was split into a modeling subsample and a holdout sample. Table 10 includes a predictive validation of the model 1 that appears in the table. In Table 10 the patterns of complex antecedents conditions are con-sistent indicators of high scores in service outcome, arouse plea-sure, using the first half of cases in the sample of 435 cases. The findings for testing model 1 predictions on the data in the second sample appear below Table 10. The findings indicate a highly consistent model (C1 = 0.923) and high coverage (C2 = 0.597). Additional predictive test findings support the conclusion that the highly consistent models for subsample 1 have high predictive abilities for subsample 2 and vice versa (available upon request).

GENERAL CONCLUSION

The bringing together of complexity theory, fsQCA, and pattern research in service dominant logic is a fit-like-a-glove union for advancing theory, method, and practice in service research. Complexity theory is a useful lens for seeing that simple antece-dent conditions relate to an outcome condition of interest positively, negatively, and not at all — which of these three rela-tionships occur depends on the observed complex antecedent conditions in which the simple antecedent conditions occur. Individual service facets in service performances with successful service outcomes do not have to be all positive ingredients in all possible complex but parsimonious patterns.

Acknowledgment

The authors gratefully acknowledges permission granted by the publisher, Elsevier, to reuse content in this chapter original appearing in Wu, Yeh, Huan, and Woodside (2014).

References

Babin, B. J., & Darden, W. R. (1995). Consumer self-regulation in a retail environment. *Journal of Retailing*, 71(1), 47–70.

Baker, J., Parasuraman, A., Grewal, D., & Voss, G. B. (2002). The influence of multiple store environment cues on perceived merchandise value and patronage intentions. *Journal of Marketing*, 66(2), 120–141.

Barber, K. (2008). The well-coiffed man: Class, race, and heterosexual masculinity in the hair salon. *Gender and Society*, 22(4), 455–476.

Bass, F. M., Tigert, D. J., & Lonsdale, R. T. (1968). Market segmentation: Group versus individual behavior. *Journal of Marketing Research*, 5(3), 264–270.

Beauty Salon Business Overview & Trends. (2012). Retrieved from http://www.sbdcnet.org/small-business-research-reports/beauty-salon-2012

Big Five Statistics. (2013). Retrieved from http://www.experienceispa.com/media/facts-stats/

Bitner, M. J. (1995). Building service relationships: It's all about promises. *Journal of the Academy of Marketing Science*, 23(4), 246–251.

Bloemer, J., & De Ruyter, K. (1998). On the relationship between store image, store satisfaction and store loyalty. *European Journal of Marketing*, 32(5–6), 499–513.

Chang, C.-W., Tseng, T.-H., & Woodside, A. G. (2013). Configural algorithms of patient loyalty. *Journal of Services Marketing*, 27(2), 91–103.

Chebat, J.-C., Haj-Salem, N., & Oliveira, S. (2012). *Three psychological processes explaining the impact of the shopping pal on mall shoppers*. The 12th International Research Conference in Service Management, A Londe les Maures, France. Retrieved from http://www.cerog.org/lalondeCB/SM/2012_lalonde_seminar/papers/06-P125-2012-CHEBAT-HAJ-SALEM-OLIVEIRA-REV-20-03-2012.pdf. Accessed on May 29, 30, 31, and June 1, 2012.

Cohen, J. (1977). *Statistical power analysis for the behavioral sciences*. New York, NY: Academic Press.

Donovan, R. J., & Rossiter, J. R. (1982). Store atmosphere: An environmental psychology approach. *Journal of Retailing*, 58(1), 34–57.

Donovan, R. J., Rossiter, J. R., Marcoolyn, G., & Nesdale, A. (1994). Store atmosphere and purchasing behavior. *Journal of Retailing*, 70(3), 283–294.

Fiss, P. C. (2011). Building better casual theories: A fuzzy set approach to typologies in organizational research. *Academy of Management Journal*, 54(2), 393–420.

Fiss, P. C., Marx, A., & Cambré, B. (2013). Configurational theory and methods in organizational research: Introduction. In P. C. Fiss, B. Cambré, & A. Marx (Eds.), *Configurational theory and methods in organizational research* (Vol. 38, pp. 1–22). Research in the Sociology of Organizations. Bingley, UK: Emerald Group Publishing Limited.

Gigerenzer, G. (1991). From tools to theories: A heuristic of discovery in cognitive psychology. *Psychological Review*, 98, 254–267.

Gigerenzer, G., & Brighton, H. (2009). Homo heuristics: Why biased minds make better inferences. *Topics in Cognitive Science*, 1, 107–143.

Gladwell, M. (2002). *The tipping point.* New York, NY: Little, Brown.

Goffman, E. (1959). *The presentation of self in everyday life.* New York, NY: Anchor.

Grimlin, D. (1996). Pamela's place: Power and negotiation in the hair salon. *Gender and Society*, 10(5), 505–526.

Harris, L. C., & Ezeh, C. (2008). Servicescape and loyalty intentions: An empirical investigation. *European Journal of Marketing*, 42(3–4), 390–422.

Hielscher, S., Fisher, T., & Cooper, T. (2009). The return of the beehives, Brylcreem and botanical! An historical review of hair care practices with a view to opportunities for sustainable design. In: *Undisciplined! Design Research Society Conference 2008.* Sheffield Hallam University, Sheffield, UK. Retrieved from http://shura.shu.ac.uk/549/1/fulltext.pdf. Accessed on July 16–19, 2008.

Hudson, S., & Gilbert, D. (2000). Tourism constraints: The neglected dimension in consumer behaviour research. *Journal of Travel & Tourism Marketing*, 8(4), 69–78.

Kamen, J. M. (1970). Quick clustering. *Journal of Marketing Research*, 7(2), 199–204.

Lazarsfeld, P. F. (1937). Some remarks on the typological procedures in social research. *Zeitschrift fur Socialforschung*, 6, 119–139.

Leibenstein, H. (1950). Bandwagon, snob, and veblen effects in the theory of consumers' demand. *The Quarterly Journal of Economics*, 64(2), 183–207.

Lusch, R. F., & Vargo, S. L. (Eds.). (2006a). *The service-dominant logic of marketing: Dialog, debate, and directions.* Armonk, NY: ME Sharpe.

Lusch, R. F., & Vargo, S. L. (2006b). Service-dominant logic as a foundation for a general theory. In R. F. Lusch & S. L. Vargo (Eds.), *The service-dominant logic of marketing: Dialog, debate, and directions* (pp. 406–420). Armonk, NY: ME Sharpe.

Mathwick, C., Malhotra, N., & Rigdon, E. (2001). Experiential value: Conceptualization, measurement and application in the catalog and internet shopping environment. *Journal of Retailing*, 77(1), 39–56.

Matthews, I. (2013). *Marketing trends presentations 2013 review.* Retrieved from http://www.in-cosmetics.com/en/Online-Press-Centre/Normal–Industry-articles/marketingtrends2013review/

McClelland, D. C. (1998). Identifying competencies with behavioral-event interviews. *Psychological Science*, 9, 331–3339.

Milgrom, P., & Roberts, J. (1986). Price and advertising signals of product quality. *Journal of Political Economy*, 94(4), 796–821.

Mitchell, V. W. (2001). Re-conceptualizing consumer store image processing using perceived risk. *Journal of Business Research*, *54*(2), 167–172.

Otnes, C. C., Ilhan, B. C., & Kulkarni, A. (2012). The language of marketplace rituals: Implications for customer experience management. *Journal of Retailing*, *88*(3), 367–383.

Popper, K. (1961). *The logic of scientific discovery*. New York, NY: Science.

Ragin, C. (2008). *Redesigning social inquiry*. Chicago, IL: University of Chicago Press.

Ragin, C. C. (2000). *Fuzzy-set social science*. Chicago, IL: The University of Chicago Press.

Robert, S., & Pashler, H. (2000). How persuasive is a good fit? A comment on theory testing. *Psychological Review*, *107*, 358–367.

Sharma, A., & Stafford, T. F. (2000). The effect of retail atmospherics on customers' perceptions of salespeople and customer persuasion: An empirical investigation. *Journal of Business Research*, *49*(2), 183–191.

Sharma, U., & Black, P. (2001). Look good, feel better: Beauty therapy as emotional labour. *Sociology*, *35*(4), 913–931.

Simon, H. A. (2009). Science seeks parsimony, not simplicity searching for pattern in phenomena. In A. Zellner, H. A. Keuzenkamp, & M. McAleer (Eds.), (2009). *Simplicity, inference and modelling: Keeping it sophisticatedly simple* (pp. 32–72). Cambridge: Cambridge University Press. Retrieved from http://digitalcollections.library.cmu.edu/awweb/awarchive?type=file&item=47027

Sirgy, M. J., Grewal, D., & Mangleburg, T. (2000). Retail environment, self-congruity, and retail patronage: An integrative model and a research agenda. *Journal of Business Research*, *49*, 127–138.

Tatzel, M. (2002). "Money worlds" and well-being: An integration of money dispositions, materialism and price-related behavior. *Journal of Economic Psychology*, *23*, 103–126.

The Economist. (2014). Because it's no longer worth it. *The Economist*, January 11, p. 57.

Toerien, M., & Kitzinger, C. (2007). Emotional labour in action: Navigating multiple involvements in the beauty salon. *Sociology*, *41*(4), 645–662.

Üstüner, T., & Thompson, C. J. (2012). How marketplace performances produce interdependent status games and contested forms of symbolic capital. *Journal of Consumer Research*, *38*(5), 796–814.

Urry, J. L. (2005). The complexity turn. *Theory Culture Society*, *22*, 1–14.

Vargo, S. L., & Lusch, R. F. (2004a). Evolving to a new dominant logic for marketing. *Journal of Marketing*, *68*(1), 1–17.

Vargo, S. L., & Lusch, R. F. (2004b). The four services marketing myths: Remnants from a manufacturing model. *Journal of Service Research*, *6*(4), 324–335.

Vargo, S. L., & Lusch, R. F. (2006). Service-dominant logic: What it is, what it is not, what it might be. In R. F. Lusch & S. L. Vargo (Eds.), *The service-dominant logic of marketing: Dialog, debate, and directions* (pp. 43–56). Armonk, NY: ME Sharpe.

Vargo, S. L., & Morgan, F. W. (2005). An historical reexamination of the nature of exchange: The service-dominant perspective. *Journal of Macromarketing*, 25(1), 42–53.

Wakefield, K., & Blodgett, J. G. (1996). The effect of the servicescape on customers' behavioral intentions in leisure service settings. *Journal of Services Marketing*, 10(6), 45–61.

Woodside, A. G. (2013a). Moving beyond multiple regression analysis to algorithms: Calling for a paradigm shift from symmetric to asymmetric thinking in data analysis, and crafting theory. *Journal of Business Research*, 66, 463–472.

Woodside, A. G. (2013b). Proposing a new logic for data analysis in marketing and consumer behavior: case study research of large-N survey data for estimating algorithms that accurately profile X (extremely high-use) consumers. *Journal of Global Scholars of Marketing Science*, 22 (4), 277–289.

Woodside, A. G., Frey, L. L., & Daily, R. T. (1989). Linking service quality, customer satisfaction and behavioral intention: From general to applied frameworks of the service encounter. *Journal of Health Care Marketing*, 9(4), 5–17.

Woodside, A. G., & Sims, J. T. (1976). Retail sales transactions and customer "purchase pal" effects on buying behavior. *Journal of Retailing*, 52(3), 57–64, 95.

Woodside, A. G., & Zhang, M. (2012). Identifying X-consumers using causal recipes: 'Whales' and 'jumbo shrimps' casino gamblers. *Journal of Gambling Studies*, 28, 13–26.

Wu, P.-L., Yeh, S.-S., Huan, T. C., & Woodside, A. G. (2014). Applying complexity theory to deepen service dominant logic: Configural analysis of customer experience-and-outcome assessments of professional services for personal transformations. *Journal of Business Research*, 67, 1647–1670.

Zeithaml, V. A., Berry, L. L., & Parasuraman, A. (1996). The behavioral consequences of service quality. *Journal of Marketing*, 60(2), 31–46.

Appendix A

Table A1:   Survey Items.

Variables	Measures	
Store Ambience	Regarding the ambience, I feel — Very poor (1)/Very good (5)	
Ea1	Background music	12345
Ea2	Music volume	12345
Ea3	Luminance level	12345
Ea4	Temperature level	12345
Ea5	Aroma	12345
Eb1	Architecture	12345
Eb2	Decoration	12345
Eb3	Wallpaper	12345
Eb4	Efficient layout	12345
Eb5	Item display	12345
Ec1	Sufficient number of personnel	12345
Ec2	Professional uniform	12345
Ec3	Friendliness of personnel	12345
Ec4	Professionalism of personnel	12345
Ec5	Crowdedness level	12345
Experiential Value	Regarding the following statement of experiential value, I feel — Disagree very much (1)/Agree very much (5)	
Ev1	The experience is worth the price	12345
Ev2	Superior service quality	12345
Ev3	High esthetics value	12345
Ev4	Arouse pleasure	12345
Store Image	Regarding the following statement about store image, I feel — Disagree very much (1)/Agree very agree (5)	
Si1	Effective facial treatment	12345
Si2	Effective body treatment	12345
Si3	Effective health treatment	12345
Si4	Spatial surrounding	12345
Si5	Good ambience	12345
Si6	Nice style	12345

Table A1:   (*Continued*)

Variables	Measures	
Si7	Politeness	12345
Si8	Responsiveness	12345
Si9	Initiative	12345
Si10	Good value for money	12345
Si11	Acceptable price range for the consumption level of local community	12345
Si12	Acceptable price range for me	12345
Buying Intention	Regarding the following statement about buying intention, I feel – Disagree very much (1)/Agree very much (5)	
	I will visit again	12345
	This will be my first choice	12345
	I will spend more time here	12345
	I will purchase more service here	12345

Appendix B

Table B1: Beauty Salon/Spa Facets: (1) Architecture; (2) People_Quality; (3) Aroma, Temp, Lighting; (4) Music; (5) Displays; (6) Personnel_Numb.

		Component					
		1	2	3	4	5	6
1. Architecture (touch)	Architecture	.850					
	Wallpaper	.764					
	Decoration	.748					
2. People quality	Professionalism of personnel		.790				
	Friendliness of personnel		.778				
	Crowdedness level		.673				
	Professional uniform		.641				
3. Aroma, temp, light	Aroma			.835			
	Temperature level			.691			
	Luminance level			.587			
4. Music	Background Music				.830		
	Music Volume				.801		
5. Product displays	Efficient layout					.746	
	Item display					.663	
6. People number sufficient	Sufficient number of personnel						.839
	Rotated Sums of Squared						
	Loadings	2.71	2.61	1.89	1.88	1.53	0.99
	% variance	18.04	17.42	12.61	12.52	10.19	6.60

Note: This table includes only factor loadings having values above 0.50.

Table B2: Service Outcomes: (1) Responsiveness; (2) Price_Acceptance; (3) Spatial; (4) Treatment; (5) Arousal_Pleasure; (6) Service_Quality.

		Component					
		1	2	3	4	5	6
1. Responsiveness	Responsiveness	.870					
	Politeness	.757					
	Initiative	.755					
2. Price-acceptable	Acceptable price range for the consumption level of local community		.861				
	Acceptable price range for me		.812				
	Good value for money		.749				
3. Ambience	Spatial surrounding			.820			
	Good ambience			.751			
	Nice style			.729			
4. Effective treatment	Effective health treatment				.855		
	Effective facial treatment				.691		
	Effective body treatment				.655		
5. Arouse pleasure	Arouse pleasure					.773	
	High aesthetics value					.753	
6. Service quality	The experience is worth the price						.778
	Superior service quality						.723
	Rotation Sums of Squared Loadings	2.49	2.45	2.22	2.07	1.72	1.60
	% of Variance	15.54	15.34	13.90	12.91	10.72	9.99

Note: This table includes only factor loadings having values above 0.50.

7

Complexity Theory and Human Resources Management: Transcending Variable and Case-Based Perspectives of Service Employees' (Un)happiness and Work Performance

Chyi Jaw, James Po-Hsun Hsiao,
Tzung-Cheng (T. C.) Huan and
Arch G. Woodside

ABSTRACT

This chapter describes and tests the principles of configural theory in the context of hospitality frontline service employees' happiness-at-work and managers' assessments of these employees' quality of work performances. The study proposes and tests empirically a configural asymmetric theory of the antecedents to hospitality employee happiness-at-work and managers' assessments of employees' quality of work performance. The findings confirm and go beyond prior statistical findings of small-to-medium effect sizes of happiness-performance relationships. The method includes matching cases of data from surveys of employees ($n = 247$) and surveys completed by their managers (n = 43) and uses qualitative comparative analysis via the software program fsQCA.com. The findings support the four principles of configural analysis and theory construction: recognize equifinality of different solutions for the same outcome; test for asymmetric solutions; test for causal asymmetric outcomes for very high versus very low happiness and work performance; and embrace complexity. The theory and findings confirm that configural theory and research resolves perplexing happiness–performance conundrums. The study provides algorithms involving employees' demographic characteristics and their assessments of work facet-specifics which are useful for explaining very high happiness-at-work and high quality-of-work performance (as assessed by managers) – as well as algorithms explaining very low happiness and very low quality-of-work performance.

Keywords: Configuration; customer-directed extra role performance; demographics; employee happiness-at-work; in-role performance; work facet-specifics

Introduction

> Relationships between variables can be non-linear with abrupt switches occurring, so the same "cause" can, in specific circumstances, produce different effects.
>
> Urry (2005)

Warr (2007) emphasizes three principal domains of happiness: context-free or a person's chronic state of happiness (see Hellen & Sääksjärvi, 2011); domain-specific happiness covering only feelings in a targeted domain (e.g., happiness at home with family members, happiness at work), and "facet-specific" happiness focusing on particular aspects of a domain, such as your pay, physical surroundings at work, or your boss. "Many publications appear to be based on the assumption that causes and consequences are the same at each level of scope. They are not, and must be distinguished from each other" (Warr, 2007, p. 726).

This chapter focuses on the relationships between the second and third domains of happiness — how they relate to each other among hospitality front-line service employees (HFSE) as well as work-domain and work facet-specific happiness associating with managers' assessments of work performances of HFSEs. The study advances theory for solving the major research happiness-performance conundrums. The conundrums include estimates indicating a small-to-medium effect size (Cohen, 1977) of the relationship of employee work-domain happiness and managers' assessment of employee work-performance with some studies indicate no significant relationship as well as occurrence of a number of cases of employees very low in work-domain happiness with very high performance assessments and employees with high work-domain happiness with very low performance assessments. The theory and empirical findings in this report serve to increase understanding and explanation of the contexts when the positive effect sizes for happiness–performance associations are small versus large as well as the contexts when work-domain happiness and work performance associate negatively.

This study includes an empirical test of the theory via the collection and merging of two data files — HFSEs' of facets-specific and work-domain happiness and their managers' assessments of these employees' work in-role performance (IRP) and their customer-directed extra-role performance (CDERP). Bettencourt and Brown (1997), Bettencourt, Gwinner, and Meuter (2001), and Karatepe (2013) suggest that CDERP is the extra effort of employees when providing service to customers that raises the quality and positive perception of the service given. While the relationship between IRP and CDERP is positive and the effect size is large for this relationship, hospitality managers in the present study emphasized the need to assess both — and managers and employees were able to distinguish between IRP and CDERP as overlapping but unique domains.

Following this introduction, the next section provides a brief review of relevant literature on employee work-domain happiness and managers' performance assessments. After this, a configural theory of alternative antecedent recipes associating with high employee work-domain happiness, IRP, and CDERP is introduced. The section "Method" describes the method of the empirical study to test the theory. Findings of the study are presented next. The section that follows is a discussion of the findings, includes limitations of the empirical study, and concludes with implications to theory and practice and suggestions for future research.

Employee Work-Doman Happiness and Managers' Assessment of Employee Performance

Lyubomirsky, King, and Diener (2005) provide an extensive meta-analysis of general and specific categories of happiness and success. Their overall assessments of work-life happiness and success indicate a small-to-medium effect size (a weighted mean $r = .20$ for 19 cross-sectional studies and a weighted $r = .05$ for 11 longitudinal studies).

The Lyubomirsky et al. (2005) meta-analysis summarizes findings across all three levels of happiness and various domains of work-related success. Drilling down to the relationship between work-related happiness and managers' assessments of employee work performance indicates a small effect size. Work performance may be more strongly predicted by general well-being than by job satisfaction. "In two studies, Wright and Cropanzano (2000) report that job performance, as judged by supervisors, was significantly correlated with well-being (r's of .32 and .34, respectively), but uncorrelated with measures of job satisfaction (r's of $-.08$ and .08, respectively)" (Lyubomirsky et al., 2005, p. 822). Adopting the perspective that "job satisfaction" and "employee-at-work happiness" are analogous concepts, Lyubomirsky et al.'s (2005) general conclusion of a "robust" positive relationship between happiness and success ("robust" appears eight times in their meta-analysis) fails to hold for the nitty-gritty findings for employee work-happiness and managers' assessment of employee work performance.

Additional reviews (Iaffaldano & Muchinsky, 1985; Judge, Thoresen, Bono, & Patton, 2001; Vroom, 1964) confirm that the uncorrected relationship between job satisfaction and performance is modest. However, Fisher (2010) emphasizes that when corrections for unreliability and sampling error are applied, meta-analytic studies show moderate relationships between job satisfaction and both core and contextual performance (Judge et al., 2001; LePine, Erez, & Johnson, 2002).

Rather than continuing to examine the issue of how large is the effect size between employee job happiness and managers' evaluations of employee job performance, the study here proposes redirecting focus on examining the complex antecedent conditions associating with very high and low happiness-at-work as an outcome as well as the configural conditions that include very high (low) happiness and manager's assessments of very high (low) job performance as an outcome condition.

Configurational Theory of Antecedents and Outcomes of Employee Happiness-at-Work and Manager's Assessment of Job Performance

Heretofore happiness-success research and modeling makes use almost exclusively of symmetric tests of statistical hypotheses — tests such as analysis of variance (ANOVA), multiple regression analysis (MRA), and structural equation modeling (SEM). Such statistical tools implicitly assume and test symmetrical theory, that is, a high value in an independent variable (i.e., X, one construct or an equation containing several constructs) relates closely with a high value in a dependent variable (Y) and low value in the same independent variable relates closely with a low value in the same dependent variable. The symmetric perspective builds from the assumption of sufficiency and necessity of the relationship between X and Y — for Y to be high, X must be high; for Y to be low, X must be low.

GENERAL CONFIGURAL THEORY

Most real-life contexts include asymmetrical relationships quite often and only rarely symmetrical ones (Ragin, 2008). Figure 1b illustrates the symmetrical stance. Figures 1c and d illustrate two symmetrical stances. Figure 1c illustrates the sufficiency but not necessary relationship. Figure 1d illustrates the necessary but not sufficiency stance. (Figure 1a shows a rectangular distribution of cases, that is, no relationship other than a random distribution of Y's for X's.)

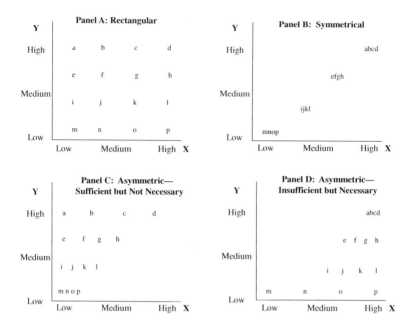

Figure 1. Rectangular, Symmetrical, and Asymmetrical Relationships: Hypothetical Plots of 16 Cases (a through p) for Outcome *Y* and Complex or Simple Causal Statement *X*.

The insight, "Scientists' tools are not neutral" (Gigerenzer, 1991, p. 19) and the limitations of examining theoretical relationships empirically using symmetric statistical tests have lead researchers in marketing (Bass, Tigert, & Lonsdale, 1968), in psychology (Doyle, O'Connor, Reynolds, & Bottomley, 1999; McClelland, 1998), in sociology (Ragin, 2008), in management (Fiss, 2007, 2011), and in tourism (Woodside, Hsu, & Marshall, 2012) to call for building and testing theory using algorithms from an asymmetric stance. For example, in building models which predict success at work McClelland (1998) advocates focusing theory and tests on "competency-qualification algorithms" following the identification of "critical frequencies" (i.e., tipping points, see Gladwell, 1996) or levels that best distinguish between "outstanding" and "typical" executives.

Because data are noisy (i.e., construct values near the median for an independent variable associate frequently with a wide range of values for a dependent variable), quite often individual (case-level) memberships within level 5 (highest) versus level 1 (lowest) among quintiles are representative of critical frequencies (i.e., "tipping points"). For example, while the correlation for the total set of data in the current study employee happiness-at-work and job performance equals .17 ($p < .009$, a small-to-medium effect size, $n = 243$), a comparison of distributions of the critical frequencies within quintiles 1 and 5 for low/high happiness and low/high performance results in a large effect size ($\varphi = .48$, $p < .003$, $n = 38$).

Both in theory and in real-life contexts, researchers and executives seek in particular to build algorithms accurate in identifying exceptional employee outcomes (e.g., algorithms that identify individuals either very high or very low in happiness and/or job performance). McClelland (1998) emphasizes examining and reporting antecedents for high versus typical employee performance in terms of symmetrical tests (e.g., ANOVA, correlation, MRA, SEM) understate and misrepresent the significance of the focal relationship while configural statements based on tipping-points provide highly useful "competency algorithms." For a classification of "outstanding" versus "typical" performer, the competency algorithm McClelland (1998, p. 334) reports requires a case (i.e., individual executive) to achieve "for at least 1 of the 3 individual-initiative competencies, 1 of the organizational competencies, and 6 of the 12 valid competencies overall."

Ragin (2010) advances theory and provides useful software (fsQCA.com) for model-building and empirical-testing alternative algorithms that identify cases with high (or low) focal outcomes consistently. An algorithm is a conjunctive statement that requires the presence of two or more conditions in a given case for a favorable (unfavorable) conclusion or decision. For example, the following algorithm predicts high performer and is a complex antecedent condition (a recipe) that combines four simple antecedent conditions: a frontline employee who is happy-at-work, works well with other employees, never causes peer conflicts, and always arrives to work on-time is a high performer. This configural statement does not tell us that exhibiting this recipe is the only recipe that results in the identification of a high performer; the statement says only that an employee high in all four ingredients is a high performer. The statement indicates sufficiency but not necessity.

Configurational analysis stresses four principles in study of antecedent conditions affecting an outcome. The first is the principle of equifinality, that is, "a system can reach the same final state, from different initial conditions and by a variety of different paths" (Katz & Kahn, 1978, p. 30). While "unifinality" assumes the occurrence of one optimal configuration, equifinality assumes that two or more configurations can be equally effective in achieving high performance within the same context (Fiss, 2007; Galunic & Eisenhardt, 1994; Gresov & Drazin, 1997). Thus, two frontline employees may be both very happy-at-work but for different combinations of antecedents.

The principle of asymmetry (asymmetrical relationships) is the second principle of configural analysis. Statistical tests such as multiple regression, structural equation modeling, and analysis of variance test for the presence of symmetrical relationships. However, large effect sizes (e.g., correlations above .60) rarely occur and usually occur only for tests for reliability (e.g., coefficient alpha). Real-life is most often made up of asymmetric relationships between simple and complex X scores and Y scores as appearing in Figures 1c and d.

The principle of complexity is the third tenet of configural analysis. Emergence is a central idea to the principle of complexity: It is not that the sum is greater than the size of its parts – but that there are system effects that are different from their parts (Jervis, 1997; Urry, 2005). The complexity principle supports a shift from reductionist analyses to those that involve the study of complex adaptive ("vital") matter that shows ordering but which remains on "the edge of chaos" (Urry, 2005, p. 1). Thus, the configural analysis focus is a shift away from examining/deconstructing the net effect of each independent variable, interactions, moderating, mediator, and total effects to the study of alternative causal configurations or recipes that consistently result in a given outcome of interest (cf. Ragin, 1997) – such as high employee happiness or employee work performance. Ragin (1997) refers to this paradigm shift as "turning the tables: how case-oriented methods challenge variable oriented methods."

The butterfly effect is relevant for the study of operations of the complexity principle – if combined in certain configurations with other antecedents, the flapping of a butterfly wings in a nearby location contributes to a huge impact in a distant location (see Lorenz, 1961). Consequently, the relevant issue is not to focus on the net effect of each independent variable but on the totality of testing each complex combination of antecedent conditions.

The principle of complexity goes beyond the butterfly effect to include reversals of what variable-based research describes as "main effects." Reversals of influence of a simple antecedent condition on an outcome condition can occur depending upon the other ingredients in alternative configurations. Thus, high happiness may occur in six of the nine, and low happiness may occur in two of the nine, complex configurations associating with high performance — a statement that illustrates that high happiness is not a necessity for high performance among all employees. In this brief thought experiment, the state of employee happiness is irrelevant in one of the nine configurations. All nine configurations are relevant to one or more employees with high happiness-at-work uniquely or in overlapping relationships; the nine configurations may "explain" most but not all cases of high happiness among a sample of employees.

Third, configural theory also stresses the principle of causal asymmetry, that is, the causes leading to the presence of an outcome of interest may be quite different from those leading to the absence of the outcome (Ragin, 2008). The use of "cause" here refers to relevant association and not causation from the perspective of true experiments with treatment and control groups and random assignment of cases to groups. A highly negative score for one minus happiness-at-work is an indicator (but not necessarily the same concept) of high unhappiness. The principle of causal asymmetry suggests that high unhappiness is not an ingredient necessarily in all configurations that lead to low performance even if high happiness appears in nearly all algorithms associating with high performance.

HAPPINESS–PERFORMANCE CONFIGURAL THEORY

Figure 2 is a visual summary of a configural theory of complex antecedent conditions leading to high as well as low happiness and high as well as low employee work performances (IRP and CDERP). The Venn diagrams in Figure 2 are to suggest the adoption of the perspective of configural influence on outcome conditions.

The arrows in Figure 2 illustrate testable propositions of seven principal associations: (1) demographic configurations influence on facet-specific domains of work; (2) demographic configurations influence on happiness-at-work; (3) demographic configurations influence on employee IRP; (4) configurations of facet-specific domains-of-work influence on happiness; (5a) configurations of facet-specific domains-of-work influence IRP; (5b) happiness affects 5a; (6) happiness as a stand-alone antecedent influences IRP; and (7) IRP's stand-alone influences CDERP.

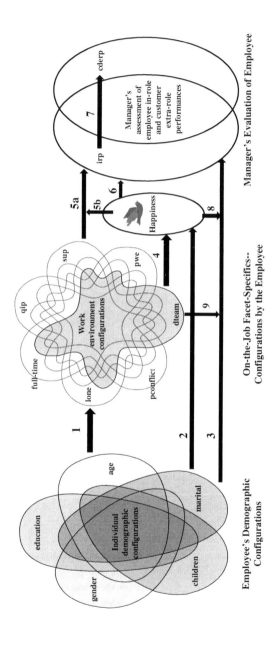

Figure 2. Configural Modeling Associations with Very High/Low Hospitality-Service Employee Work Contexts, Very High/Low Happiness, In-Role, and Customer-Directed Extra Role Performances. *Notes*: dteam = job demands of teamwork; cderp = customer-directed extra role performance; irp = in-role performance; lone = do not join social activities with my colleagues; pconflict = peer conflict; pwe = physical work environment pleasing; qip = quality of interpersonal relationships; sup = supervisor support.

THE RELEVANCY OF DEMOGRAPHICS TO HAPPINESS-AT-WORK

The literature on the net effects of employee demographic variables on work performance is vast and summaries are available (e.g., Kossek & Ozeki, 1998; Sloan, 2012; Warr, 2007). Kossek and Ozeki's (1998) meta-analytic (using effect sizes of correlations) findings show that regardless of the type of measure used (bidirectional work-family conflict, work-to-family, family-to-work); a consistent negative relationship exists among all forms of work-family conflict and job and/or life satisfaction.

Using survey response data (n = 1,380) to a questionnaire distributed to a random sample of 2,500 employees working in career service positions of one state in the southern USA ("career service jobs") are all positions in the state in which the workers do not serve the governor directly, Sloan examined how demographic and job characteristics influence self-management of job-happiness. From symmetric tests (MRA) and focusing on net effects of demographic influences on job-happiness, Sloan concludes, "... men manage their happiness at work more than women (b = $-.153$). In other words, compared to men women are more expressive of happiness at work." Sloan also reports:

> Among the demographic variables and controls, whites and married respondents reported less happiness management than the non-whites and non-married workers and older workers manage their happiness more than younger workers. Interestingly, age and race are very strong predictors of happiness management (b = .153 and b = -142, respectively). Along with men, the older workers and non-white workers put an effort into appearing emotionless (or at least, joyless) while working. In addition, income and education have significant negative associations with happiness management; however, these effects are explained with the addition of the job characteristic variables.

While the present study focuses on theory and model testing to identify hospitality service-employees very (and low) in happiness and not how well workers manage happiness, the point here is that focusing on the symmetric main effects of demographic variables on happiness management or high (low) happiness conditions provides less useful information than the asymmetric combinatory effects of demographic antecedents in identifying outcomes such as very high happiness or very high job performance.

For example, asymmetric outcomes are likely to show that the algorithm of young, unmarried, females, employee with children and low education are low in happiness at work due to the high demands and conflicts of work-family requirements. Considering quintile 1 and 5 for age and education along with two categories each for gender, employment status, and children, the total number of combinations is 32. For the expressed algorithm to be highly accurate/useful in indicating cases of low happiness, all or nearly all cases fitting into the segment (i.e., $\sim$h $\leq$ $\sim$age• children•$\sim$education• female•$\sim$married) would be low in job-happiness. In the Boolean statement, the tilde ("$\sim$") expresses negation and the mid-level dot ("•") expresses the logical "and" condition. This one statement indicates only that high scores in the negation of happiness will not occur when the complex statement scores are high and high scores in $\sim$happiness will occur for young AND female employees AND having low education AND having children, AND working part-time. The statement says nothing about cases (i.e., employees) with low scores on this one Boolean algebra statement – some of the cases not in this segment will be high and some will be low in happiness.

Because causal asymmetry occurs frequently in real-life, the assumption is often inaccurate that the mirror opposite of the complex statement indicates the opposite outcome. However, theory might suggest that older AND male employees AND high education, AND working full-time are high in happiness (with children not contributing (being unnecessary) in predicting high happiness accurately. (The following empirical study does support both models – the first for not happy-at-work ($\sim$h) and the second for happy-at-work (h).)

The theory and analysis does not claim that all employees who are very high (or very low) in job-happiness are identifiable by complex statements of demographic conditions. The theory and analysis only states that some complex statements are accurate in identifying employees who are very high (or very low) in job-happiness. For some cases of the data, complex demographic-statements alone may be insufficient or irrelevant in identifying very high (low) happy employees or employees with very high (low) job performances; antecedents other than demographics (e.g., emotions relating to job facet-specifics) may be necessary and informative in providing necessary information for identifying such cases.

In general terms, considering highest and lowest quintiles and two categories of gender and the absence and presence of children, the inclusion of five demographics in a study of configural influences of demographics on happiness and job performance implies that combinations of two-to-five of these simple antecedents will be useful in predicting very high (low) happiness-at-work and very high (low) work performance. An "accurate parsimonious configural model" indicates that fewer than all the available antecedents are necessary for accurately predicting an outcome of interest – such as the model indicating that older-married-males working full-time are very high in happiness-at-work with no need to consider whether or not they are fathers.

WORK FACET-SPECIFICS

The study proposes configurations of seven work facet-specifics influence happiness-at-work and work performance. The seven appear in a flower-like Venn diagram in the center of Figure 2; this diagram illustrates all possible two-way to seven-way combinations of the seven simple antecedent conditions. Thus, theory includes the proposition that parsimonious models (most likely of three-to-six very high and low combinations of the seven facet-specific antecedents) associates with very high (low) happiness and very high (low) work performance.

For example, the study proposes and tests the following work facet-specific statements. Very high happiness associates with the combination of full-time employment, low peer conflict, highly pleasing work environment, high-quality interpersonal relationships, and high supervisory support. Very low happiness associates with part-time employment, not joining social activities with colleagues at work (lone), and not having a pleasing work environment. The following Boolean statements represent these two propositions:

$h \leq$ full-time•~conflict•pleasing•high-quality-interpersonal•high-supervisory-support

~$h \leq$ ~full-time•lone•~pleasing

Considering two levels of part versus full-time and quintile 1 versus 5 for the other six antecedents, a total of 128 combinations are possible theoretically for the seven antecedents – but additional combinations can be relevant if only two to six simple antecedents are necessary for predicting high scores in happiness and/or job performance. The general proposition for work facet-specific antecedents is that a few configurations of these antecedents are useful for predicting very high (low) happiness and very high (low) work performance.

The following literature review serves as the basis of the selection of work facet-specific antecedents for the current study. Certainly, additional facet-specific antecedents may be relevant and are worthy of attention in future research.

Physical Work Environment

Scholars advocate that the physical work environment (PWE) of services of the entity can impact behavior and can be conducive to marketing services (Kotler, 2000; Shostack, 1985) and should therefore be properly planned and designed. The PWE in service sector likely enters several configural models impacting happiness and job performance because customers and employees are both present during hospitality service enactments. The implications of the physical environment are observable service providers and recipients which can influence strategic planning and space design greatly in comparison (Crosby, Evans, & Cowles, 1990; Lovelock, 1996). Thus, many scholars discuss the physical environment's impact on customers (Babin, Darden, & Griffin, 1994; Baker, 1986; Bitner, 1990; Donovan & Rossiter, 1982; Foxall & Greenley, 1999; Machleit & Eroglu, 2000; Turley & Milliman, 2000; Wart, Robertson, & Zielinski, 1992; Wirtz & Bateson, 1999; Yoo, Park, & MacInnis, 1998). Environment awareness can cause employees to have a different perspective on the companies they work for and can affect their emotional responses (Russell & Lanius, 1984; Russell & Pratt, 1980).

Quality of Interpersonal Relationships

Howton (1963) refers to interpersonal relations as one of the resulting factors of an organization's work environment while Schutte et al. (2001) propose that interpersonal relations relate closely to emotional intelligence. Interpersonal relations are the interactions between human beings, and in the context of the service industry, refer to an individual's relations (service contact employee) with management, subordinates (such as probationary service personnel) and colleagues (such as those whose collaborative work or duties are the same). Interpersonal relation quality refers to employees' attitude towards themselves, their bosses and colleagues, in addition to their relation quality awareness and satisfaction.

Interpersonal relation is a dynamic type of relation that can affect an organization's members' mood and attitudes, which affects each individual's performance in the organization. Thus, employees' self-awareness of their interpersonal relations can affect their performance in their organization. In the service industry, management, subordinates and colleagues need interpersonal interactions to communicate and overcome problems that arise in the work place. For a service employee, positive interpersonal relations can allow a person to dispel negative moods and can add to a positive performance.

Employees who have a high quality of interpersonal relations can cause a rise in positive moods. Service contact employees in an organization who are able to perceive the quality of interpersonal relationships can have a positive impact on their emotions.

Peer Conflicts

In the large and dense tourism industry, the first line of employees has people from all sorts of working environments and backgrounds with different values and beliefs. These differences are plausible causes of conflicts in an organization. Those organizations that have positive interpersonal relations can raise moods of employees, yet working situations that often have employee conflicts can have a negative impact on moods.

In different organizations different types of conflicts that occur. As Slack (1997) points out, participants can have different levels of conflict, which include personal conflict, interpersonal conflict, group (the organization) conflict, and inter-group (inter-organizational) conflict. The study uses Slack's interpersonal conflict to discuss peer conflict and its effect on employee moods.

Gibson, Ivancevich, and Donnelly (1994) and Slack (1997) propose that conflicts within organizations can arise from factors such as resource limitations, differences in goals, lack of cooperation, communication distortion, differences in pay compensation, power inconsistencies in decision-making. Some studies identify interpersonal conflict behavior triggering negative reactions (Hepbur, Loughoin, & Barling, 1997; Terry, Tonge, & Callan, 1995). Spector and Jex (1998) point out that frequency of interpersonal conflicts that take place in an organization have a correlation with negative work attitude and dissatisfaction. Frone (2000) offers a similar conclusion in a second empirical study.

As a majority of services require different co-workers, peer conflict may not be avoidable. These conflicts with their peers may affect the mood of employees and a drop in service performance. Thus, for modeling the negation of happiness ($\sim$h) and very low in-role performance evaluations ($\sim$irp), configurations of facet-specific antecedents are likely to often include service staff employees' conflicts with their peers.

Teamwork

Teamwork refers to the need for cooperation in order to achieve a set goal, which brings about a certain type of interaction between two or more employees; therefore, teamwork requires a high degree of interaction among its members, in attempts to reach common goals (George & Jones, 2002). The team may also as a result face more and perhaps complex interpersonal challenges.

The interaction within members of the team can have a great impact on employees' happiness. As Frijda (1988) describes, happiness within an organization or group can play the role of signaling, which means the transmission of how members of the group feel about their interpersonal relations with others (Hess & Kirouac, 2000). The display of emotions can have a great deal to do with the status of members in the group (Clark, 1999; Collins, 1990; Lovaglia & Houser, 1996; Lucas & Lovaglia, 1998). As a result of constant interaction between team members, members may mimic emotions and the spread of emotions is inevitable; in related research of organization literature, scholars have pointed out that emotions of the team can be transferred, and different types of teams can have different emotional effects on their members (Barsade, 2000, 2002; Bartel & Saavedra, 2000).

Hospitality frontline services often need teamwork to complete tasks, and teamwork indeed may affect team members' interpersonal and emotional link. Service employees need high degrees of teamwork and thus interpersonal conflict with their peers or the quality of the management staff can affect emotions; if the demand for teamwork is less, then it minimizes the interpersonal interaction. Hence, teamwork is likely to be integral in configurations in modeling happiness as well as IRP.

HAPPINESS-AT-WORK AND JOB PERFORMANCE

Is high happiness-at-work sufficient and/or necessary for high job performance? Given that the literature on happiness-at-work and job performance indicates a small-to-medium effect size for their relationship (Choi & Kim, 2012; Lyubomirsky et al., 2005; Zelenski, Murphy, & Jenkins, 2008), the study here proposes that happiness-at-work by itself is insufficient and unnecessary for high job performance.

Thus, assuming that arrow 6 in Figure 2 indicates either sufficiency or necessary, the evidence in the following study does not support the existence of arrow 6. However, the configural theory includes the proposition that happiness in recipes with work facet-specific (arrow 5b in Figure 2) and/or demographic antecedents (arrow 8 in Figure 2) are sufficient in predicting very high work performance.

Note also that arrow 9 appears in Figure 2. Arrow 9 represents the proposition that a one or a few facet-specific work antecedents influence IRP in conjunction with a few configurations of demographics and happiness. Such a proposition suggests consideration of very complex configurations is useful for explaining and describing very high (low) IRP.

IN-ROLE PERFORMANCE AND CUSTOMER-DIRECTED EXTRA-ROLE PERFORMANCE

Effective interaction between service employees and customers may contribute to maintaining a firm's customers, with the feedback from existing customers possessing the potential to attract new customers. Netemeyer, Maxham, and Pullig (2005) define this performance as "in-role performance" (IRP) and "extra-role performance" (ERP). Arrow 6 in Figure 2 indicates more than just a direct relationship between IRP and customer-directed extra-role performance (CDERP). In the present study arrow 6 implies sufficiency and necessary — employees with very high scores in IRP will have very high scores in CDERP and employees with very low scores in IRP will have very low scores in CDERP. (The findings below do support the sufficiency implication but not the necessity implication.)

The concept of IRP includes three perspectives. First, Motowidlo and Van Scotter (1994) propose that IRP reflects an organization's performance demands from its employees, which relates to a company's service objectives and critical techniques. Second, Singh, Verbeke, and Rhoads (1996) suggests that the operational definition of IRP comprises items such as product, customer requests, time management efficiency, company resources, customer service volume, and other factors that affect performance quality. Third, Singh (2000) proposes IRP as product production capabilities and quality, with product production capabilities referring to a quantifiable output (such as customers contracting a specific amount) and product quality referring to employees (the management of interaction between customers and employees).

This study also explores CDERP. Borman and Motowidlo (1993) propose that a customer's evaluation of an organization's performance has something to do with contextual customer performance that does not relate to the demands of the employee's IRP. Bettencourt, Gwinner, and Meuter (2001) and Bettencourt and Brown (1997) suggest that CDERP is the extra effort of employees when providing service to customers that raises the quality and positive perception of the service given.

Methods

The main study includes the use and merging of two files of survey data. Employees and their immediate supervisors of a large-size hospitality service business-group participated in the study. Employees completed a survey covering demographics, work facet-specific information, and a happiness-at-work scale; their supervisors completed IRP and CDERP scales on the performance assessments of these same employees. All surveys were coded by a matched employee-supervisor number and all completed surveys were collected by a team of university professors in person and did not go through the business group's mail distribution center.

Janfusan Fancyworld, the largest (in revenues and number of employees) tourism business group in Taiwan, was the business-group participating in the study. Janfusan Fancyworld includes tourist hotels, amusement parks, restaurants, and other related service sectors. The anonymity in participating in the study was assured by letter from the CEO to all participants – both front-line employees and their supervisors and by letter by the professors (the authors) directing the study.

SURVEY INSTRUMENTS

Except for full versus part-time question item, the work facet-specific questions included 7-point Likert scales, ranging from 1 (strongly disagree to 7 (strongly agree). The IRP and CDERP item responses ranged from 1 to 10, with 10 reflecting the best quality and 1 reflecting the worst quality). Table 1 includes these items and the item-to-total scale correlations and coefficient alphas for the scales.

Table 1:   Construct Scale and Coefficient Alpha (Corrected Item to Total Correlations) (Decimal Points Omitted).

Work Facet-Specific Antecedents (and Outcomes)	Outcomes

• Supervisor support (supsup) (65)
  − When I encounter difficult, my supervisor gives me support. (48)
  − My supervisor clearly understands what I think and how I feel. (48)
 	
• Quality of interpersonal relationships (qip) (74)
  − I feel very happy about working with my colleagues. (58)
  − Most of colleagues are very nice that they help each other actively. (58)
 	
• Physical work environment (pwe) (77)
  − Overall, the present working environment is what I want. (62)
  − I work at a pleasant environment. (62)
 	
• I seldom join social activities with my colleagues. (lone)
 	
• Peer conflict (pconflict) (56)
  − I usually have a conflict with my colleagues because of issues of work. (38)
  − There is usually an argument between colleagues and me. (31)
  − Colleagues always ascribe problems of work to me. (41)
 	
• Demands of teamwork (dteam) (78)
  − The assistance from colleagues can help me collect useful information and suggestion on my job. (55)
  − Teamwork eases the loading of responsibility on job. (60)
  − In order to achieve goal, I have to cooperate closely with my colleagues. (69)
	• Happiness-at-work (hap) (96)
	  − Happy/unhappy (87)
	  − Pleasant/unpleasant (88)
	  − Satisfied/unsatisfied (85)
	  − Content/discontent (83)
	  − Enjoyable/non-enjoyable (80)
	  − Comforting/uncomforting (82)
	  − Gratifying/non-gratifying (86)
	  − In-role performance (irp)(83)
	
	• This employee is qualified with the knowledge of the company, and competitors' products/service. (58)
	  − Overall job performance is approved to reach the set goal. (78)
	  − This employee is accurately accomplishing job regulations. (59)
	  − Follows requirements of the company to serve customers. (66)
	
	• Customer-directed extra-role performance (cderp) (89)
	  − The degree of this employee is willing to pay extra time or efforts to make a customer satisfied. (68)
	  − Even if beyond job requirements, this employee still takes initiatives to assist a customer. (83)
	  − How often does this employee voluntarily go out of his/her way to make customer contented? (71)
	  − How often does this employee goes above and beyond job expectation or "call of duty" while serving customers? (78)

To learn whether or not the questions and topics of the survey were understood and answered by the survey takers, two pre-tests were done. The respondents for first pre-test included key professionals. The respondents for second pre-test included service employees and management staff. Careful revision steps were taken to keep the respondents from making the wrong interpretations and thus altering the accuracy of the data.

WORK FACET-SPECIFIC SCALES

The survey scale for service working environment adopted the measurements in Bitner (1992). After the reliability analysis, two items were deleted and two items were kept and tested (α = 0.77). See Table 1 for details.

The assessment of quality of interpersonal relationship was based upon measurements developed by Lin (1998) and further revised. The original measurements of Lin included 6 items. After the pre-test, four items were deleted, and two items remained and tested (α = 0.74).

The assessment of peer conflicts combines the measurements of interpersonal conflicts developed by Spector and Jex (1998) and Frone (2000). Three items were selected after the pre-test. Also, the content of items was revised and tested (α = 0.56) in order to reflect realistic situations.

The study uses Van de Vliert and Euwema's (1994) "Job Dependence Scale" to evaluate the degree of dependency on teamwork by the employees. Items were revised based on the results of the pre-test and five items were selected and tested (α = 0.78) following reliability analysis.

For measuring happiness-at-work, the survey uses the emotional reaction measurements by Havlena and Holbrook (1986) which comprises seven items (α = 0.96). For performance outcomes this study adopts two performance indicators in-use by the business group's appraisals of frontline employees for IRP and CDERP. IRP (α = 0.83) and CDERP (α =0.89) include four items respectively, scaling included choices of 1 to 10 to measure service performance levels of employees.

DATA COLLECTION PROCEDURE

The two respective surveys were taken had 406 frontline employee respondents and 48 management supervisory respondents. Five supervisors turned-in incomplete surveys consistently which rendered 43 effective sets of supervisor surveys; in addition to eliminating the five management staff participant surveys and the 32 employee participant surveys that they were paired with, seven other employee surveys were filled incompletely or incorrectly. In total, there were 367 fully completed and useable employee surveys. The manager sample is less than the employee respondents; each manager provided employee performance measures for several employees and this study combines the data from the two sets of sample sources.

Therefore, the management staff and employee pairings totaled 367. A total of 247 of the 367 cases were available for data analysis in this study. Unfortunately, data for 120 cases were carried-away as refuse accidently and were not reclaimable. Twenty-four of the 43 staff management group were women, making up 55.8% of the group while 83.7% of the group were 30 years or older, 39.5% of the group received an education level of beyond college, and 60% of the group was married and had children. The majority of the staffs (approximately 81.4%) were employed full-time, with more than five years of service.

Two-thirds of the 367 person employees were women. This gender bias is possibly due to the fact that many service enterprises employ more females than males (such as restaurants). Unmarried individuals comprised 54.8% of the group, with 31.1% of the group between the ages of 26 and 30 while 39.8% of the group had received their highest level of education at the high school level, 29.7% and 27.5% received degrees from colleges and professional schools, respectively and 76.8% of the employees worked full-time, with most employees, around 40.5%, having one to five years of service.

DATA ANALYSIS

Data analyses include both symmetric statistical tests via correlations, regression analysis, and analysis of variance as well as asymmetric algorithm construction and testing using the software program fsQCA.com (fsQCA = "fuzzy set Qualitative Comparative Analysis"). Testing by fsQCA requires calibration all variable scales into calibrated scales with scores ranging from endpoints of 0.00 for full non-membership to 1.00 for full membership. The fsQCA program provides calibrated scores. Fuzzy-set calibration makes use of external information on the degree to which cases satisfy membership criteria and not inductively derived determination criteria (e.g., not using sample means). To perform fuzzy-set calibration, criteria are necessary for three breakpoints — 0.05 for threshold for full non-membership; 0.50 for the crossover point of maximum membership ambiguity; and 0.95 for the threshold of full membership. Specifying the original values for these three breakpoints, permits the software to calibrate all remaining scores. Calibrated scores are membership scores and not probabilities.

For the present report the following simple procedure was used to calibrate the original multiple-value scales. Scores for cases in the highest quintile equal 0.95; calibrated scores for cases in the middle quintile were set at 0.50; calibrated scores for cases in the lowest quintile were set at 0.05. Consequently, the fsQCA software set scores for the second quintile to 0.81 and the fourth quintile to 0.82. Table 2 reports the original and calibrated scores for happiness using this procedure.

Using the fuzzy set calibration method did not change any of the results in the findings section below. Fuzzy set scores for all original scores also appear in Table 2. The complete coverage of the range for possible scores (from 7 to 49) on the original happiness scale as well as the closeness in values for the mean, median, and mode offers support of the discriminating usefulness of the scale.

Ragin (2008) and Woodside (2013) provide numerical examples for calculating consistency and coverage – both researchers stress the first importance of achieving high consistency over high coverage. The primary importance of consistency relates to the equifinality principle; the existence of multiple configurations of antecedent conditions useful in predicting high scores of an outcome condition means that any one configuration will have a low coverage of cases.

In fsQCA, the consistency and coverage indexes are the metrics indicating the useful of a given model of a simple antecedent condition or a set of complex antecedent conditions for predicting scores in an outcome condition. The consistency index gauges the degree to which the cases share the antecedent condition (simple or complex) in displaying the outcome in question – consistency is analogous to correlation in statistical analysis. The coverage index in fsQCA assesses the degree a simple or complex antecedent condition (recipe) "accounts for" instances of an outcome condition – coverage is analogous to r^2 in statistical analysis.

The score for a complex antecedent condition is equal to the lowest score for the simple antecedent conditions within the complex statement. Using a thought experiment (hypothetical fuzzy set score data) for five employees, the appendix numerical examples of computing membership scores for complex antecedent conditions.

Table 2:   Original and Calibrated Happiness Scales and
Frequency of Cases by Scores.

Observed Original	Using 5 Scores Calibrated	Using Fuzzy Scores Calibrated	Frequency	Percent	Cumulative Percent
7.00	.05	.01	6	2.5	2.5
13.00	.05	.03	1	.40	2.9
14.00	.05	.04	9	3.7	6.6
15.00	.05	.05	1	.40	7.0
16.00	.05	.06	2	.80	7.8
18.00	.05	.07	6	2.5	10.3
20.00	.05	.08	2	.80	11.1
21.00	.05	.09	14	5.8	16.9
22.00	.05	.16	6	2.5	19.3
23.00	.18	.23	2	.80	20.2
24.00	.18	.24	10	4.1	24.3
25.00	.18	.25	5	2.1	26.3
26.00	.18	.28	4	1.6	28.0
27.00	.18	.32	9	3.7	31.7
28.00	.50	.36	27	11.1	42.8
29.00	.50	.37	10	4.1	46.9
30.00	.50	.45	6	2.5	49.4
31.00	.50	.50	9	3.7	53.1
32.00	.50	.57	8	3.3	56.4
33.00	.50	.65	8	3.3	59.7
34.00	.82	.71	7	2.9	62.6
35.00	.82	.77	16	6.6	69.1
36.00	.82	.82	12	4.9	74.1
37.00	.82	.86	5	2.1	76.1
38.00	.82	.90	7	2.9	79.0
39.00	.95	.92	9	3.7	82.7
40.00	.95	.94	8	3.3	86.0
41.00	.95	.95	6	2.5	88.5
42.00	.95	.96	12	4.9	93.4
43.00	.95	.97	3	1.2	94.7
44.00	.95	.98	3	1.2	95.9

Table 2:   (*Continued*)

Observed Original	Using 5 Scores Calibrated	Using Fuzzy Scores Calibrated	Frequency	Percent	Cumulative Percent
45.00	.95	.99	2	.80	96.7
46.00	.95	.99	2	.80	97.5
47.00	.95	.99	2	.80	98.4
48.00	.95	1.00	1	.40	98.8
49.00	.95	1.00	3	1.2	100.0
Total			243	100.0	100.0
Mean					30.53
Std. error of mean					0.58
Median					31.00
Mode					28.00

Notes: The use of either set of calibration scores resulted in nearly identical findings in the study. The fuzzy set scores results from the use of the calibration sub-routine in the software fsQCA with the original to fuzzy set scores: 41 = 0.95; 31 = 0.50; 15 = 0.05.
The findings in the main analysis follow from the use of the 5 scores calibrations.

The guidelines used in the study here is that an fsQCA model is useful when its consistency is equal to or above 0.85 and its coverage is above 0.00. A high consistency score (e.g., consistency = 0.85) indicates high membership scores in the outcome condition for nearly all cases with high scores in the simple or complex antecedent condition with most other cases fitting an asymmetric sufficiency distribution (i.e., Figure 1c). See Ragin (2008) for detailed training on using fsQCA.

Findings

The findings here do not include responses for four cases of data. The four cases are employees in the oldest age group (≥ 56 years of age). The four members in the oldest age group had significantly lower happiness, IPR, and CDERP scores in comparison to the cases in the three age groups prior to this group. Age as an antecedent condition in the configural analyses plays no role in the models with the inclusion of the above 55 years of age group.

Possibly the findings for the oldest age group members indicates that business group needs to devote special attention and nurturing to the oldest aged frontline employees. The XY plots for happiness, IRP, and CERP with the other demographics and work facet-specific scales exhibited linear significant and non-significant relationships.

From the dominant logic perspective of statistical analysis, the findings for the present study are similar to the findings in prior studies on employees' happiness-at-work and supervisors' assessments of employees' performances – the relationships are significant but the effect size is small. The correlations of happiness-at-work and IRP and CDERP equal 0.17 and 0.18, respectively.

From a group level perspective, the quintile analysis in Table 3 indicates happiness does not relate significantly to IRP. However, testing only the highest and lowest quintiles indicates a significant and medium-to-large effect size relationship (φ^2 = .228, a medium-to-large effect size). But, examining Table 3 supports the conclusion that very high happiness (quintile 5) does not associate consistently with very high (quintile 5) IRP; in fact, 7 of the 49 cases in Q5 have very low IRP assessments.

The similar lack of consistency occurs for very low happiness and very low performance. Four cases occur whereby very unhappy employees have very high happiness.

The findings do not support a strong symmetric relationship between employee happiness-at-work and performance assessments. Rather than ending the analysis with statistical analysis, transcending a net effects view to analysis by algorithms considers causal recipes that do provide high consistency of cases in all four corners of Table 3.

Conclusion: Arrow 6 in Figure 2 receives insufficient support – high happiness-at-work alone does not predict high performance consistently. High happiness may be a contributing factor to high performance in some configurations with additional antecedents – the findings below do support this perspective.

FINDINGS FOR MODELS FOR VERY HIGH HAPPINESS AND VERY HIGH PERFORMANCE

Figure 3 presents many findings of the propositions of the study that appear in Figure 2. Figure 3 includes three complex antecedent demographic models (L, T, and X) that associate with high

Table 3: Hospitality Employees' Happiness and Managers' Evaluations of Employees' In-Role Performances.

			Very Low	In-Role Performance Quality (IRP)			Very high	Total
			1.00	2.00	3.00	4.00	5.00	
Very low	1.00	Count	14	8	13	10	4	49
		% within happy_segs	28.6	16.3	26.5	20.4	8.2	100.0
	2.00	Count	12	14	10	11	13	60
		% within happy_segs	20.0	23.3	16.7	18.3	21.7	100.0
	3.00	Count	10	9	9	4	7	39
Happiness Quintiles for Hospitality Employees		% within happy_segs	25.6	23.1	23.1	10.3	17.9	100.0
	4.00	Count	9	10	14	6	11	50
		% within happy segs	18.0	20.0	28.0	12.0	22.0	100.0
Very high	5.00	Count	7	6	10	12	14	49
		% within happy segs	14.3	12.2	20.4	24.5	28.6	100.0
		Count	52	47	56	43	49	247
		% within happy segs	21.1	19.0	22.7	17.4	19.8	100.0

Notes: Gray shaded boxes indicate possibly surprising findings: cases do occur of very unhappy employees with very high IRP scores and vice versa. Table 1 reports a quintile analysis of hospitality employee happiness and their managers' in-role performance (IRP) evaluations. Even though the findings for the total sample are not significant statistically, note the modest positive relationship—14 versus 4 employees very low in happiness are very low versus very high in IRP, respectively. The distribution of the 49 very happy employees includes 14 with very high IRP scores and only 7 with very low IRP scores. However, the fsQCA shows how different configurations of complex antecedent conditions for very unhappy versus very happy hospitality employees associate with high IRP scores as well as how different complex antecedent conditions for very happy hospitality employees associate with very low versus very high IRP scores. Total sample: ($\varphi = .259$; $p < .413$; ($\varphi^2 = .07$ (very small effect size). Q1 and Q5 happiness and five quintiles for IRP: $9 = .299$, $p < .068$; ($p^2 = .09$ (medium effect size). Comparing Q1 and Q5 for both happiness and IRP: $\varphi = .478$, $\varphi^2 = .228$ (medium-to-large effect size).

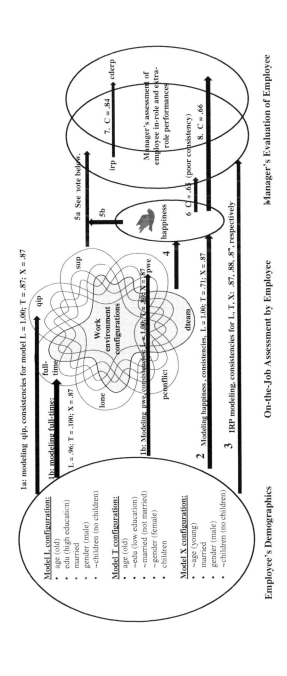

Figure 3. Consistencies of Configural Models for Hospitality-Service Employee Context Outcomes, *Very High* Happiness, and *Very High* In-Role and *Very High* Customer-Directed Extra Role Performances. *Notes*: C = consistency; for highly consistent model in associating antecedent configuration with the outcome, $C \geq .85$. dteam = job demands teamwork; cderp = customer-directed extra role performance; irp = in-role performance; lone = do not join social activities with my colleagues; pconflict = peer conflict; pwe = physical work environment pleasing; qip = quality of interpersonal relationships; sup = supervisor support; yservice = years of service; • = logical "and" condition; ~ = negation. *Notes on findings*: For arrow 4 findings, see Table 6a; high scores for a few facet-specific configurations predict high happiness. Happiness alone does *not* offer a consistent model for explaining high irp or cderp. Arrows 5a, 5b include seven highly consistent models, five for high happiness; one for unhappiness; one without happiness entering the model. An example model for arrows 5a and 5b: high IRP $\leq$ pwe•dteam•~pconflict •~lone•supsup•~qip•~yservice•happy; $C = .90$.

happiness — two models include males (one for young and one for older male employees) and one model includes females (older, not married, low in education, with children — but not necessarily at home).

These three demographic models associate consistently with high scores in several work facet-specific conditions (not all of facet-specific conditions were tested). All three demographic models associate with high scores in full-time, physical-work environment pleasing (pwe), and high quality of interpersonal relationships (qip).

The three demographic models associate with high happiness consistently and high IRP consistently. The following two models are additional models associating consistently with high happiness ("+" include Boolean algebra means "or"; "gender" means male and "~gender" means female): ~age•married•gender)• ~children + age•edu•married•gender. Thus, young males with no children who are married and older males with high education who are married are happy-at-work consistently.

Arrow 6 in Figure 3 shows high happiness does not associate consistently with high IRP (consistency = 0.65). What additional ingredients are necessary to be present for very high or very low happiness to associate consistently with very high IRP?

Tables 4a and 4b includes the complex antecedent models resulting in very high in-role performance assessments by managers (IRP). High supervisory support appears among the ingredients in six of the seven models in Tables 4a and 4b. High happiness appears in five, low happiness appears in one, and happiness is not an ingredient in one of the seven.

VERY LOW HAPPINESS AND VERY HIGH IRP

Note in Table 4a that model 4 includes the negation of happiness with additional ingredients that predict high IRP consistently. These cases are employees with many years of service, experiencing low peer conflict, high team work demand, who do not join in social activities with colleagues, and have low supervisory support.

Table 4b sheds additional light on low happiness and high IRP. Table 4b includes models of demographics and happiness associating with high IRP. Two of the nine models in Table 4b include very low happiness and additional ingredients associating with very high IRP.

Table 4a: Configurations of On-Job Happiness and Additional On-Job Antecedents Associating with Managers' Judgments of Employees' High In-Role Performances (IRP) (Arrows 5a and b in Figure 4).

Model		Raw Coverage	Unique Coverage	Consistency
1	pwe13_c*~dteam_c*~pconflict_c*lone_*supsup_c*qip_c*yservice_c	0.125820	0.020845	0.911004
2	hap_c*pwe13_c*dteam_c*~pconflict_c*~lone_c*supsup_c*~qip_c*~yservice_c	0.155635	0.053567	0.903133
3	hap_c*pwe13_c*~dteam_c*~ pconflict_c*~lone_c*supsup_c*~qip_c*~yservice_c	0.111951	0.003737	0.929015
4	~hap_c~pwe13_c*~dteam_c*~ pconflict_c*lone_c*~supsup_c*qip_c*yservice_c	0.110290	0.015032	0.949250
5	hap_c*pwe13_c*dteam_c*~pconflict_c*~lone_c*supsup_c*qip_c*yservice_c	0.129973	0.024998	0.975686
6	hap_c*pwe13_c*~ dteam_c*~pconflict_c*~lone_c*supsup_c*qip_c*yservice_c	0.114609	0.007474	0.981508
7	hap_c*pwe13_c* dteam_c*~pconflict_c*~lone_c*supsup_c*qip_c*yservice_c	0.104394	0.004817	0.955893

solution coverage: 0.249481
solution consistency: 0.862970

Table 4b: Configurational Models for Demographics and Happiness for Very High In-Role Performance.

Model	Raw Coverage	Unique Coverage	Consistency
1 ~yservice_c*~age_c*~edu_c*married*~gender*children*~fulltime	0.041608	0.022257	0.939961
2 yservice_c*age_c*~edu_c*married*fulltime*~hap_c	0.122498	0.084046	0.923607
3 yservice_c*age_c*edu_c*married*gender*fulltime*hap_c	0.067021	0.027988	0.932948
4 ~yservice_c*~age_c*edu_c*~married*~gender*children*fulltime*~hap_c	0.027822	0.006395	0.912807
5 ~yservice_c*~age_c*edu_c*married*gender*~children*~fulltime*hap_c	0.026078	0.006727	1.000000
6 yservice_c*~age_c*~edu_c*~married*~gender*~children*fulltime*hap_c	0.056889	0.036708	0.938356
7 ~yservice_c*~age_c*edu_c*married*~gender*children*fulltime*hap_c	0.045844	0.026493	0.924623
8 ~yservice_c*~age_c*edu_c*married*~gender*children*fulltime*hap_c	0.025828	0.003737	0.906705
9 ~yservice_c*age_c*~edu_c*married*~gender*children*fulltime*hap_c	0.051491	0.012790	0.932331

solution coverage: 0.270908

solution consistency: 0.894435

The first of these models includes older employees with many years of service, low in education, married, with children and working full-time, without gender relevancy to the model. The second of these two models includes unhappy females with children at home, not married, low in education, and young with few years of service – a configuration that likely highly relates to high family-job stress. Both models may associate with low salaries (a guess here because education is very low). The main point here is that modeling such complex configurations helps to clarify the low happiness and high performing employees.

IRP AND CDERP

The findings in IRP indicate that high IRP alone associates consistently with high CDERP (consistency = 0.84). However, a few (n = 9) cases occur where employees score low on IPR but high on CDERP. These nine cases appear in the top left corner of the XY plot in Figure 4. Space is not devoted here to examining such

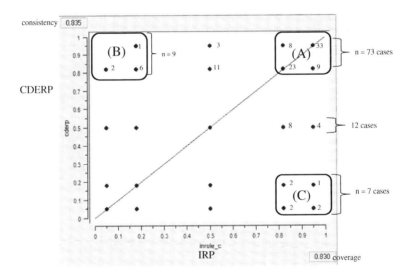

Figure 4. Impact of Managers' Evaluations of Hospitality Service Workers' In-Role Performance (IRP) on Managers' Evaluations of Customer-Directed Extra-Role Performance (CDERP) (*n* = 243 cases). *Notes*: Numbers indicate the number of cases for each dot. **(A)** While high IRP is informative in explaining high CDERP; **(B)** nine cases exhibit high CDERP and low IRP. Thus, high IRP is not necessary for high CDERP. Also, the few cases that are **(C)** high IRP and low in CDEREP indicates that IRP is not completely sufficient for explaining high CDERP – seven cases occur with high IRP and very low CDERP.

cases but such a finding indicates that case level analysis is possible while generalizing to the total sample — a particular advantage of using qualitative comparative analysis.

Figure 4 shows that more than three-fourths of the cases very high in IRP are very high in CDERP ($n = 92$). Thus, consistency for very high IPR in predicting very high CDERP equal to 0.835 indicates that the simple antecedent condition of high IRP alone is sufficient for estimating high CDERP. Even higher consistency is achievable by including facet-specific, happiness, and/or demographics with IRP in modeling high CDERP. (This report does not include this level of complexity.)

FINDINGS FOR MODELS FOR VERY LOW HAPPINESS AND VERY LOW PERFORMANCE

Figure 5 includes two complex demographic antecedent models with consistency for high happiness and high IRP. Model D represents young married males low in education. Model G represents young single females who are low in education with children.

Models D and G also relate consistently to the negation of finding their physical work environment please (~pwe) but do not relate consistently to full versus part-time employment status.

As appearing in Figure 4, the negation of IRP (~IRP) relates to the negation of CDERP (~CDERP) consistently. Given these findings and the findings for IRP and CDERP, the IRP and CDERP tends toward being symmetrical for the substantial majority of cases.

WORK FACET-SPECIFIC AND HAPPINESS CONFIGURATIONAL MODELS RELATING TO NEGATION OF IRP

Table 5a includes four models of work facet-specific models that relate consistently to high ~IRP (i.e., very low performance). All four of these models include the negation of full-time employment (i.e., high part-time employees) with very few years of service (~yservice). Three of the four models include low happiness as an ingredient; one includes high happiness.

High Happiness and Low Performance

The one complex model for ~IPR that includes high happiness also includes low supervisory support, low quality of interpersonal relationships (~qip), and very few years of service (~yservice), ~lone, high peer conflict, and high job teamwork demands

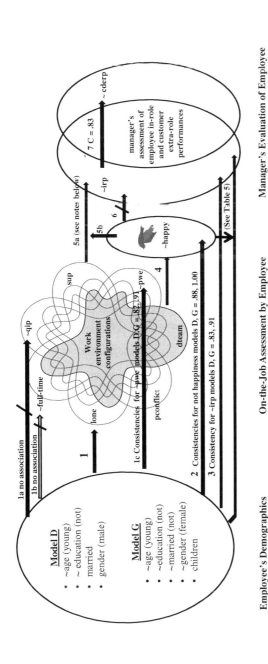

Figure 5. Configural Modeling Associations with Hospitality-Service Employee Work Contexts, *Very Low* Happiness, *Very Low* In-Role, and *Very Low* Customer-Directed Extra Role Performances. *Notes:*dteam = job demands of teamwork; cderp = customer-directed extra role performance; irp = in-role performance; lone = do not join social activities with my colleagues; pconflict = peer conflict; pwe = physical work environment pleasing; qip = quality of interpersonal relationships; sup = supervisor support; yservice (not shown in figure).*Notes on findings:* (1) For arrow 4: five work environment configurations have high consistencies in associating with not happiness.For example, ~happy ≤ ~yservice•~qip•~pwe–dteam •pconflict•lone•~sup, consistency = .93. See Table 6b for detailed findings.For arrows 5a and 5b, six of seven models predicting high membership in low irp (i.e., ~irp) very well include ~yservice. Example model:~irp = ~fulltime•~happy•~pwe•~dteam•~pconflict•lone•~supsup_c• ~yservice•qip_c (consistency = 0.982).

Table 5a: Configurations of On-Job Happiness and Additional On-Job Antecedents Associating with Managers' Judgments of Employees' Very Low In-Role Performances (~IRP) (Arrows 5 and 5b in Figure 4).

Model	Raw Coverage	Unique Coverage	Consistency
1 ~qip_c*~yservice_c*~hap_c*~pwel3_c*~dteam_c*~pconflict_c*~lone_c*~supsup_c*~fulltime	0.058733	0.018354	0.982265
2 ~qip_c*~yservice_c*hap_c*~pwel3_c*~dteam_c*pconflict_c*~lone_c*~supsup_c*~fulltime	0.042989	0.008402	0.975926
3 qip_c*~yservice_c*hap_c*~pwel3_c*~dteam_c*pconflict_c*~lone_c*~supsup_c*~fulltime	0.052451	0.009952	0.934592
4 qip_c*~yservice_c*hap_c*~pwel3_c*dteam_c*~pconflict_c*~lone_c*~supsup_c*~fulltime	0.137940	0.118280	0.919022

solution coverage: 0.197487

Solution consistency: 0.921233

Table 5b: Configurational Models for Demographics and Happiness for *Very Low* In-Role Performance.

Model	Raw Coverage	Unique Coverage	Consistency
1 ~hap_c*~yservice_c*~age_c*~edu_c*~married*~children*~fulltime	0.066400	0.026185	0.913580
2 ~yservice_c*~age_c*~edu_c*~married*gender*~children*~fulltime	0.057509	0.017293	0.901535
3 ~hap_c*~yservice_c*~age_c*~edu_c*~married*~gender*children*fulltime	0.027327	0.006281	0.912807
4 ~hap_c*~yservice_c*age_c*~edu_c*~married*~gender*children*fulltime	0.050575	0.030916	0.922619
5 ~hap_c*~yservice_c*age_c*~edu_c*~married*gender*~children*fulltime	0.053430	0.033771	0.926450
6 hap_c*~yservice_c*age_c*~edu_c*~married*~gender*children*fulltime	0.025369	0.003671	0.906705

solution coverage: 0.161025

Solution consistency: 0.876944

(dteam). Thus, part-time employees experiencing little supervisor support, high peer conflict, and new to the job, with high requirements for team work, and poor quality of interpersonal relationships are one answer to the conundrum of very high happiness and very low performance. This new employee may be very happy just to be receiving a salary. However, this recipe that predicts very low performance accurately remains unclear and requires additional study.

Table 5b sheds additional light on the occurrence of high happiness and low performance. Table 5b includes one such model (model 6). Model 6 includes females new to the job, older, working full-time, unmarried, with (most likely grown) children, with low education. Being new to the job may be a principal ingredient in their very low IRP scores as well as being high in happiness.

WORK FACE-SPECIFIC CONFIGURATIONS FOR VERY HIGH AND VERY LOW HAPPINESS

High scores for five work contexts associate with very high happiness. All the configurations that do so include high supervisory support as an ingredient. Details for each of the five work facet-specific configurations appear in Table 6a. High quality of interpersonal relationships (qip) occurs in five of the six models; the negation of qip (~qip) does not occur in any of the models. These models support the importance of carefully designing specific aspects of the workplace to achieve the objective of high happiness.

High scores for five work contexts associate with very low happiness. All five include either ~qip and/or the negation of pleasing working environment (~pwe). Details appear in Table 6b. These work facet-specific findings for the configurations affecting the negation of happiness are not mirror opposites of the configurations affecting happiness. This general finding supports the principle of causal asymmetry — the configurations of conditions serving to increase happiness are distinct from the configurations of conditions serving to increase unhappiness.

Discussion, Limitations, and Contributions

The study here contributes to moving beyond the issues of whether or not happiness-at-work influences job performance,

Table 6a: On-Job Antecedent Configurations Associating with Very High Happiness-at-Work (Arrow 4 in Figure 4).

Model		Raw Coverage	Unique Coverage	Consistency
1	~pconflict_c*pwe13_c*dteam_c*supsup_c*~lone_c*fulltime	0.221722	0.077981	0.920395
2	qip_c*pwe13_c*~dteam_c*supsup_c*lone_c*fulltime	0.262792	0.069750	0.921452
3	pconflict_c*qip_c*pwe13_c*supsup_c*lone_c*fulltime	0.207722	0.023420	0.924471
4	pconflict_c*qip_c*~pwe13_c*dteam_c*supsup_c*~lone_c*~fulltime	0.050318	0.016377	0.919380
5	~pconflict_c*qip_c*pwe13_c*dteam_c*supsup_c*lone_c*~fulltime	0.069410	0.035469	1.000000
solution coverage: 0.438184				
solution consistency: 0.907238				

Note: High supervisory support is an ingredient in all models which indicates its necessity for very high happiness-at-work.

Table 6b: On-Job Antecedent Configurations Associating with Very Low Happiness-at-Work (Findings for Arrow 4 in Figure 4).

Model		Raw Coverage	Unique coverage	Consistency
1	~qip_c*~pwe13_c*~dream_c*~supsup_c*fulltime	0.335357	0.060408	0.927514
2	qip_c*~pwe13_c*~lone_c*~supsup_c*fulltime	0.338953	0.056333	0.910300
3	~qip_c*~pwe13_*c~dteam_c*~pconflict_c*lone_c*~supsup_c	0.230843	0.017978	0.937378
4	qip_c*~pwe13_c*dteam_c*pconflict_c*~supsup_c*fulltime	0.240271	0.012305	0.898148
5	qip_c*~pwe13_c*~dteam_c*pconflict_c*lone_c*~supsup_c*~fulltime	0.055134	0.014383	0.981508
6	~qip_c*pwe13_c*~dteam_c*~pconflict_c*~lone_c*supsup_c*fulltime	0.162685	0.028366	0.900088

solution coverage: 0.538953

solution consistency: 0.859126

Note: Five of the six models include the negation of supervisory support – for many cases having very low supervisory support associates with very low performance but not always.

the size of the effect of this relationship, and whether or not the impact is always positive. The study contributes to theory and research by proposing that the impact of employee happiness-at-work on manager's assessment of employee performance depends on configurations of employee demographics and employees' judgments of work facet-specific factors.

Rather than looking narrowly at happiness-at-work and managers' assessments of employee work performance, a more complex in-depth stance is necessary to learn the combinations of conditions whereby high happiness associates with very high as well as very low performance. Separately, theory and empirical reports need to consider the configurations associating with very low happiness and very low versus very high managers' assessments of employee work performance.

Frontline, middle, and senior managers may seek to focus on all the complex antecedent conditions associating with high versus low quality of employee performances. These complex conditions are likely to include recipes with very high happiness, very low happiness, and happiness not in one or more of the recipes. Identifying these alternative complex configurations is possible and a worthy objective of theory, research, and practice.

The high importance of happiness-in-many-contexts relating to very high (low) quality of work assessments by managers is a key finding of the present study. Research to advance theory of how happiness affects performance is worthwhile but needs to embrace moving beyond a net-effects symmetric perspective to the construction of useful algorithms for predicting happiness as well as for predicting the conditions when happiness associates with very high (low) quality of work performance.

Figure 6 is an additional method for visualizing findings of demographic configurations associating with high versus low happiness-at-work — these findings are limited to the data in the present study and should be taken to suggest that unhappiness-at-work usually follows for young unmarried females with low education and children. Figure 6 is a way of illustrating the importance in advancing theory to focus on conditional statements that go beyond attempting to combine main and interaction effects in multiple regression models (Woodside, 2013). Such tree diagrams as Figure 6 can be drawn for high and low performance as well.

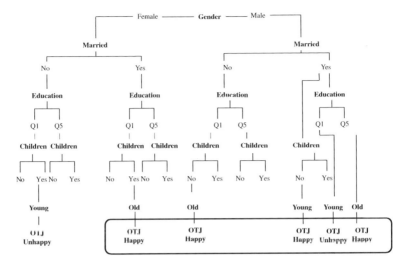

Figure 6. Demographics-Only Causal Asymmetry Configurations Associating with On-the-Job (Un)Happiness. *Notes:* Q1 = Lowest education quintile; Q5 = highest education quintile. OJJ = on-the-job. The associations are relevant only for the data in the present study do not necessarily hold for other data sets.

CONFIRMING THE FOUR PRINCIPLES OF CONFIGURAL THEORY

The findings support the four principles of configural theory. The multiple configurations associating (leading to) high values in happiness and in-role performances confirm the principle of equifinality. Consequently, a single configuration may be sufficient but it is not necessary for accurately predicting high employee happiness or high employee quality of work performance.

The findings confirm the second principle of configural theory – configural relationships that are accurate in predicting very high happiness and very high quality of work performance are symmetric and indicate sufficiency but not necessity. Low scores on these configurations associate with both low and high scores on the two outcome conditions (very low and very high happiness or performance). This perspective is another way of saying that linear causality is rare in real-life and researchers should discard the view of single-model sufficiency and necessary. Thus, researchers should end reporting in terms of "critical importance" and "key success factors" since no one condition is likely to be both sufficient and necessary.

The findings confirm the third principle of configural theory. Achieving very high happiness and very high quality work performance are complex undertakings. The examination of net effect and two and three-way interactions are insufficient in describing and understanding very high happiness and performance. Useful models in describing and understanding such outcome conditions likely requires embracing a configural stance such as crafting and testing algorithms via fsQCA.

The findings confirm the fourth principle. The findings support a causal asymmetry perspective – the configurations associating very high quality of work performance are not the mirror opposites of the configurations associating with very low work performance – the same conclusion applies for happiness-at-work. Having a deep accurate understanding of what brings about high quality of work performance only provides partially accurate hints of the causes of very low quality of work performance. Modeling both very high and very low quality of work performances and happiness are necessary.

THE EMPLOYEE HAPPINESS-AT-WORK AND MANAGER'S ASSESSMENT OF QUALITY OF EMPLOYEE PERFORMANCE RELATIONSHIP

From the stance of statistical testing of the hypothesis, the present study confirms both the small and medium-to-large effect size of the relationship of employees' happiness-at-work and managers' assessment of quality of employees' work performance. The relationship effect size is likely small but significant when taking into account the total sample of data in a study; the relationship is likely to be medium when limiting the analysis to the very low and very high quintiles of respondents for happiness-at-work and managers' assessments of quality of employees' work. These findings complement the findings for configural analysis.

From the stance of configural analysis, high happiness-at-work is insufficient is explaining high quality of work as assessed by managers. However, incorporating work facet-specific antecedents or demographics with happiness-at-work results in several complex configurations that are sufficient in explaining and predicting high quality of work as assessed by managers – and for some employees, low quality of work performance. If theory and practice seeks to understand how happiness affects high work performance, scholars' and practitioners' insight will improve by including work facet-specific contextual and/or demographic information in crafting complex statements along with happiness to explain high work performance.

The same perspective applies for increasing insight for explaining very low work performance. Unhappiness alone is not informative sufficiently to adequately explain very low work performance. However, the negation of happiness in combination with facet-specific simple antecedents combines into complex statements (algorithms) that do adequately explain very low work performance.

HAPPINESS, IRP, AND CDERP

Happiness alone is insufficient for predicting CDERP. However, IRP is sufficient alone for explaining CDERP. The findings of the study support the perspective that employees need to perform the basic in-role work requirements very week to achieve high evaluations in customer-directed extra role performances.

While not included in this study, additional analyses indicate that the inclusion of a few work facet-specific antecedents with IRP does improve the configural power in explaining CDERP. These findings are available from the authors by request.

LIMITATIONS AND SUGGESTIONS FOR FUTURE RESEARCH

The study here develops and explores configural theory of hospitality service employees' happiness and work performance. A general confirmation of the theory and findings for alternative configurations requires going beyond one empirical study in one industry in one country. One helpful step is to replicate the survey one within the same industry to additional firms in the same country as well as additional country contexts.

The predictive accuracy of configural models useful in this study needs to be tested using holdout samples of cases. This step can be taken by splitting the present sample into two subsamples randomly and repeating the analyses along with using the models useful for the first subsample to test their predictive accuracy on the cases in the second sample, and vice versa. This second step was taken in the present study and the findings proved substantial support for the usefulness of the models in the present study. (Details of predictive validity tests are available by request to the authors.)

KEEPING ONE EYE ON CASES AND THE SECOND ON THE SAMPLE

As McClelland (1998) emphasizes, the focus on creating and testing theories based on algorithms permits generalizing beyond the individual case in data set and yet permits the examination of individual cases in the analytical output. Both executives and employees benefit and will usually appreciate being able to receive feedback on performances at the individual, case, level rather than the dominant scholarly practice of reporting findings only at the level variables.

The use of qualitative comparative analysis to study causal complexity in employee happiness-at-work and quality of work performance offers breakthroughs in formulating theory and understanding how contexts affects work outcomes. The present study confirms Ragin's (1999, p. 1228) tenet, "It is much more fruitful to allow for the possibility that a given outcome may follow from a variety of different combinations of theoretically relevant causal conditions" (than limiting one's perspective and testing to a single theoretical statement).

Acknowledgment

The authors gratefully acknowledges the permission granted by the publisher, Emerald, to reuse content originating from Po-Hsun Hsiao et al. (2015).

References

Babin, B. J., Darden, W. R., & Griffin, M. (1994). Work and/or fun: Measuring hedonic and utilitarian shopping value. *Journal of Consumer Research*, 20(4), 644–656.

Baker, J. (1986). The role of the environment in marketing services: The consumer perspective. In J. A. Czepiel, C. Congram, & J. Shanahan (Eds.), *In the services challenge: Integrating for competitive advantage* (pp. 79–84). Chicago, IL: American Marketing Association.

Barsade, S. (2000). *The ripple effect: Emotional contagion in groups.* Working Paper. Yale University Press, Hew Haven, CT. Retrieved from http://papers.ssrn.com/abstract=250894. Accessed on February 7, 2011.

Barsade, S. (2002). The ripple effect: Emotional contagion and its influence on group behavior. *Administrative Science Quarterly*, 47(4), 644–676.

Barte1, C. A., & Saavedra, R. (2000). The collective construction of work group moods. *Administration Science Quarterly*, 45(2), 197–231.

Bass, F. M., Tigert, D. J., & Lonsdale, R. T. (1968). Market segmentation: Group versus individual behavior. *Journal of Marketing Research*, 5(3), 264–270.

Bettencourt, L. A., & Brown, S. (1997). Contact employees: Relationships among workplace fairness, job satisfaction, and pro-social service behaviors. *Journal of Retailing*, 73(1), 39–61.

Bettencourt, L. A., Gwinner, K. P., & Meuter, M. L. (2001). A comparison of attitude, personality, and knowledge predictors of service-oriented organizational citizenship behaviors. *Journal of Applied Psychology*, 86(1), 29–41.

Bitner, M. J. (1990). Evaluating service encounters: The effects of physical surroundings and employee responses. *Journal of Marketing*, 54(4), 69–82.

Bitner, M. J. (1992). Servicescapes: The impact of physical surroundings on customers and employees. *Journal of Marketing*, 56(2), 57–71.

Borman, W. C., & Motowidlo, S. J. (1993). Expanding the criterion domain to include elements of contextual performance. In N. Schmitt & W. C. Borman (Eds.), *Personnel selection in organizations* (pp. 71–98). San Francisco, CA: Jossey-Bass.

Choi, H. J., & Kim, Y. T. (2012). Work-family conflict, work-family facilitation, and job outcomes in the Korean hotel industry. *International Journal of Contemporary Hospitality Management*, 24(7), 1011–1028.

Clark, B. H. (1999). Marketing performance measures: History and interrelationships. *Journal of Marketing Management*, 15(8), 711–732.

Cohen, J. (1977). *Statistical power analysis or the behavioral sciences.* New York, NY: Academic Press.

Collins, P. H. (1990). *Black feminist thought: Knowledge, consciousness, and the politics of empowerment.* Boston, MA: Unwin Hyman.

Crosby, L. A., Evans, K. R., & Cowles, D. (1990). Relationship quality in services selling: An interpersonal influence perspective. *Journal of Marketing*, 54, 68–81.

Donovan, R. J., & Rossiter, J. R. (1982). Store atmosphere: An environmental psychology approach. *Journal of Retailing*, 58(1), 34–57.

Doyle, J. R., O'Connor, D. J., Reynolds, G. M., & Bottomley, P. A. (1999). The robustness of the asymmetrically dominated effect: Buying frames, phantom alternatives, and in-store purchases. *Psychology & Marketing*, 16, 225–243.

Fisher, C. D. (2010). Happiness at work. *International Journal of Management Reviews*, 12(4), 384–412.

Fiss, P. (2011). Building better causal theories: A fuzzy set approach to typologies in organization research. *Academy of Management Journal*, 54, 393–420.

Fiss, P. C. (2007). A set theoretic approach to organizational configurations. *Academy of Management Review*, 32(4), 1180–1198.

Foxall, G. R., & Greenley, G. E. (1999). Consumers' emotional responses to service environments. *Journal of Business Research*, 46(2), 149–157.

Frijda, N. (1988). The laws of emotion. *American Psychologist*, 43(5), 349–358.

Frone, M. R. (2000). Interpersonal conflict at work and psychological outcomes: Testing a model among young workers. *Journal of Occupational Healthy Psychology*, 5(2), 246–255.

Galunic, D. C., & Eisenhardt, K. M. (1994). Reviewing the strategy-structure-performance paradigm. *Research in Organizational Behavior, 16,* 215–255.

George, J. M., & Jones, G. R. (2002). *Understanding and managing organizational behavior* (3rd ed.). Upper Saddle River, NJ: Prentice Hall.

Gibson, J. L., Ivancevich, J. M., & Donnelly, J. H., Jr. (1994). *Organizations: Behavior, structure, processes.* Burr Ridge, IL: Richard D. Irwin.

Gigerenzer, G. (1991). From tools to theories: A heuristic of discovery in cognitive psychology. *Psychological Review, 98,* 254–267.

Gladwell, M. (1996). *The tipping point: How little things can make a big difference.* New York, NY: Little, Brown.

Gresov, C., & Drazin, R. (1997). Equifinality: Functional equivalence in organization design. *Academy of Management Review, 22,* 403–428.

Havlena, W. J., & Holbrook, M. B. (1986). The varieties of consumption experience: Comparing two typologies of emotion in consumer behavior. *Journal of Consumer Research, 13*(3), 394–404.

Hellen, K., & Sääksjärvi, M. (2011). Happiness as a predictor of service quality and commitment for utilitarian and hedonic services. *Psychology & Marketing, 28,* 934–957.

Hepbur, V. G., Loughoin, C. A., & Barling, J. (1997). Coping with chronic work stress. In B. H. Gottlieb (Ed.), *Cooping with chronic stress* (pp. 343–366). New York, NY: Plenum.

Hess, U., & Kirouac, G. (2000). Emotion expression in groups. In M. J. Lewis & M. Jeannette (Eds.), *Handbook of emotions* (pp. 489–497). New York, NY: The Guilford Press.

Howton, F. W. (1963). Work assignment and interpersonal relations in a research organization: Some participant observations. *Administrative Science Quarterly, 7*(4), 502–520.

Iaffaldano, M. T., & Muchinsky, P. M. (1985). Job satisfaction and job performance: A meta-analysis. *Psychological Bulletin, 97,* 251–273.

Jervis, R. (1997). *System effects.* Princeton, NJ: Princeton University Press.

Judge, T. A., Thoresen, C. J., Bono, J. E., & Patton, G. K. (2001). The job satisfaction—Job performance relationship: A qualitative and quantitative review. *Psychological Bulletin, 127,* 376–407.

Karatepe, O. M. (2013). High-performance work practices and hotel employee performance: The mediation of work engagement. *International Journal of Hospitality Management, 32,* 132–140.

Katz, D., & Kahn, R. L. (1978). *The social psychology of organizations* (2nd ed.). New York, NY: Wiley.

Kossek, E. E., & Ozeki, C. (1998). Work-family conflict, policies, and the job-life satisfaction relationship: A review and directions for organizational behavior-human resources research. *Journal of Applied Psychology, 83*(2), 139–149.

Kotler, P. (2000). *Marketing management: Planning, implementation, and control* (10th ed.). Englewood Cliffs, NJ: Prentice Hall.

LePine, J. A., Erez, A., & Johnson, D. E. (2002). The nature and dimensionality of organizational citizenship behavior: A critical review and meta-analysis. *Journal of Applied Psychology, 87,* 52–65.

Lin, J. C. (1998). *The influence of meditation to business employee's emotion management and personal relationship.* Unpublished doctoral dissertation.

Lorenz, K. (1961). *Arithmetik und Logik als Spiele.* Dissertation. Kiel: Universitat Kiel.

Lovaglia, M. J., & Houser, J. A. (1996). Emotional reactions and status in groups. *American Sociological Review*, 61(5), 867–883.

Lovelock, C. H. (1996). *Services marketing* (3rd ed.). Upper Saddle River, NJ: Prentice Hall.

Lucas, J. W., & Lovaglia, M. J. (1998). Leadership status, gender, group size, and emotion in face-to-face groups. *Sociological Perspectives*, 41(3), 617–637.

Lyubomirsky, S., King, L. A., & Diener, E. (2005). The benefits of frequent positive affect: Does happiness lead to success. *Psychological Bulletin*, 131, 803–855.

Machleit, K. A., & Eroglu, S. A. (2000). Describing and measuring emotional response to shopping experience. *Journal of Business Research*, 49(2), 101–111.

McClelland, D. C. (1998). Identifying competencies with behavioral-event interviews. *Psychological Science*, 9, 331–3339.

Motowidlo, S. J., & Van Scotter, J. R. (1994). Evidence that task performance should be distinguished from contextual performance. *Journal of Applied Psychology*, 79(4), 475–480.

Netemeyer, R. G., Maxham III, J. G., & Pullig, C. (2005). Conflicts in the work-family interface: Links to job stress, customer service employee performance, and customer purchase intent. *Journal of Marketing*, 69(2), 130–143.

Po-Hsun Hsiao, J., Jaw, C., Huan, T. C., & Woodside, A. G. (2015). Applying complexity theory to solve hospitality contrarian case conundrums. *International Journal of Contemporary Hospitality Management*, 27(4), 608–647.

Ragin, C. (2008). *Redesigning social inquiry: Fuzzy sets and beyond.* Chicago, IL: Chicago University Press.

Ragin, C. C. (1997). Turning the tables: How case-oriented methods challenge variable oriented methods. *Comparative Social Research*, 16(1), 27–42.

Ragin, C. C. (1999). Using qualitative comparative analysis to study causal complexity. *Health Services Research*, 34(5, Pt. 2), 1225–1239.

Ragin, C. C. (2010). *Constructing social research.* Thousand Oaks, CA: Sage.

Russell, J. A., & Lanius, U. F. (1984). Adaptation level and the affective appraisal of environments. *Journal of Environmental Psychology*, 4(2), 119–135.

Russell, J. A., & Pratt, G. (1980). A description of the affective quality attributed to environments. *Journal of Personality and Social Psychology*, 38(2), 311–322.

Schutte, N. S., Malouff, J. M., Bobik, C., Coston, T. D., Greeson, C., Jedlicka, C., ... Wendorf, G. (2001). Emotional intelligence and interpersonal relations. *Journal of Social Psychology*, 141(4), 523–536.

Shostack, L. G. (1985). Planning the service encounter. In J. A. Czepiel, M. R. Solomon, & C. F. Surprenant, (Eds.), *The service encounter* (pp. 243–254). New York, NY: Lexington Books.

Singh, J. (2000). Performance productivity and quality of frontline employees in service organizations. *Journal of Marketing*, 64(4), 15–34.

Singh, J., Verbeke, W., & Rhoads, G. K. (1996). Do organizational practices matter in role stress processes? A study of direct and moderating effects for marketing-oriented boundary spanners. *Journal of Marketing*, 60(6), 69–86.

Slack, T. (1997). *Understanding sport organizations: The application of organization theory*. Windson, ON: Human Kinetics.

Sloan, M. M. (2012). Controlling anger and happiness at work: An examination of gender differences. *Gender, Work & Organization*, 19(4), 370–391.

Spector, P. E., & Jex, S. M. (1998). Development of four self-report measures of job stressors and strains: Interpersonal conflict at work scale, organizational constraints scale, quantitative workload inventory, and physical symptoms inventory. *Journal of Occupational Health Psychology*, 3(4), 356–367.

Terry, D. J., Tonge, L., & Callan, V. J. (1995). Employee adjustment to stress: The role of coping resources, situational factors and coping responses. *Anxiety, Stress, and Coping*, 8(1), 1–24.

Turley, L. W., & Milliman, R. E. (2000). Atmospheric effects on shopping behavior: A review of the experimental evidence. *Journal of Business Research*, 49(2), 193–211.

Urry, J. (2005). The complexity turn. *Theory Culture Society*, 22(5), 1–14.

Van de Vliert, E., & Euwema, M. C. (1994). Agreeableness and activeness as components of conflict behaviors. *Journal of Personality and Social Psychology*, 66(4), 674–687.

Vroom, V. H. (1964). *Work and motivation*. New York, NY: Wiley.

Warr, P. (2007). Searching for happiness at work. *The Psychologist*, 20(12), 726–729.

Wart, S., Robertson, T. S., & Zielinski, J. (1992). *Consumer behavior*. Chicago, IL: Scott, Foresman and Company.

Wirtz, J., & Bateson, J. E. G. (1999). Consumer satisfaction with service: Integrating the environment perspective in services marketing into the traditional disconfirmation paradigm. *Journal of Business Research*, 44(1), 55–66.

Woodside, A. G. (2013). Moving beyond multiple regression analysis to algorithms: Calling for a paradigm shift from symmetric to asymmetric thinking in data analysis and crafting theory. *Journal of Business Research*, 63, 463–472.

Woodside, A. G., Hsu, S.-Y., & Marshall, R. (2012). General theory of cultures' consequences on international tourism behavior. *Journal of Business Research*, 64, 785–799.

Wright, T. A., & Cropanzano, R. (2000). Psychological well-being and job satisfaction as predictors of job performance. *Journal of Occupational Health Psychology*, 5, 84–94.

Yoo, C., Park, J., & MacInnis, D. J. (1998). Effects of store characteristics and in-store emotional experiences on store attitude. *Journal of Business Research*, 42(3), 253–263.

Zelenski, J. M., Murphy, S. A., & Jenkins, D. A. (2008). The happy-productive worker thesis revisited. *Journal of Happiness Studies*, 9, 521–537. Retrieved from http://link.springer.com/article/10.1007/s10902-008-9087-4#page-2

Appendix: Examples of Computing Scores for Complex Antecedent Conditions

Consider the following descriptions of five employees. Bob is very young with little education, he is unmarried with no children, he works part-time, he is a new employee, he is very happy-at-work; Bob's manager rates Bob's job performance to be very low.

Edwina is very young with little education, unmarried, children at home, she works full-time, three years of working in the firm, she is very unhappy-at-work; Edwina's manager rates Edwina's job performance to be very high.

Helen is 54 years old, married, grown children, 18 years working in the firm, working full-time, very little education, very happy at work; Helen's manager rates her job performance to be very high.

Linda is new to the firm, 24 years old, university graduate, married, no children, working full-time, very happy-at-work; Linda's manager rates her performance to be acceptable but not high, "she has a long way to go but she shows promise."

Consider the following complex antecedent conditions:

Model D: ~age•~education•~married•~children•gender
Model R: ~age•~education•~married•children•~gender
Model V: ~age•education•married•~children•~gender
With ~age = the negation of age (i.e., high score means very young);
~education = very low education score
~married = not married
~children = no children
~gender = female (thus, gender = male).

Using the logical "AND" in Boolean algebra, the membership score for the complex statement is equal to the lowest score among the scores for the simple antecedents in the complex statement.

Bob's score for ~age = .0.99; his score for ~education = 0.99; his score for ~married = 0.99; his score for ~children = 0.99; his score for gender = 0.99. Thus, Bob's score for model D equals 0.99 – the lowest score among the five simple antecedent

Table A1: Computing the Complex Antecedent Scores for Models D, R, and V, for the Four Employees.

Case	Age	Education	Married	Children	Gender	D	R	V
Bob	.01	.01	.01	.01	.99	.99	.01	.01
Edwina	.01	.01	.01	.99	.01	.01	.99	.01
Helen	.72	.01	.99	.99	.01	.01	.01	.01
Linda	.06	.82	.99	.01	.01	.01	.01	.82

conditions. Here are Linda's scores for the simple antecedent conditions in Model V: ~age = .94; education = 0.82; married = 0.99; ~children = 0.99; ~gender = 0.99; Linda's score for model V is equal to the lowest score among the five values (i.e., .82).

Construction of XY plots by hand is possible with the each set of scores for models D, R, and V on the X-axis and the scores for full-time, happiness, and job performance on the Y-axis. Note that full-time equals 0.00 and part-time equals 0.01; "very happy" equals 0.99 and very unhappy equals 0.01; very high performance equals 0.00 and very low performance equals 0.01. With five demographic antecedent conditions, all possible combinations include 32 models for the complex combinations

Index